Beethoven

Symphony No. 1 in C Major
Op. 21

Creation, Origins and Reception History
Incorporating
Contextual Accounts of Beethoven and His Contemporaries

BEETHOVEN
As depicted by the life mask taken by Franz Klein in 1812
(derived from a copy in the author's possession)

BEETHOVEN
SYMPHONY NO. 1 IN C MAJOR OP. 21

CREATION ORIGINS AND RECEPTION HISTORY

Incorporating contextual accounts of Beethoven and his contemporaries

Terence M. Russell

Jelly Bean Books

The right of Terence Russell to be identified as the
Author of the Work has been asserted by him in accordance
with the Copyright, Designs and Patents Act 1988.

Copyright © Terence M. Russell 2025

Published by
Jelly Bean Books
136 Newport Road
Cardiff
CF24 1DJ

ISBN: 978-1-917022-72-9

www.candyjarbooks.co.uk

All rights reserved.
No part of this publication may be reproduced, stored in a
retrieval system, or transmitted at any time or by any means,
electronic, mechanical, photocopying, recording or otherwise
without the prior permission of the copyright holder. This book is
sold subject to the condition that it shall not by way of trade or
otherwise be circulated without the publisher's prior consent in any
form of binding or cover other than that in which it is published.

CONTENTS

AUTHOR'S NOTE	I
INTRODUCTION	IX
EDITORIAL PRINCIPLES	XVIII
BEETHOVEN'S FINANCIAL TRANSACTIONS	XX

SYMPHONY NO. 1 – SELECTED WRITINGS

Allgemeine musikalische Zeitung	1
Wilhelm Altmann	4
Paul Bekker	5
John Blacking	7
Leon Botstein	8
Joseph Braunstein	9
Barry Cooper	10
Basil Deane	12
Philip G. Downs	13
Donald Jay Grout, and Claude V. Palisca	14

(Sir) George Grove	15
George Hogarth	16
David Wyn Jones	17
William Kinderman	19
Gustav Mahler	20
Stedman Preston	21
Maynard Solomon	22
Michael Steinberg	23
Coriander Stuttard	24
Donald Francis Tovey	25
Paul Webster	26
Ralph Vaughan Williams	27
BEETHOVEN AND BONN	29
BEETHOVEN AND VIENNA	38
BEETHOVEN: A CONTEMPORARY PORTRAIT	69
BEETHOVEN: A NEW PATH	92
SYMPHONY NO. 1: CREATION ORIGINS	111
PUBLISHERS AND PUBLICATION	130
SYMPHONY NO. 1: RECEPTION HISTORY	148
SYMPHONY NO. 1: MUSICOLOGY: SELECTED WRITINGS	198
	130
BIBLIOGRAPHY	223
INDEX	258
ABOUT THE AUTHOR	262

AUTHOR'S NOTE

I have cherished the idea of making a study of the life and work of Beethoven for many years. This statement requires a few words of personal reflection. I first encountered Beethoven in my early piano lessons — Minuet in G major, WoO 10, No. 2. At the same time I became acquainted with his piano pupil Carl Czerny — *Book One, Piano Studies*. My heart sank when I discovered the rear cover advertised a further *99* books in the same series — scales, arpeggios studies for the left hand, studies for the right hand — all the way to his Op. 824! By coincidence, my *Czerny Book One* was edited by Alec Rowley — who had the same surname as my music teacher. In my childish innocence, I often wondered why *he himself* never appeared to give me a lesson!

In my teenage years I found myself drawn ever closer to

Beethoven's music in the manner that ferromagnetic materials are ineluctably held captive in the sway of a magnetic field. The impulse to which I yielded is well described in words the conductor Bruno Walter gave in one of his rare public addresses:

> 'It is my belief that young people at that age are more easily impressed by what is heroic and grandiose; that they more easily understand works of art in which passionate feelings are violently uttered in raised accents, and that the lighter sounds of cheerfulness are less impressive to them.'

I do indeed recall the stirring effect made on me on first hearing the Overture *Egmont*, the unfolding drama of the Fifth Symphony and the declamatory opening chords of the *Emperor* Piano Concerto.

I resolved to read everything I could about Beethoven, starting with Marion Scott's pioneering English-language study of the composer in *The Master Musicians series*. My father took out a subscription for me for *The Gramophone* magazine, enabling me to read reviews of the new 'LP' recordings — none of which though I could afford! The LP was then — 1950s — beginning to supplant the 78 rpm shellac records, stacks of which could be purchased for as little as six pence each in 'old' money. I listed to the radio to hear Anthony Hopkins 'Talking about music' and to other musicological luminaries including Howard Fergusson, Hans Keller, Paul Hamburger, Denis Matthews, and Peter Stadlen.

At this same time, I had the privilege of hearing Beethoven's music performed by the *Hallé Orchestra* under the baton of Sir John Barbirolli, and experienced the *Carl*

Rosa Opera Company perform the composer's only opera *Fidelio*, I borrowed the piano-reduction score from the City Library to become better acquainted with this moving work — only to find the score's fists full of notes were well beyond my capabilities. Nonetheless, since then *Fidelio's* every note has been woven into my DNA. I also recall the period when the *London Promenade Concerts* were designated 'Friday night is Beethoven night'.

Through these influences I resolved to visit Vienna to see where Beethoven had lived and worked. But how? The support for such travel was beyond the means of my family. Fortunately in my final year at school (1959) an opportunity presented itself. I saw a poster that stated *WUS — World University Service* — required volunteers to work in the Austrian town of Linz to help relocate refugees who were living there in improvised wooden shacks — displaced and dispossessed victims of the Second World War. To those participating all expenses would be paid together with free accommodation — in one of the crumbling wooden shacks! From Linz, I planned to make my way to Vienna.

I applied to *WUS* and, despite being a mere school-leaver, I was accepted. The *WUS* authorities doubtless reasoned the building-trade skills I had acquired during my secondary education in the building department of a technical school would be useful. This proved to be the case. At the refugee camp I dug trenches and was allowed to assist as a bricklayer. All about me were wide-eyed children eager to help but mostly getting in the way. I recall one afternoon when a reporter from *The Observer* newspaper paid a visit to our construction site to gather material for an article he was writing on European post-war recovery — he generously admired my trenches and brickwork!

Of lasting significance was another visit, this time from a Belgian priest. He took a group of us to the nearby

Mauthausen Concentration Camp, recently opened as a silent and solemn memorial to those who had perished there. It was a deeply moving experience. Years later I learned of the views of the ardent Beethovenian Sir Michael Tippet. After the horrors of the *Holocaust*, he posed the question for mankind: 'What price Beethoven now?' He posited: 'Could we any longer find solace in Beethoven's setting of Schiller's *Ode to Joy* and its utopian vision – "Be embraced you Millions"?'

My refugee contribution duly came to end and Vienna beckoned. On arrival there I found scenes reminiscent of *The Third Man* and *Harry Lime*. I recall, for example, encountering cobblestones piled high in the streets waiting to be replaced after having been disturbed by the heavy armoured vehicles that had so recently passed over them. But Vienna was welcoming. I visited the houses where Beethoven had lived and worked and paused outside others associated with him that were identified by a commemorative plaque and the Austrian flag. A particularly memorable occasion was attending a recital in the great salon within the palace of Beethoven's noble patron Prince Lobkowitz – the very one where the *Eroica* Symphony had been premiered. Ultimately, my steps led me to the composer's first resting place in the *Währinger Ortsfriedhof*. I paid silent homage to the great man and, as I did so, discovered nearby the resting place of Franz Schubert to whom Beethoven was an endless source of admiration and inspiration.

I felt a youthful impulse to discover yet more about Beethoven and his music. But absorption in musicology would have to take second place. My chosen career beckoned in the guise of architecture – 'the mother of the arts' and 'the handmaid of society'. There was room though for Beethoven's music and from that time on it has been my constant companion through attendance at recitals, in concerts and music-making in the home. And at home a reproduction of Franz Kline's 1812 study of the composer has greeted me each day for more than half a century.

On my retirement from a career in architectural practice, research and university teaching, the opportunity finally presented itself for me to devote time to researching Beethoven musicology. Having attained my eightieth year also emboldened me to make progress with my good intentions!

With these autobiographical remarks outlined I will say a few remarks about my working method— see also the comments made in *Editorial Principles*.

As a member of staff of The University of Edinburgh, I had the good fortune to have access to the *Reid Music Library*, formed from a nucleus of books bequeathed by General John Reid and augmented over the years by such custodians as Sir Donald Francis Tovey, sometime *Reid Professor of Music* and renowned Beethoven scholar. Over a period of three years, I made a survey of the many works in the Reid collection. I consulted each item in turn making records on paper slips — many hundreds — that I deemed to be relevant for my researches. I confined my searches to book-publications, as reflected in my accompanying bibliography. All of this was quite some years ago, the cut-off date for my researches being 2007. Beyond this date I have not surveyed any further works. I am mindful though that Beethoven musicology and related publication continue to be a major field of endeavour in the manner of the proverbial 'ever rolling stream'.

In the intervening years since completing my archival researches, personal tribulations associated with family illness and bereavement slowed my progress in giving expression to my projected intentions. Latterly, however, with renewed energy, and more time at my disposal, I have been able to make progress. My studies take the form of a set of monographs. The first set of these, trace the creation origins and reception history of each of Beethoven's piano sonatas and string quartets. The resulting texts also incorporate contextual accounts of Beethoven and his contemporaries. Also included in my musicological surveys are two related Beethoven anthologies. The set of monographs in question, identified by short title, are:

Beethoven: An anthology of selected writings.
Beethoven: The piano sonatas: An anthology of selected writings.

The Piano Sonatas:
Op. 2–Op. 28
Op. 31–Op. 81a
Op. 90–Op. 111

The String Quartets:
Op. 18, Nos. 1–6
Op. 59, Nos. 1–3 (Razumovsky); Op. 74 (The Harp); Op. 95 (Quartetto serioso)
Op. 127, Op. 132 and Op. 130 (Galitzin)
Op. 131, Op. 135; Grosse Fuge, Op. 133 and Op. 134 (Fugue transcription)

I provide further information about these studies in the introduction to each individual monograph. Suffice it for me to state here the basic premise upon which my work is founded. I believe it is rewarding, concerning the life of a great artist, to find connections between who he *was* and what he *did*; in Martin Cooper's words 'between his personality, as expressed on the one hand in human relationships, and on the other in artistic creation'. (*Beethoven, The Last*

Decade) That is not to say I consider it essential to the enjoyment of Beethoven's music to know this or that fact about it. His music can be enjoyed, as millions do, with — in Robert Simpson's apt phrase —'an innocent ear', for what it is and how it reaches out to us in purely musical terms without any prejudging of its merits based upon extra-musicological facts. Maynard Solomon expresses similar thoughts:

> 'It is doubtless true that we need have no knowledge whatever of a composer's biography, or knowledge of any other motivating factor of any kind, to appreciate the artwork on some fundamental level.' (*Beethoven Essays*, 1988, p. 116)

I must make a further point. I am mindful that a scholar who ventures into a field of study that is not rightly his may be regarded with some suspicion. In this regard I can but ask the reader to place his or her trust in me in the following way. I have attempted to bring to my work the care which publishers and their desk editors have required of me in my book writings relating to architecture — listed elsewhere.

As inferred, it is now more than sixty years since I paid homage to Beethoven in Vienna's *Währinger Ortsfriedhof* and my warmth of feeling towards the composer and his music have grown with the passing of the years. My studies are not intended to be propaedeutic — that would be pretentious. However, if in sharing with others what I have to say contributes to their knowledge and understanding of the composer, and thereby increases their own feelings towards him and his works, my own pleasure in bringing my work to completion will be all the more enhanced.

When Beethoven arrived in Vienna, he was unknown. He was armed though with a note of encouragement from his youthful friend and benefactor Count Ferdinand Waldstein. It contained the often-quoted words: 'Receive Mozart's spirit from Haydn's hands.' Some forty years later Beethoven passed away in the House of the black-robed Spaniards at 200 *Alservorstädter*, the *Glacis* where he had lived since the autumn of 1825. Soldiers had to be called to secure the doors to the inner courtyard of the house from the pressure of onlookers. His body was blessed in the *Alservorsttädt Parish Church*, schools were closed and perhaps as many as 10,000 people formed a funeral procession — an honour ordinarily reserved for monarchs. The *Marcia Funebre* from the composer's Op. 26 Piano Sonata was performed at the funeral ceremony. Franz Grillparzer read the funeral oration. Franz Schubert, who, as remarked in life so admired Beethoven, was one of the pallbearers. The composer's mortal remains were lowered into a simple vault. Beethoven now belonged to history.

Dr Terence M. Russell
Edinburgh 2020

To the foregoing I am pleased to add the following works:

The Piano Concertos
The Symphonies: An Anthology of Selected Writings
Symphony No. 1 In C Major, Op. 21
Symphony No. 2 in D Major, Op. 36
Symphony No. 3 in E-flat Major, Op. 55 (Eroica)
Symphony No. 4 in B-flat Major, Op. 60

TMR
2024

INTRODUCTION

Beethoven considered composing a symphony from around 1795, the period when he was preparing his three Piano Trios Op 1 for publication; a symphony would be his most ambitious orchestral work to date. Evidence of his wish to realize such a challenging composition is apparent insofar as he worked on various drafts over the next three years. It has been suggested Beethoven entertained the hope of presenting a symphony at one of the annual concerts of the Tonkünstler-Societät — 'Society of Musicians'.[1] Haydn, then at the height of his powers, had already presented some of his symphonies at the Society's concerts and it would only be natural for Beethoven, his pupil, to emulate his master. Two such concerts were announced for 29 and 30 March 1795. At the first of these Beethoven made his début public-appearance as both a virtuoso of the keyboard and composer, performing his B-flat major Piano Concerto —

but no symphony of his was forthcoming. Between February and July 1796, Beethoven made a concert tour of Prague, Dresden, Leipzig, and Berlin, during which he made extensive sketches for a symphony. Some authorities consider he had the possibility of performance in mind, but he was evidently not yet satisfied with the work he had so far undertaken. This consisted of extensive sketches for the first three movements and ideas for a finale.

Setting aside such extra-musicological considerations as the foregoing, we need to bear in mind that Beethoven, in the 1790s, was not yet the colossus he was to become. In taking time to write a symphony, he would not commit to such an undertaking until he felt he was sufficiently equipped to endow such a work with the intensity of feeling characteristic of his nature. He also had to contend with the legacy of his forebears, Haydn and Mozart. It is not surprising, therefore, that he should wait until he felt himself well-equipped to undertake the endeavour. As Paul Mies observes: 'Just as Haydn's and Mozart's symphonies impelled Beethoven to severe self-criticism, his own works had the same effect on his successors.'[2][3] When Beethoven did start to give public orchestral concerts, he gave new status to them by making them a vehicle by means of which he could present his largest and most ambitious works that, as we shall see, would challenge both players and audience.

An interesting question arises as to which period, in Beethoven's evolving musical style, does his First Symphony belong? Following his death, attempts were made to formulate his music into clearly identifiable periods. As Maynard Solomon remarks, early chroniclers of his works were confronted by an immense range of formal and expressive problems, bearing on the qualitative changes in his style, each one of which constitute no less than turning points in the history of music.[4] In his *Biographie Universelle des Musiciens et Bibliographie Générale de la Musique (Brussels, 1833-44, 8 vols.)*, the Belgian composer, music critic and musicologist Joseph Fétis, made pioneering attempts to categorise Beethoven's music into three identifiable periods that he called 'classes of production': He considered the first period to extend from Op. 1 (Piano Trios) to the *Waldstein* Piano Sonata, Op. 53 – thereby including the First Symphony; the second period from the Piano Sonata, Op. 54 to the Seventh Symphony, Op. 92; and the third period from the Eighth Symphony, Op. 93 to the Fugue for String Quintet in D major, Op. 137. In his *Beethoven et ses Trois Styles* (1855), the musicologist Wilhelm von Lenz, is accredited with formulating the hypothesis of 'three-stages' of Beethoven's compositions that may be described chronologically as 'early, middle, and late'. Others, have attempted to capture what we have just described as Beethoven's 'evolving musical style' in the tripartite formulation of works that are considered to be 'imitative, heroic, and introspective'.[5]

Douglas Johnson remarks it is too late now to seek to modify the concept of 'three periods' on the grounds:

> 'The broad stages of Beethoven's creative life – *imitative, heroic,* and *introspective* – [italics added] have been assimilated into the basic popular vocabulary from which all discussion of his music now proceeds.'

He adds: 'And not without reason, for the division does associate important changes in his style with what have been perceived as crises in his life.'[6] In his schematization, Lenz placed the First Symphony at the close of Beethoven's first period. Beethoven's early biographer Anton Felix Schindler, however, demurred and placed the C major Symphony, Op. 21 at the start of the composer's second period.[7] Perhaps the devoted Beethovenian, Donald Tovey, struck the right note in his *Essays in Musical Analysis* where he describes the First Symphony as being 'Beethoven's "farewell" to the classical period'.

On the occasion of Beethoven's Death Centenary (1827), Richard Wagner sought to place the composer's early compositions in the context of his musical forebears: 'Beethoven's earlier works are not incorrectly held to have sprung from Haydn's model; and a closer relationship to Haydn than Mozart may be traced even in the later development of his genius ... As regards form, he agreed with his teacher but the unruly demons of his inner music, fettered by that form, impelled him to a disclosure of his power, which, like everything else in the doings of the gigantic musician, could only appear incomprehensibly rough.' He elaborates with typical Wagnerian enthusiasm:

> 'We see young Beethoven ... facing the world at once with that defiant temperament which, throughout his life, kept him in almost savage independence: his enormous self-confidence, supported by haughtiest courage, at all times prompted him to defend himself from the frivolous demands made upon music by a pleasure-seeking world ... He was the soothsayer of the innermost of the innermost world of tones, and he had to vary forms in which music was displaying itself as a merely diverting art.'[8]

The Swiss-American conductor, educator, and scholar Leon Botstein regards Beethoven's early symphonic achievement as a contribution to the transformation of the tradition of the 'sublime and the dignified' — as quintessentially exemplified in the symphonies of Mozart — 'towards monumentality, dramatic intensity, and universality, conceived in a political and social as well as an aesthetic sense'. He cites the pioneering writings of the German musicologist Paul Bekker, who placed emphasis on the 'monumentality' in Beethoven's orchestral music — 'with its anticipations of the extended symphonies of Bruckner and Mahler'. Similarly, he invokes the spirit of the multi-faceted Ernst Theodor Amadeus Hoffmann for whom Beethoven's instrumental music 'unveils before us the realm of the mighty and the immeasurable ... it sets in motion the machinery of awe, of fear, of terror'.[9]

In more restrained and musicological terms, Beethoven authority David Wyn Jones writes:

> 'The key, C major, could not be more conservative, chosen not because it was the key of Mozart's last symphony or one of the latest symphonies by Haydn that he would have known, No. 97 (1792), but because it enabled the Symphony to take its place amongst any number of C major works with trumpets and timpani composed in the eighteenth century; other recent examples include two by [Adelbert] Gyrowetz (C1 and C4), one by [Franz Anton] Hoffmeister (C2), three by [Ignaz] Pleyel (B128, B 131, and B143), four by Paul Wranitzky (P2, P5, and P14), and two by Anton Wranitzky (C1, and C2).'[10]

Towards the end of his life, support for Beethoven was expressed in 1826 in the pages of the Leipzig journal *Allgemeine musikalische Zeitung* ('General musical Magazine'). The subscriber remarked:

> '[Some] critics believed Beethoven had abandoned well-known ideas such as unity, simplicity, beauty, clarity, melody, and nature when he ceased to follow the path of Mozart, others saw his discoveries not as a departure from Mozart but as an "artistic deed" that "opened the romantic world in which Mozart's dramatic music moves, for instrumental music too".'

In the sister journal, the Berliner *Allgemeine musikalische Zeitung*, the composer-theorist Gottfried Wilhelm Fink enthused, in figurative prose characteristic of the period:

> 'Beethoven ascended like a youth decorated with all the colours of spring. He seats himself upon mountains. Wildly his steeds rush forth: brooding, he holds the reins firmly so that they rear at the precipice. He, however, peers into the abyss as if he had buried something down there. Then he bounds across the gaping crevices and proceeds home, playing as if in mockery or blustering as if in a storm.'[11]

The American musicologist Raymond Knapp has written about the challenge Johannes Brahms had to confront, in the genre of symphonic composition, following on from Beethoven's inheritance. Regarding the latter, Knapp maintains:

> '[The] symphony ... after Beethoven had come to represent, to both its champions and detractors, the pinnacle of absolute music. Beethoven's symphonies were, for the nineteenth century, his most important and vital legacy, demonstrating more than any other body of work both the power

and, for doubters, the limitations of "pure" discourse.'

He further asserts:

> 'The symphonies themselves provided ample justification for either perspective, with a funeral march, bird calls, a storm, and an eventual recourse to words testifying to Beethoven's own discontent with pure musical expression on the one hand, countered on the other by a fervent conviction that such intrusions were overwhelmed by and absorbed into the larger musical argument.'[12]

It is often remarked how Beethoven is a bridge that links the eighteenth century and the nineteenth and, thereby, that he spans the Classical and Romantic periods of music. In this context, we cite Paul Mies once more:

> '[Beethoven] stands, at least superficially, in the eighteenth-century relationship of the composer to his patron. His patrons were, to begin with, the Electoral Court in Bonn; Count Waldstein [with his note of encouragement] for his journey to Vienna ["Receive Mozart's spirit from the hands of Haydn"]; and subsequently the noble families of that city, in whose house he gave concerts and lessons and also found [influential] friends.'[13]

Soon after his arrival in Vienna, Beethoven began to publish. He issued piano works that would appeal to amateur pianists, notably sets of piano variations and, through the medium of the keyboard, he exploited popular melodies; consider, for example, his Twelve Variations on *Si vuol ballare* (WoO 40) from Act One of Mozart's *Figaro*. Through his prowess at the keyboard, Beethoven quickly established a position as a social favourite amongst the nobility. His reputation, in 1795, was assisted by his publication, by subscription, of his Piano Trios, Op. 1. The subscription list carried a hundred and twenty-three names representing the social, intellectual, and musical élite of Vienna's high society; the names included those of Prince Kinsky, Prince Lichnowsky, Prince Lobkowitz, Count Rasumovsky, and Count Waldstein.

With regard to publishers, the Vienna house of Artaria & Co. brought out Beethoven's first works, following long-established dealings with such other composers as Haydn and Mozart. Others soon followed. These included Nikolaus Simrock, who conducted his business transactions from Beethoven's home town Bonn, and Franz Anton Hoffmeister, who is perhaps best remembered today for being the dedicatee of Mozart's String Quartet in D major, K. 499 – the *Hoffmeister* Quartet. In 1802, Breitkopf and Härtel collaborated with Beethoven as did the newly formed *Kunst- und Industrie-Comptoir* – also known as the *Bureau des Arts et d'Industrie*. By 1805, Beethoven could ask 700 gulden for his *Eroica* Symphony, the *Waldstein* Piano Sonata, and the Piano Sonatas Opp. 54 and 55. In 1808, he demanded 900 gulden from Breitkopf and Härtel for his Mass in C, the Fifth and Sixth Symphonies, and the Sonata for Cello and Piano, Op. 69. In general, Beethoven set his fees according to the scale and complexity of the work he had in hand. Later in life, as publishers vied amongst each other for his compositions; he was prepared to set off one against another – sometimes nefariously!

With his Symphony in C major, Op. 21, Beethoven gave inception to a genre of orchestral music that is still today central to orchestral-music performance-culture. In his own lifetime he was acknowledged as the composer whose music most embodied the concept of heroic genius. We cite once more the words of E. T. A. Hoffman:

> 'The genius-artist lives only for the work which he understands as the composer understood it and which he now performs ... All his thoughts and actions are directed towards the bringing into being all the wonderful, enchanting pictures and impressions the composer sealed in his work with magical power.'[14]

---

[1] David Wyn Jones, *The symphony in Beethoven's Vienna*, .2006, pp. 158–59. See also: Elliot Forbes, editor *Thayer's Life of Beethoven*, 1967, pp. 173–74.

[2] Paul Mies, *Beethoven's Orchestral Works* in: *The Age of Beethoven, The New Oxford History of Music, Vol. VIII*, Gerald Abraham, editor, 1988, p. 120.

[3] Perhaps a parallel can be drawn here with Brahms who similarly delayed the composition of his first symphony – in part intimidated by Beethoven's legacy in the genre. And when he did so he had to suffer the ignominy of having his creation declared as 'Beethoven's Tenth'!

[4] Maynard, Solomon, *Beethoven Essays*, 1988, pp. 116–17. The words cited have been slightly adapted.

[5] See, for example, the writings of Barry Cooper, 1990 *Beethoven and the Creative Process*, and 2000, *Beethoven: The Master Musicians*.

[6] Douglas Johnson in: Alan Tyson, editor, *Beethoven Studies 3*, 1982, p. 1.

[7] Anton Felix Schindler, *Beethoven as I Knew Him*, edited by Donald W. MacArdle and translated by Constance S. Jolly from the German edition of 1860, 1966, p. 177.

[8] Richard Wagner, *Beethoven: With [a] Supplement from the Philosophical Works of A. Schopenhauer, translated by E. Dannreuther*, 1893, p. 39.

[9] Leon Botstein, *Sound and Structure in Beethoven's Orchestral Music* in: Glenn Stanley, editor, *The Cambridge Companion to Beethoven*, 2000, p. 166.

[10] David Wyn Jones, *The symphony in Beethoven's Vienna* 2006, p. 159.

[11] As quoted in: William M. Senner, Robin Wallace and William Meredith, editors, *The Critical Reception of Beethoven's Compositions by his German Contemporaries*, 1999, Vol. 1, p. 2.

[12] Raymond Knapp, *Brahms and the Challenge of the Symphony* c.1997, pp. 195–96.

[13] Paul Mies, *Beethoven's Orchestral Works* in: *The Age of Beethoven, The New Oxford History of Music, Vol. VIII*, Gerald Abraham, editor, 1988, p. 124.

[14] E. T. A. Hoffman, quoted by Alain Frogley, *Beethoven's Music in Performance: Historical Perspectives* in: Glenn Stanley, editor, *The Cambridge Companion to Beethoven*, 2000, p. 261.TMR

EDITORIAL PRINCIPLES

By its very nature a study of this kind draws extensively on the work of others. Every effort has been made to acknowledge this in the text by indicating words quoted or adapted with single quotation marks. Wherever possible, for the sake of consistency, I have retained the orthography of quoted texts making only occasional silent changes of spelling and capitalization. Deleted words are identified by means of three ellipsis points ... and interpolations are encompassed within square brackets [ ]. Quoted words, phrases and longer cited passages of text remain the intellectual property of their copyright holders.

I address the reader in the second person notwithstanding that the work is my own — produced without the benefit of a desk editor. It follows that I must bear the responsibility for any errors of misunderstanding or misinterpretation for which I ask the reader's forbearance. A collaboration I must acknowledge is the help I received from the librarians of the *Reid Music Library* at the University of Edinburgh. Over the three-year period it took me to compile my reference sources, they served me with unfailing courtesy, often supplying me with twenty or more books at a time. In converting my manuscript into book-format, I wish to thank my editorial coordinator, William Rees, for his support and painstaking care. I would also like to thank Shaun Russell (no relation) for his work designing the covers for each of the volumes.

My admiration for Beethoven provided the initial impulse to commence this undertaking and has sustained me over the several years it has taken to bring my enterprise to completion. That said I am no Beethoven idolater. I am mindful of the danger that awaits one who ventures to chronicle the work of a great artist. I believe it was Sigmund Freud who suggested that biographers may become so disposed to their subject, and their emotional involvement with their hero, that their work becomes an exercise in idealisation. In response to such a putative charge let me say. First, I am no biographer. I do however make occasional reference to Beethoven's personal life and his relationships with his contemporaries. Second, I acknowledge Beethoven has his detractors. Accordingly, I have not shrunk from allowing dissentient voices critical of Beethoven and his work to be heard. These, however, are few and are silenced amidst the adulation that awaits the reader in support of the endeavours of one of humanity's great creators and one who courageously showed the way in overcoming personal adversity.

TMR

BEETHOVEN'S FINANCIAL TRANSACTIONS

Beethoven's negotiations with his music publishers make many references to his compositions. Today they are recognised for what they are — enduring works of art — but referred to in his business correspondence they appear almost as though they were mere everyday commodities — for which he required an appropriate remuneration. Beethoven resented the time he had to devote to the business-side of his affairs. He believed an agency should exist, for fellow artists such as himself, from which a reasonable sum could be paid for the work (composition) submitted, leaving more time for creative enterprises. In the event Beethoven, like Mozart before him, had to deal with publishers largely on his own. Beethoven, though, did benefit in his business dealings from the help he received from his younger brother Kasper Karl (Caspar Carl). From 1800, Carl worked as a clerk in Vienna's Department of Finance in which capacity he found time to correspond with publishers to offer his brother's works for sale and — importantly — to secure the best prices he could. In April 1802 Beethoven wrote to the Leipzig publishers Breitkopf & Härtel: '[You] can rely entirely on my brother who, in general, attends to my affairs.' Whilst Carl promoted Beethoven's interests with determination, he appears to have lacked tact and made enemies. For example, Beethoven's piano pupil Ferdinand Ries — who for a while also helped the composer with his business negotiations — is on record as describing Carl as being 'the biggest skinflint in the world'.

The currencies most referred to in Beethoven's correspondence are as follows:

> Silver gulden and florin: these were interchangeable and had a value of about two English shillings.
> Ducat: 4 1/2 gulden / florins: valued at about nine shillings.
> Louis d'or: This gold coin was adopted during the Napoleonic wars and the French occupation of Vienna and Austria more widely. It had a value of about two ducats or approximately twenty shillings or one-pound sterling.

Beethoven was never poor — in the romantic sense of 'an artist starving in a garret'. On arriving in Vienna in 1792, he was fortunate to receive financial support from his patron Prince Karl Lichnowsky who conferred on him an annuity of 600 florins — that he maintained for several years. Between the months of February and July of 1796, Beethoven undertook a concert tour taking in Prague,

Dresden, Leipzig and Berlin. He was well-received and wrote to his other younger brother Nikolaus Johann: 'My art is winning me friends and what more do I want? ... I shall make a good deal of money.' Later on, in 1809, Napoleon Bonaparte's youngest brother Jérôme Bonaparte offered Beethoven an appointment at his Court with the promise of an income of 4,000 florins. Alarmed at the prospect of losing Beethoven — now the most celebrated composer in Europe — three of Vienna's most notable citizens, namely, the Archduke Rudolph (Beethoven's only composition pupil), Prince Kinsky and Prince Lobkowitz settled on the composer the same sum of 4,000 florins. Inflation, however, brought about by the Napoleonic wars, soon eroded its value; personal misfortune to Lobkowitz and Kinsky also took its toll.

Beethoven undoubtedly had to work hard to secure a reasonable standard of living. Notwithstanding, despite his occasional straitened circumstances, he contributed generously to the needs of others. For example, he allowed his works to be performed at charitable concerts without seeking any benefit to himself; in 1815 his philanthropy earned for him the honour of Bürgerrecht — 'freedom of the City'.

Beethoven earned a great deal of money when his music was performed, to considerable acclaim, at several concerts held in association with the Congress of Vienna (1814–15). He did not, though, benefit from it personally; he invested it on behalf of his nephew Karl. It is one of the misfortunes of Beethoven's life that in money-matters he was in somewhat culpably improvident. This is poignantly evident in a letter he wrote on 18 March 1827 to the Philharmonic Society of London — just one week before his death; the Society had made him a gift of £100. He sent the Society 'his most heartfelt thanks for their particular sympathy and support'.

In 1806, the music correspondent to the Allgemeine musikalische Zeitung reflected on Beethoven's First Symphony that had now become established in Vienna's concert repertoire. He remarked:

Beethoven wrote his First Symphony in C Major, a masterpiece that does equal honour to his inventiveness and his musical knowledge. Being just as beautiful and distinguished in its design as its execution, there prevails in it such a clear and lucid order, such a flow of the most pleasant melodies, and such a rich, but at the same time never wearisome, instrumentation that this Symphony can justly be placed next to Mozart's and Haydn's

As cited in Wayne M. Senner, Robin Wallace and William Meredith editors, The Critical Reception of Beethoven's Compositions by his German Contemporaries, Lincoln: University of Nebraska Press, in association with the American Beethoven Society and the Ira F. Brilliant Center for Beethoven Studies, San José State University, 1999. Vol. 1, pp. 168-69.

SELECTED WRITINGS

We open our account of Beethoven's First Symphony in C major, Op. 21 with a selection of writings that convey the regard for this composition as variously expressed by musicologists and musicians. The texts selected derive from various periods and reflect the differing styles of expression and register of language characteristic of their time. Thereby, they convey the evolving estimation felt for this work from the period of its first appearance to closer to the present day.

ALLGEMEINE MUSIKALISCHE ZEITUNG (AMZ)
The *Allgemeine musikalische Zeitung* (*General music newspaper*) was a German language periodical that commenced publication in 1798 under the direction of its owner and

founder Gottfried Christoph Härtel. Its publisher was Breitkopf & Härtel of Leipzig with whom Beethoven had many negotiations. The periodical reviewed musical events taking place in the German-speaking nations and in other countries. As such, it was amongst the first to bring to the attention of the musically minded public an awareness of Beethoven's compositions and of their originality — that the periodical's contributors frequently found to be disturbing. In 1800 the *AmZ* published a review ostensibly in celebration of Joseph Haydn to whom it accorded 'the first place' with regard to his symphonies and quartets, 'wherein no one has yet surpassed him'. Beethoven, a still relatively unknown composer, is not, however, overlooked; the reviewer comments how he may even usurp the venerable master 'if he calms his wild imaginings'. In due course the *Allgemeine musikalische Zeitung* received news of Beethoven's compositions with increasing respect. A music critic, writing in issue XXVI of the *AmZ* of 1824, acknowledged Beethoven's works 'engendered hostility on the way' but conceded 'all that is now stilled for today no other can touch this great spirit'.

Commenting on the first performance of the First Symphony, that had taken place on 2 April 1800, the *AmZ* critic's remarked:

> '[The Symphony] contained considerable art, novelty and a wealth of ideas. The only flaw was that the wind instruments were used too much so that there was more harmony than orchestral music as a whole.'

After hearing Beethoven's First and Second Symphonies and his Oratorio *Christus am Ölberg*, performed at the Theater-an-der-Wien on 4 April 1803, the *AmZ's* music correspondent enthused:

> 'It confirms my long-held opinion that Beethoven in time can effect a revolution in music like Mozart's. He is hastening towards this goal with great strides.'

Elliot Forbes editor, *Thayer's Life of Beethoven*, Princeton, New Jersey: Princeton University Press, 1967, p. 255 and p. 330.

In 1806, the music correspondent to the *AmZ* reflected on Beethoven's First Symphony that had now become established in the concert repertoire:

> 'Beethoven wrote his First Symphony in C Major, a masterpiece that does equal honour to his inventiveness and his musical knowledge. Being just as beautiful and distinguished in its design as its execution, there prevails in it such a clear and lucid order, such a flow of the most pleasant melodies, and such a rich, but at the same time never wearisome, instrumentation that this symphony can justly be placed next to Mozart's and Haydn's.'

The editors add:

> 'There is no need to discuss the work here. Since its first appearance, it has been a favourite piece for all full orchestra ... and therefore is renowned and sufficiently recommended.'

On 13 November 1822 the *AmZ* announced the first, continental, publication of the C major Symphony in full score:

'We are familiar with the beautiful Paris edition of Haydn's symphonies engraved by Pleyel in full score. Beethoven's First Symphony appears here in the same format, in the same arrangement, and engraved just as beautifully.'

The edition referred to was that by the Bonn publisher Nikolaus Simrock; an edition had already appeared in January-February 1809 by the London publishers Cianchettini & Sperati, although without Beethoven's knowledge.

In the May 1824 issue of the *Berliner Allgemeine musikalische Zeitung*, the German musicologist Adolf Bernhard Marx reflected on Beethoven's achievement in the symphonic repertoire. He made passing reference to the composer's earliest works in the genre:

'The First [Symphony] can be called Mozartian without hesitation; the Second is written in a similar spirit, but is expanded more and therefore goes beyond Mozartian symphonies.'

Wayne M. Senner, Robin Wallace and William Meredith, editors, *The Critical Reception of Beethoven's Compositions by his German Contemporaries*, Lincoln: University of Nebraska Press, in association with the American Beethoven Society and the Ira F. Brilliant Center for Beethoven Studies, San José State University, 1999, Vol. 1 p. 64, p. 164, and pp. 171–72.

WILHELM ALTMANN
Wilhelm Altmann was a German historian and musicologist who held the post of Librarian at the Royal (later State)

Library in Berlin, where he was also Director of its Music Department. He was the author of several books on music but is perhaps now best remembered for his scholarly introductions to the editions of miniature scores by such publishers as Eulenburg. From one of these we cite the following:

> 'Beethoven had already conceived the plan of a symphony in his early Bonn period. Gustav Nottebohm (*Zweite Beethoveniana*, 1887, p. 567) prints from sketches the opening of a C minor movement labelled "Sinfonia" that corresponds to the beginning of the first Allegro of the Second Quartet [Op. 18, No. 2], composed in 1785. The same scholar (p. 228) also found sketches for a Symphony in C major on which Beethoven must have been working in 1794 and early 1795, but never completed. These sketches, which Nottebohm (*Beethoveniana*, p. 202) at first erroneously connected with the Symphony published as No. 1, have no relation to the Symphony in C major published by Fritz Stein in 1911 from old parts of the Akademisches Konzert in Jena, founded in 1780.'

Wilhelm Altmann, *Beethoven: Symphony No. 1 in C major*, Introduction to Score, Dover Publications, 1976 (reprint).

PAUL BEKKER

The German music critic and musicologist Paul Bekker is remembered for his study of Beethoven (1911). Placing Beethoven in the context of other composers, he contends:

'Compared with the works of other musicians of the first rank, Beethoven's compositions are few in number and restricted in kind; a glance at the collected works of Bach, Handel, Haydn and of the short-lived Mozart and Schubert confirms this. But to deduce that Beethoven was therefore less creatively fertile would be wrong. The explanation lies in the peculiar nature of his genius as an artist. He was first a thinker and poet, and secondarily a musician. He never subordinated his ideas to the limitations of tone or of his craft. His whole work is ever a struggle of idea with tone-material, which he made for ever more adaptable, more expressive as a vehicle of thought, It is this process, with its many difficulties, which accounts for Beethoven's slow development and the comparative fewness of his works. The thought-infused nature of his art and the types of problem which he chose for artistic treatment demanded evolution and continuous refinement of style.'

Of Beethoven's First Symphony Bekker avers:

'The music bears unmistakably the stamp of Beethoven, but has not the tremendous power of his later work. It is however, greatly in advance of contemporary productions, and its grave yet cheerful manliness must prevent us from calling it a "youthful work" in any sense ... The immediate and widespread success of the C major Symphony goes to show that Beethoven's contemporaries overlooked the germs of promise for the future in the work and were principally concerned with those features which accorded with the taste of the period ... Many ... critics of the time made Beethoven's First Symphony the measure of the value of those which followed, and always upon the ground of its conservative elements.'

Paul Bekker, *Beethoven*, London: J. M. Dent & Sons, 1925, p. 149, pp. 150–51 and pp. 337–39. (See also the entry to Leon Botstein relating to Paul Bekker)

JOHN BLACKING
In his essay 'Expressing Human Experience through Music', the British ethnomusicologist and anthropologist John Blacking expressed his views on the nature of artistic creations — bearing upon his wider belief in music's social and cultural virtues:

'Artistic products are not simply semi-ritualized, abstract expressions of cultural forms: they are conscious comments on the human condition, expressing the dynamic relationships between nature and humanity, and between people, as they exist in different cultures at different moments ... The purpose of art is to capture force with form: the force of individual human experience and the form of collective cultural experience, of certain given orders of relationships, social, musical, and otherwise. If artists want to communicate the force of their experience to others, they must base their work on given forms of expression even if they find it necessary to revise the rules.'

*

Having outlined his intellectual construct, Blacking then makes reference to the C minor Symphony:

> 'There was nothing new about the dominant seventh chord on C when Beethoven wrote his First Symphony; but to begin a symphony in C major on that chord, and promptly to resolve it with the chord of F minor, was a cultural shock to a contemporary audience, and an imposition of Beethoven's personal vision on the forms of his society.'

As cited in: Reginald Byron, *Music, Culture, & Experience: Selected Papers of John Blacking*. Chicago, 1995, p. 52.

LEON BOTSTEIN

The Swiss-American Leon Botstein is an educator, music scholar and President of Bard College. In writing about Beethoven's First Symphony he recognised the composer's debt to Mozart and Haydn. However, even in this early symphonic work, Botstein, making reference to the writings of Paul Bekker, argued Beethoven had wider musical agendas than his predecessors:

> 'Symphony No. 1 ... has suffered by comparison, owing to its reputation as being Haydnesque and less truly Beethovenian in the sense established by Symphonies Three and Five ... Beethoven opened up the sonic power implicit in the orchestral forces of Mozart and Haydn, and the symphony now became more than a sonata for orchestra. [Paul] Bekker [*Beethoven*, 1925]

suggested that Beethoven composed with a new "idealized picture of the space and listening public" in mind; his goal was to reach a "mass" public with the symphony, and to create a "community" through the act of shared listening. That community was far reaching, representing humankind, a spectrum of listeners that extended beyond the aristocracy and embraced those liberated from the shackles of the past by the ideas and events surrounding the French Revolution ... He did not strive to emulate "beauty" in music in a manner readily appreciated by a public convinced of its refined sensibilities ... [He] departed from a reliance on Mozartian melodies as thematic subjects in the symphony and showed a marked preference for "easily grasped" and "riveting" motivic gestures.'

Leon Botstein, *Sound and Structure in Beethoven's Orchestral Music* in: Glenn Stanley, editor, *The Cambridge Companion to Beethoven*, Cambridge; New York: Cambridge University Press, 2000, p. 165 and p. 169.

JOSEPH BRAUNSTEIN

Joseph Braunstein was a Viennese-born American musicologist who lived to the great age of 104. He was born when Johannes Brahmas was still alive and, as a young violinist and violist, played at the Vienna State Opera in performances of *Salome, Elektra, Der Rosenkavalier* and *Die Frau Ohne Schatten* under the baton of their composer Richard Strauss. For a generation of musically inclined Americans, Braunstein will be remembered for the programme notes for the Chamber Music Society of the Lincoln Center and, most notably, for the Chamber Orchestra *Musica Aeterna*; in published form they fill three volumes. Braunstein's writings have been described as 'combining scholarly detail and analysis with a sense of atmosphere that conveyed something of a composer's milieu'.

Writing of Beethoven's First Symphony, he opens with the following remarks:

> 'The lustrum between Haydn's last symphonies (1795) and Beethoven's first (1800) represents a vacuum in the development of the symphony. During this time no symphony was produced that could secure a place in the orchestral repertory, although hundreds of symphonies were written in the closing years of the eighteenth century ... Beethoven's First is still an eighteenth-century symphony as is also his second. The starting point of the road that led to the symphonies of Brahms, Bruckner, and Mahler, and which was still to be reached. Beethoven arrived at it in the *Eroica*, his third.'

Joseph Braunstein, *Musica Aeterna, Program Notes for 1971–1976*, New York: *Musica Aeterna*, 1978, pp. 29–30.

BARRY COOPER

The British musicologist Barry Cooper is internationally recognised for his scholarly studies of the life and work of Beethoven. In addition, Beethovenians have him to thank for his reconstruction of a performing edition of the composer's 10th Symphony — from the many surviving sketches that were left incomplete at the time of his death. Pianists are no less in debt to Cooper for his recently released edition of the Piano Sonatas for The Associated Board of the Royal Schools of Music (ABRSM).

Commenting on Beethoven's First Symphony, Cooper bears testimony to the composer's attachment to the style of symphonic writing he inherited from Mozart and Haydn

> 'Although he did not complete his First Symphony until the age of twenty-nine, Beethoven's style of orchestral writing was close to that of his Viennese predecessors and did not change radically over the next quarter-century, certain passages and effects notwithstanding. The strings still dominate the texture, as they had done in Haydn's and Mozart's symphonies; and if the woodwind appear to be more prominent as early as the First Symphony, this can perhaps be traced to the orchestral textures of Mozart's mature piano concertos (a repertory Beethoven knew intimately), where the wind collectively contribute as much as the keyboard soloist to the concertante style.'

Cooper, elaborates:

> 'One notes an early interest in the cello (often doubled by the violas) as an important melodic voice; this too can be traced via the string quartet tradition, back to Mozart. Perhaps the most important "new" feature of Beethoven's orchestration lies in the designing of themes for instruments incapable of playing melodies; thus, some of the most memorable moments in Beethoven's orchestral compositions feature instruments not normally given solo parts by

Haydn and Mozart, viz. the horns (in virtually every symphony from the *Eroica* onwards) and the tympani (in exposed passages from the last three symphonies).'

Barry Cooper, *The Beethoven Compendium: A Guide to Beethoven's Life and Music*, London: Thames and Hudson, 1991, pp. 203–04.

BASIL DEANE

Samuel Basil Deane was an Irish musicologist and held a number of high-level academic posts including those of professor of music at the Universities of Sheffield, Manchester and Birmingham. He was also the author of a number of composers' biographies and other writings on music. He considered Beethoven's First Symphony already revealed the hallmarks of the composer's individuality:

'Beethoven's First Symphony (C major, Op. 21, 1800) has been dismissed as derivative or timid: Edwin Evans, for example, referred to "the composer's hesitation to trust himself too far ahead of his compeers". [Edwin Evans, *Beethoven's Nine Symphonies, fully Described and Annotated,* London, 1924, I, p. 19] But Beethoven never hesitated to advance beyond his contemporaries on his own path, as some of the earliest works show, and the First Symphony, in fact, declares its individuality from the opening bars of the *Adagio molto* introduction. Its originality does not reside in the opening chord itself — a dominant seventh on C — which is reputed, wrongly, to have offended contemporary critics;

but rather in the nature and fusion of the introduction as a whole and in its motivic structure and instrumentation.'

Basil Deane, *The Symphonies and Overtures* in: Denis Arnold and Nigel Fortune editors, *The Beethoven Companion*, London, Faber and Faber, 1973, pp. 281–82.

PHILIP G. DOWNS

The American musicologist Philip G. Downs remarks on 'the spacious grandeur' to be found in Beethoven's music:

'The tendency towards the grandiose was always a pronounced feature of the Beethoven style. In the earliest published works there is an obvious enlargement of the scale of operations of Haydn and Mozart which undoubtedly is prompted by the fashion of the times, but which one cannot help suspecting is also partly a conscious assertion of Beethoven's independence, if not superiority.'

Of Beethoven's First Symphony he maintains:

'To many listeners today the First Symphony sounds so orthodox – so like the symphonies of Haydn and Mozart in structure – that it is all too easy to forget the work's first critic found it "full of art and novelty, and rich in ideas". [This is a reference to the music correspondent of the *Allgemeine musikalische Zeitung* of October 1800] That first critic was perceptive when he wrote "the wind instruments were used far too much, so that it sounded more like wind-band music than music for the full orchestra". Before the turn of the century, Beethoven had grasped one of the ways of the future, and his first novelty lies in the strength of his writing for the winds, wood and brass, and in the consequent diminishing of the role of the strings.'

Philip G. Downs, *Classical Music: The Era of Haydn, Mozart, and Beethoven*, New York: W.W. Norton, 1992, p. 592 and pp. 597–98.

DONALD JAY GROUT, AND CLAUDE V. PALISCA
The American born Donald Grout and the Italian born Claude Palisca — both musicologists — position the musicological character of Beethoven's First Symphony:

'The First [Symphony] is the most Classic of the nine symphonies. Its spirit and many of its technical features stem from Haydn; all four movements are so regular in form that they might serve as textbook models. Beethoven's originality is evident not in the large formal outlines but in the details of his treatment, and also in the unusual prominence given to the woodwinds, in the character of the third movement — a scherzo, though labelled a minuet — and especially in the long and important codas of the other movements.'

Donald Jay Grout, and Claude V. Palisca, editors, *A History of Western Music*, London: J. M. Dent, 1988, p. 634.

SIR GEORGE GROVE

The name Grove is familiar to generations of music lovers through association with *Grove's Dictionary of Music and Musicians* of which Grove was the inspiration and source. Sir George Grove, however, did not receive a formal education in music and trained as a structural engineer, being admitted as a graduate of the Institution of Civil Engineers. Following a change of career, he was appointed in 1849 to the Secretaryship of the Society of Arts — at the period of gestation of the Great Exhibition of 1851. When the exhibition relocated to Sydenham, in the guise of The Crystal Palace, it was as a result of the actions of Grove that the German-born August Manns was appointed, first as bandmaster and later as the conductor of a full-size orchestra. Manns presided over regular concerts for more than forty years, Grove providing numerous programme notes that later formed the basis for his *Dictionary*.

Many of Beethoven's works were performed at The Crystal Palace under the direction of August Manns including overtures, concertos, symphonies and choral works. *Fidelio* received a concert performance in 1859 and in 1866 the resident orchestra had to be augmented for a rendering of the *Eroica* Symphony that was billed as 'a special event'. The occasion of Queen Victoria's Diamond Jubilee in 1894 offered *The Musical Times* the chance to review some of the significant musical activities that had taken place at The Crystal Palace in its preceding forty-or-so years of concert life. Sir George Grove was singled out for being a 'very natural exhibitor' and for promoting the works of Beethoven amongst others including Mendelsohn and Schubert. The following year was the 125th anniversary of Beethoven's birth, an event that was commemorated in a special concert devoted entirely to works by the composer, namely: Overture *Prometheus*; First Symphony, slow movement; *Emperor* Piano Concerto;

Ah! Perfido, *Eroica* Symphony; a selection of songs; and to conclude the Overture *Leonora* No. 3.

Writing about Beethoven's First Symphony, Grove remarked:

> 'On hearing this Symphony, we can never forget that it is the first of that mighty and immortal series which seem destined to remain the greatest monuments of music, as Raphael's best pictures are still the monuments of the highest point reached by the art of painting, notwithstanding all that has been done since. Schuman has somewhere made the just remark that the early works of great men are to be regarded in quite a different light from those of writers who never had a future. In Beethoven's case this is most true and interesting, and especially so with respect to the First Symphony. Had he died immediately after completing it, it would have occupied a very different position from what it now does. It would have been judged and loved on its merits; but we should never have guessed of what grander beauties and glories it was destined to be the harbinger, or have known the pregnant significance of its Minuet.'

George Grove, *Beethoven and his Nine Symphonies*, London: Novello, Ewer, 1896, p. 1.

GEORGE HOGARTH

George Hogarth was a Scottish, Age of Enlightenment Polymath. He was an accomplished cellist, composer, music critic, musicologist, newspaper editor, lawyer, and the author of seven volumes of music biography and criticism. He was music critic to The Harmonicon and later served as Secretary to the Royal Philharmonic Society. In his Musical History, Biography and Criticism (1838) he wrote discerningly of Beethoven:

> 'As a musician, Beethoven must be classed along with Handel, Haydn, and Mozart. He alone is to be compared to them in the magnitude of his works, and their influence on the state of the art ... In his music there is the same gigantic grandeur of conception, the same breadth and simplicity of design ... In Beethoven's harmonies the masses of sound are equally large ...As they swell in our ears, and grow darker and darker, they are like the lowering storm-cloud on which we gaze ... Such effects he has especially produced in his symphonies.'

George Hogarth, as quoted in: Denis Arnold and Nigel Fortune, editors, *The Beethoven Companion*, London: Faber and Faber, 1973, pp. 502–03.

DAVID WYN JONES

David Wyn Jones is a British musicologist who has made a special study of the music of the Classical period with particular regard to the works of Haydn and Beethoven. He suggests Beethoven's First Symphony should be regarded as being primarily a work of consolidation of the legacy of the symphonic writing of his teacher Haydn:

> 'People have always scrutinized the First Symphony for prophetic hints of the later and greater

Beethoven, of which there are undoubtedly many, but looked at in context as the culmination of a decade of exploration of instrumental composition, it is a cautious work. Less ambitious than many other earlier instrumental works by Beethoven, including the aborted C major Symphony, it shows the composer writing well within himself. The *London* Symphonies (Nos. 93–104) of Joseph Haydn, in particular No. 97 in C, provided the stimulus for Beethoven: the challenge he accepted was to compose in this up-to-date manner.'

David Wyn Jones, Liner notes to *Beethoven, Symphonies 1 & 6*, The London Classical Players, EMI CDC 7497462, 1988. (See also David Wyn Jones later writings cited below)

In his later writing about Beethoven's First Symphony Jones places the composer's use of its key of C major within the genre of its use by other of his contemporary composers:

'The key, C major, could not be more conservative, chosen not because it was the key of Mozart's last symphony or one of the latest symphonies by Haydn that he would have known, No. 97 (1792), but because it enabled the Symphony to take its place amongst any number of C major works with trumpets and timpani composed in the eighteenth century; other recent examples include two by [Adelbert] Gyrowetz (C1 and C4), one by [Franz Antonn] Hoffmeister (C2), three by [Ignaz] Pleyel (B128, B 131, and B143), four by Paul Wranitzky (P2, P5, and P14), and two by Anton Wranitzky (C!, and C2) ... No-one would wish to deny the striking craftsmanship and energy of the First Symphony, even more so the composer's ability to play consequences with the language of music.'

David Wyn Jones, *The Symphony in Beethoven's Vienna*, Cambridge: Cambridge University Press, 2006, p. 159 and p. 161.

WILLIAM KINDERMAN

The American pianist and musicologist William Kinderman expresses his admiration for Beethoven's first attempt at symphonic composition:

'One of the first significant works in which the brilliant young pianist-composer staked a claim to the universal legacy of the Viennese Classical style was his Symphony in C major, Op. 21, completed in 1800. Stylistically, the First Symphony is firmly rooted in the eighteenth century, especially the graceful *Andante cantabile con moto* in F major, with its rococo rhetoric, and the playfully humorous Haydnesque Finale. Bolder and more progressive are the first movement, with its impressive slow introduction and resourceful orchestration highlighting the woodwinds, and especially the dance movement, in the penultimate position.'

William Kinderman, *Beethoven*, Oxford: Oxford University Press, 1997, pp. 52–53.

GUSTAV MAHLER

During a conversation about Beethoven, Mahler is reported to have said:

> 'In order to understand and appreciate Beethoven fully, we should not only accept him for what he means to us today, but must realize what a tremendous-revolutionary advance he represents in comparison with his forerunners. Only when we understand what a difference there is between Mozart's G minor Symphony and the Ninth can we properly evaluate Beethoven's achievement. Of geniuses like Beethoven, of such sublime and most universal kind, there are only two or three among millions. Among poets and composers of more recent times we can, perhaps, name but three: Shakespeare Beethoven and Wagner.'

In the 1900–01 concert season, Gustav Mahler celebrated Beethoven's birthday by conducting his First and Fourth Symphonies and the *Coriolan* Overture. Natalie Bauer-Lechner, a violist and devoted admirer of Mahler, writes:

> 'Of the First, he said to me on the eve of the performance that it was Haydn, raised to the highest degree of perfection. And that it was Beethoven's good fortune! For precisely this fact gave him access to his contemporaries. They could find a link with what they already understood — whereas he himself, the later, totally individual Beethoven, would have seemed to them completely incomprehensible.'

Bauer-Lechner further remarks:

> 'In answer to a question of mine, he called Beethoven the father and true founder of humour in music, exclaiming: "What humour there is in his C major Symphony and the *Pastoral!*" '

Natalie Bauer-Lechner, *Recollections of Gustav Mahler*, London: Faber Music, 1980, pp. 29–30, p. 174, p. 161 and p. 179.

WILLIAM STEDMAN PRESTON

William Stedman Preston is an American music educator, composer and musicologist. Throughout his long life — at the time of writing he is approaching his centenary — he has held a number of important offices in America's music life including that of Director of Western Opera, San Francisco Opera and Vice President of the Pacific Symphony Orchestra.

Writing of Beethoven's First Symphony, Preston positions the composition in the genre of the classical symphony:

> 'The composer's First Symphony is one of his more classically oriented symphonies. Scored for the classical orchestra of winds in pairs (including clarinets), the work conforms to the classical symphonic outline with the exception of its use of sonata-allegro form in its second movement, the appearance of a scherzo-like minuet third movement, and the addition of lengthy coda to the Finale.'

Stedman Preston, *The Symphony*, Englewood Cliffs, New Jersey; London: Prentice-Hall, 1979, p.65.

MAYNARD SOLOMON

The American musicologist Maynard Solomon is recognised for being an authority on Beethoven. His work, although not without its critics, is characterised by a scholarly presentation of the available evidence and the construction of plausible hypotheses. In his Introduction to his *Beethoven*, he writes:

> 'The proper study of Beethoven is based on contemporary documents — on letters, diaries, Conversation Books, court and parish records, autograph manuscripts and sketches, music publications reviews, concert programmes, and similar materials. These may be utilized by a biographer with relative confidence as to their authenticity, although even they ... must be approached with some caution. A second major source of material bearing significantly on Beethoven's life and personality consists of the reminiscences of his contemporaries. Here more serious questions arise as to the validity of anecdotes, reports, and memoirs that were written down long after the fact by a wide variety of individuals.'

Of the origins of Beethoven's First Symphony Solomon comments:

> 'Sketches from the mid-1970s for an unwritten Symphony in C major survive [In footnote 19, Solomon directs the reader to Kerman, *Autograph Miscellany*, II, pp. 166–74, 1900–91], but it was not until 1800 that Beethoven ventured to complete his First Symphony, Op. 21. It was then

five years after Haydn's final effort in this form, and twelve years after Mozart's *Jupiter* Symphony ... In light of the risks involved, as well as the newness of the task, it was natural that Beethoven's First Symphony, scored for the standard orchestra of Haydn and Mozart, with clarinets added, should lean heavily on the traditional inheritance. Perhaps this is why it became one of the most popular of Beethoven's symphonies in his lifetime.'

Maynard Solomon, *Beethoven*, New York: Schirmer, 1977, pp. xi–xii and p. 103.

MICHAEL STEINBERG
The American scholar Michael P. Steinberg is Professor of history, music and German studies at Brown University and was President of the American Academy in Berlin from March 2016 to August 2018. He has written at length about Beethoven, notably in collaboration with fellow American, the musicologist Scott G, Burnham (*Beethoven and his World*, 2000.) In his discussion of Beethoven's début Symphony, Op. 21, he suggests the composer's personality is already evident:

'[Beethoven's First Symphony] is not aggressively "new" music like, for example, the famous *Pathétique* Piano Sonata of 1799, but even in Beethoven's most mannerly works of the first Viennese decade, detail after detail, strategy after strategy, attest to the presence of a personality not at all like Haydn's or Mozart's, and for that matter, to a technical command ever more equal to the task of providing that personality with a voice.'

Michael Steinberg, *The Symphony: A Listener's Guide*, Oxford; New York: Oxford University Press, 1995, p. 6.

CORIANDER STUTTARD

Coriander Stuttard is a London-based freelance writer with a particular interest in Classical music, informed by her graduate studies in violin at the Guildhall School of Music and Drama. In June 2005, she served as Content Producer to BBC Radio Three when all of Beethoven's music was performed in a single week. On that occasion she wrote:

'Beethoven's First Symphony was completed at the beginning of 1800 when he was 30. He had already made several sketches for a symphony but this was the first completed version. The influence of Mozart's wind music led to a critic at the first performance claiming that the wind instruments were used too much, especially as they were not played with any energy. However, for this first performance in Vienna, it was placed alongside a Mozart symphony, an aria from Haydn's *Creation*, Beethoven's Septet Op. 20, and his First Piano Concerto, so that it is not surprising that the musicians perhaps appeared to be lacking in energy by the time it came to the Symphony.'

Coriander Stuttard, *Beethoven: Symphony No. 1 in C major, Op. 21*; *Notes to the BBC Radio Three Beethoven Experience*, Monday 6 June 2005, www.bbc.co.uk/radio3/Beethoven

DONALD FRANCIS TOVEY

The British musicologist, composer, pedagogue and conductor Sir Donald Francis Tovey is best known for his *Essays in Musical Analysis*. They had their origins as programme notes written by him to accompany the concerts given by the Ried Orchestra, Edinburgh — performed largely under Tovey's direction. The *Essays* were published in six volumes with each volume focusing on a particular category of Beethoven's music. Volumes I and II were devoted to the symphonies; Volume III, the concertos; Volume IV, illustrative music, Volume V, vocal music; and Volume VI, supplementary essays. A seventh volume was published posthumously dealing with chamber music. These writings are still respected today for their musicological erudition that Tovey interspersed with passages of wit and mordant humour. His musical analyses seek 'to facilitate the listener's appreciation of [the music's] artistic content and technical merits'. In addition to the *Essays*, Tovey paid tribute to Beethoven and his music in a series of articles that were published in the 1911 edition of the *Encyclopaedia Britannica*.

Writing of Beethoven's First Symphony, Tovey maintains:

> 'Beethoven's First Symphony, produced in 1800, is a fitting farewell to the eighteenth century. It has more of the true nineteenth-century Beethoven in its depths than he allows to appear upon the surface. Its style is that of a Comedy of Manners, as translated by Mozart into the music of his operas and of his most light-hearted works of symphonic and chamber music. The fact that it is comedy from beginning to end is prophetic of changes in music no less profound than those which the French Revolu-

tion brought about in the social organism. But Beethoven was the most conservative of revolutionists; a Revolutionist without the R; and in his First Symphony he shows, as has often been remarked, a characteristic caution in handling sonata form for the first time with a full orchestra ... It is solemn impertinence to suppose that there is anything early or primitive in Beethoven's technique in this symphony. In at least twenty works in sonata form he had already been successful in a range of bold experiments far exceeding that covered by Haydn and Mozart: and it now interested him to write a small and comic sonata for orchestra.'

Donald Francis Tovey, *Essays in Musical Analysis*, London: Oxford University Press, H. Milford, Vol.1, 1935, p. 21 and p. 23.

PAUL WEBSTER

Paul Webster's career in music has embraced a diversity of roles including that of festival director, coach and accompanist, choir master, writer on music, arranger and composer, and teacher of composition. In his capacity as author he remarks:

> 'Beethoven's First Symphony is very familiar to concert-goers, and it's a very easy work for them, but it was very difficult for Beethoven's contemporaries. One of the things he did right at the beginning was to start with a chord that would have not been a permissible way to start a composition if one were Haydn or Mozart. It shocked

his listeners — and he meant it to — because they remembered how a piece of music is supposed to start. So, when you listen to a piece of music for the first time, you're not *really* listening to it for the first time because you are acculturated in the style of that work. A composer of the kind we're talking about plays with surprise and expectations. Sometimes your expectations are fulfilled, sometimes not.'

Paul Webster, *Memory and the Mind* in: Michael Oliver, editor, *Settling the Score: a Journey through the Music of the Twentieth Century*, London: Faber and Faber, 1999.

RALPH VAUGHAN WILLIAMS
Vaughan Williams recalls his first encounter with Beethoven's First Symphony:

'I remember my first practical lesson in orchestration. The school band was playing the slow movement of Beethoven's First Symphony. The violas were quite close to the only horn in the orchestra and my first lesson in orchestral texture came from hearing the holding note on the horn which accompanies the reiterated figure of the violas. I believe I should have made quite a decent fiddler, but the authorities decided that if I was to take up music at all the violin was too "doubtful" a career and I must seek safety on the organ stool, a trade for which I was entirely unsuited; indeed, I have the distinction of being the only pupil who entirely baffled Sir Walter Parratt [organist at St. George's Chapel, Windsor

Castle], though I must add, for my own credit, that I later on passed the F.R.C.O. examination. Sir Hugh Allen [Director of the Royal College of Music, London] always insisted that I must have bribed the examiners!'

Ralph Vaughan Williams, *A Musical Autobiography* in: *Some thoughts on Beethoven's Choral Symphony, with Writings on other Musical Subjects*, London; Oxford University Press, 1953, p. 134.

BEETHOVEN AND BONN

The earliest accounts of the youthful Beethoven derive from the recollections of Gottfried Fischer. His family owned a house in the Rheingasse in Bonn (destroyed in 1944) in which Beethoven lived from about 1775. Fischer recalls Beethoven having lessons on the violin, viola and piano, becoming particularly proficient in the case of the latter. Such was his precocity at the keyboard that, to the annoyance of his father, he was prone to 'playing after his own fashion' — that years later would find its fullest expression in his powers of extemporisation at which his contemporaries acknowledged he was without equal.[1] By June 1784 Beethoven was an official member of the Electoral musical establishment at Bonn. As such he was eligible — one might say obliged — to wear the court musician's livery consisting of a sea-green frock-coat, green knee-breaches, stockings, shoes with bows, a gold embroidered waistcoat, hat — and a sword! The artist Joseph Neesen made a silhouette portrait of the youthful composer that is thought to date from about 1786 when the composer would have been sixteen years old. His lace-trimmed neckerchief and pigtail perruque are clearly discernible. The silhouette most probably derived from an ink drawing that is said to have been created one evening in the house of the prestigious von Breuning family who rendered many services to the young Beethoven — he was almost treated as a member of the family. Beethoven considered the Breunings to be 'the guardian angels of his youth'.[2]

Notwithstanding the reference to Beethoven as violist, it was the piano — more correctly the keyboard — that was central to his musical development both as composer and emerging virtuoso. Under the tutelage of his teacher Christian Gottlob Neefe, at an early age Beethoven mastered *The Well-Tempered Clavier* of J.S. Bach — 'Bach was to be a presence, a beneficent spirit, all his life'.[3] Moreover, such was the youthful Beethoven's prowess that Neefe occasionally allowed his protégé to deputise for him as Court Organist and *cembalist* that involved directing the orchestra from the keyboard and playing at sight from the score. It was Neefe who arranged for the publication of Beethoven's Variations for Piano on a March by Dressler (WoO 63, 1782). Other compositions created under the aegis of Neefe were:

> the three *Kurfürsten* Sonatas, WoO 47 (1783) — published with a dedication to Maximilian Friedrich; the Piano Concerto in E-flat major, WoO 4 (1784);
> the three Piano Quartets, WoO, 36 (1785), between 1782–85;

> the Rondos in C major, WoO 48 and in A major, WoO 49;
> and the Minuet WoO 82.

Beethoven's first major commission though at this period was the Cantata on the Death of the Emperor Joseph II, WoO 87 (1790). In its intensity of feeling it is prophetic of the later Beethoven – and remarkable testimony to the composer's formative years spent as an orchestral player. Although it was intended to be performed at a memorial service, the orchestration proved too challenging for the players and the work was not premiered until 1884. Its sombre tones, however, found expression some years later in the darker passages of the composer's Opera *Leonora / Fidelio*.

In 1791 Carl Ludwig Junker heard Beethoven improvise at the keyboard. Junker had some standing as a dilettante composer and musical pedagogue and served as Chaplain to Prince Hohenlohe at his residence at Kirchberg. He relates:

> 'I heard ... one of the greatest pianists – the dear, good Bethofen [sic] ... I heard him extemporize in private ... I was even invited to propose a theme for him to vary. The greatness of this amiable, light-hearted man, as a virtuoso, may in my opinion be safely estimated from his almost inexhaustible wealth of ideas, the altogether characteristic style of expression in his playing, and the great execution which he displays ... His style of treatment of his instrument is so different from that usually adopted, that it impresses one with the idea, that by a path of his own discovery he has attained that height of excellence whereon he now stands.'[4]

*

We recall Neefe once more. He wrote the first public notice about Beethoven that was published in the 2 March 1783 issue of Cramer's *Magazin der Musik*. He introduced Beethoven as a boy of 'the most promising talent' — giving himself worthy mention as well! Neefe continues:

> 'He plays the clavier very skilfully and with power, reads at sight very well ... plays chiefly *The Well Tempered Clavichord* of Sebastian Bach ... Whoever knows this collection of preludes and fugues in all keys ... will know what this means. So far as his duties permitted, Herr Neefe has also given him instruction in thoroughbass. He is now training him in composition ... The youthful genius is deserving of help to enable him to travel. He would surely become a second Wolfgang Amadeus Mozart were he to continue as he has begun.'[5]

When Beethoven eventually left Bonn for Vienna, to commence his studies with Haydn, he did not forget the debt he owed to his former teacher. On 26 October 1793 he found time to write:

> 'I thank you for the advice you have very often given me about making progress in my divine art. Should I ever become a great man, you too will have a share in my success.[6]

Beethoven's musical appointment, to which we have made reference, was significant. The Elector, Maximilian Franz, was resident at Bonn and was also Archbishop of Cologne. The Electoral Court at Bonn embraced the affairs of the church and state in a fusion of musicians' duties in the genres of music for the church, the theatre, and the concert room. Beethoven's name appears in the Court Calendar of 1788 where he is listed as a viola player. As the composer's pioneering biographer Alexander Wheelock Thayer remarks: Thus, for a period of full four years, he had the opportunity of studying practically compositions in the best of all schools — the orchestra itself.'[7]

The Court orchestra was a large one by contemporary standards and consisted of some forty players. The symphony formed a central part of its repertoire and surviving records list some 650 works, including symphonies by Dittersdorf, Haydn, Mozart, Pleyel, and the now largely forgotten Paul Wranitzky. It is known Beethoven began work on two symphonies during his time in Bonn, one In C minor and one in C major. Writing of these youthful ventures into the symphonic genre, David Wyn Jones comments:

> '[They] reveal the composer's acquaintance with the nervously energetic *Sturm und Drang* idiom ... Although these two symphonies, and perhaps others for which there is no surviving evidence, were not completed, it was only a matter of time before the Bonn composer would have completed a symphony for the Court orchestra.'[8]

Beethoven's writing church cantatas requires further remarks, bearing on his future pupil-teacher relationship with Joseph Haydn. Thayer relates:

> 'When Haydn first came back from England [from his first concert tour], a breakfast was given him by the Electoral Orchestra at Godesberg, a resort near Bonn. At this occasion Beethoven laid

before him a cantata which was noticed especially by Haydn and which made him urge Beethoven to continue his studies [with him in Vienna]. Later this cantata was supposed to be performed in Mergentheim, but several places were [found to be] so difficult for the wind players that some musicians explained that they couldn't be played and the performance was cancelled.'[9]

The cantata in question was probably the Funeral Cantata WoO 78, written in the spring of 1790 in memory of the death of Emperor Joseph II; alternatively, it could have been the cantata written later in the same year in honour of the elevation of Emperor Leopold II, WoO 88.[10] As we shall in due course relate, Beethoven departed Bonn for Vienna in November 1792 to receive the anticipated instruction from Haydn. Meanwhile, his position as Court Organist was kept open and he continued to receive financial support from the Elector. The expectation was that Beethoven would eventually return to Bonn, a more experienced and proficient composer, perhaps even as a future kapellmeister. Our account will reveal the outcome would be very different.

Beethoven's leaving his home town was not without some ceremony. When news of it became more widely known, several of the composer's closest friends inscribed his *Stammbuch* — family album. We supply the names of a selection of these; their aristocratic and social standing is a measure of the esteem already felt for the young composer:

Eleonore von Breuning — for whom Beethoven had written the twelve Piano and Violin Variations WoO 64 — wrote in verse:

> 'Oh, may your good fortune
> Be exactly as I wish for you!

> Then, this year, it will
> Reach its highest goal.'

Johann Joseph Eichoff, the Mayor of Bonn wrote:

> 'So travel forth fine youth! And God's blessing go before you! For my dear Beethoven, with wishes for a prosperous journey, from his loving best friend.'

Johann Martin Degenhart, a lawyer friend and dedicatee of the composer's Duet for two Flutes, WoO 26 wrote:

> 'Yea, I always think
> Of you dearest one, with ardour!
> Sometimes, as you coax love, anger and subtle jokes,
> Mighty Master of Music!'.

Heinrich Struve, an official in the Russian Imperial Service, encouraged Beethoven:

'In the purpose of mankind — To discern *Wisdom*, to love *Beauty*,
To desire *Good*, to do the *Best*.'

These lines are believed to derive from the writings of the philosopher Moses Mendelsohn, grandfather of the composer.

Finally, from a long list of well-wishers, is an entry from Dr. J. H. Crevelt, a physician and an active member in Bonn's intellectual circle. Together with Waldstein (see following) he invoked the spirit of Mozart:

> 'Friend, in sometime at quiet midnight,

> Far from us the magic power of music
> Sinks you into gentle fantasies,
> And exultation pulses through your whole being,
> Mozart's genius hovers over you
> And smiling at you, lends its approbation.'[11]

The most significant contributor to Beethoven's *Stammbuch* was Count Ferdinand von Waldstein, whose name today we associate with the Piano Sonata in C major, Op. 53 — *The Waldstein* — of which he was the dedicatee. Waldstein was eight years older than Beethoven. The two men became acquaintances from about 1788 when Waldstein had been summoned to Bonn to perform official diplomatic duties by Maximilian Franz — the Grand Master of the *Teutonic Order* of which Waldstein was himself a knight. Beethoven's early biographer Franz Gerhard Wegeler describes Waldstein as being 'the first person to recognize Beethoven's great talent' and it is probable he may have rendered discrete financial support, and related assistance, to the young composer. Waldstein had a genuine love of music and for the *Carnival Sunday* of 6 March 1791, the two young men collaborated in writing the music required for the spring aristocratic festivities — a masked ball known as the *Ritterballet* or 'Knight's Ballet' for which the participants dressed in old-style German costume. Waldstein sent Beethoven on his way with the often-quoted words:

> 'You are now going to Vienna in fulfilment of your long-frustrated wishes. Mozart's genius still mourns and is weeping over the death of its pupil ... Through uninterrupted diligence, you shall receive *Mozart's spirit from Haydn's hands.*'[12]

It is to Beethoven and Vienna that we now direct our narrative.

[1] For a fuller account of Beethoven's youth and progress with his musical studies, see: Oscar G. Sonneck, 1927, pp. 3–10 and Peter Clive, 2001, p. 111.
[2] Beethoven House, Digital Archives, Library Document, Wegeler, W 171. Franz Wegeler and Ferdinand Ries adopted Neesen's image for the frontispiece to their pioneering study *Biographische, Notizen über Ludwig van Beethoven* that was published in Koblenz in 1838 and Oscar G. Sonneck's *Beethoven, Impressions by his Contemporaries* (1927 reprint 1967) also included the image. Neesen's silhouette is reproduced in the prefatory pages to H. C. Robbins Landon, 1992. Silhouettes of the von Breuning family can be seen by accessing the Beethoven House website, Older members of the family are depicted taking tea whilst younger members practice the violin.
[3] Michael Steinberg, 1998, p. 50.
[4] *Elliot Forbes editor, Thayer's Life of Beethoven, 1967 pp. 104–05.*
[5] The principal source for this quotation is once more Elliot Forbes editor, pp. 65–66. See also, for example: Oscar George Theodore Sonneck, *Beethoven: Impressions of Contemporaries*, 1927, p. 10 and Maynard Solomon, 1977, p. 27.
[6] Emily Anderson, editor and translator, 1961, Vol. 1, Letter No. 6, p. 9.
[7] Elliot Forbes editor, *Thayer's Life of Beethoven*, 1967 pp. 95–96.
[8] David Wyn Jones, 2006, p. 155.
[9] Elliot Forbes editor, *Thayer's Life of Beethoven*, 1967 pp. 105–06, quoting from Franz *Wegeler, Remembering Beethoven: The Biographical Notes of Franz Wegeler and Ferdinand Ries*, 1988 (reprint) pp. 15–16.
[10] *Ibid.*
[11] All the signatories who signed Beethoven's *Stammbuch*, together with other expressions of affection and esteem for Beethoven, are quoted in full by Theodore Albrecht, 1996, Vol. 1, pp. 10–29.
[12] For an account of Ferdinand Waldstein and his relationship with Beethoven, see: Elliot Forbes editor, *Thayer's Life of Beethoven*, 1967, pp. 91–2 and p. 351; Peter Clive, 2001, pp. 385–7; and Eric Blom, 1938, p. 148. For a comprehensive account of Beethoven's *Stammbuch* and its signatories, see: Theodore Albrecht editor and translator, 1996 Vol. 1, Document No. 13g, pp. 22–3.

BEETHOVEN AND VIENNA

When the Elector Maximilian granted Beethoven leave of absence from his duties in Bonn, he conferred on him an allowance of 100 Viennese thalers (about 150 florins) to cover his basic living expenses. This was about the sum he had been paid in his capacity as assistant organist to Neefe. In Vienna, the cost of living was high. For example, a bachelor living in central Vienna needed an income of at least 960 florins to cover his basic needs and 1200 florins to allow for luxuries and entertainment.[1]

Anxious to secure his continuing financial support, on 23 November 1793, Beethoven wrote a supplicatory letter to Maximilian Franz in which he stated:

> 'My sole endeavour is to render myself absolutely worthy of your Electoral Excellency's highest

favour. With this in view, I have employed this year all the powers of my soul for the benefit of music in order to be able during the coming year to send to your Electoral Excellency something that will reflect your magnanimous treatment of me.' Beethoven is referring here to the works that his teacher Haydn was about to send to Maximilian Franz as testimonies to the progress he had been making in the art of composition.[2]

On the same day, 23 November, Haydn wrote a long letter to the Elector on behalf of his pupil. He listed several compositions composed by Beethoven and offered them as proof of his diligence and application to his studies. He says, prophetically:

> 'On the basis of these pieces, expert and amateur alike cannot but admit that Beethoven will in time become one of the greatest musical artists in Europe, and I shall be proud to call myself his teacher.'

He expressed regret, though, that Beethoven would not remain his pupil for much longer; Haydn departed Vienna for his second concert tour to London on 19 January 1794. He stressed the need for his pupil to receive financial support, asking the Elector if he would allocate him an allowance of 1000 florins to provide for his subsistence and to enable him to continue with his music studies.[3]

A month later the Elector responded curtly and dismissively. He rejected Haydn's testimony, that the compositions he had received were adequate evidence of Beethoven's progress, on the grounds he considered most of them had been undertaken when Beethoven was still resident in Bonn.

He concluded:

> 'I wonder, therefore, whether he should not begin his return journey here ... for I doubt he will have made any important progress in composition and taste during his present stay.'[4]

The Elector's rebuff must have been disappointing. Beethoven's correspondence with the Bonn publisher Nikolaus Simrock indicates that by 1794 he still entertained the idea of returning to his hometown. He wrote to Simrock on 18 June referring to the publication of a set of variations he had written on a theme by his friend Count Waldstein (WoO 67). On 2 August he wrote again to Simrock suggesting he might consider returning to Bonn. Beethoven was also having to pay regard to extra-musicological considerations arising from the military conflict with France. He intimated to Simrock how circumspectly Vienna's citizens had to behave:

> 'People say that the gates leading to the suburbs are to be closed at 10.00 p.m. The soldiers have loaded their muskets with ball. You dare not raise your voice here or the police will take you into custody.'[5]

Moreover, things were little better in Bonn. Maximilian Franz, fearing for his safety, placed the Court on a war-footing and left the city in the autumn of 1794. His annuity to Beethoven had in fact ceased earlier in March. In the event, Beethoven resolved to make his own way in the world by the fruits of his labours. He remained in Vienna and never again set eyes on his native hometown.

At the time when Haydn was returning to Vienna from

England (August 1795), Beethoven played his three recently composed Piano Sonatas, Op. 2 at one of the Friday morning concerts held in the salon of Prince Karl Lichnowsky. He would become one of Beethoven's staunchest supporters and generous patrons. He was a competent pianist himself, a former pupil of Mozart, and 'a real connoisseur' with 'a great talent for music' and possessed of judgement that was 'profound and correct'.[6] Beethoven had by this time been resident in Vienna for almost three years and was well established in Vienna's musical society. We have remarked Beethoven was sent on his way to Vienna with words of encouragement from Ferdinand von Waldstein, the son of a count and princess and a knight member of the Teutonic Order. This association with the aristocracy doubtless benefitted Beethoven's entry into Vienna's aristocratic circle. Furthermore, it has been suggested his acceptance into the salons of the Austro-Hungarian aristocracy may, in part, have been due to the fact that its members may have considered *van*, in his name, to be the equivalent of *von* in theirs — a mark of distinction and nobility. Of related interest is that the Dutch-born Austrian diplomat, librarian, and government official Gottfried Freiherr van Swieten shared the same prefix as Beethoven and, thereby doubtless reinforced the composer's implied high social standing. Despite his unorthodox demeanour and unkempt appearance, Beethoven was, therefor, regarded as being 'one of theirs'.[7]

It was primarily for his performance at the keyboard, notably when extemporising, that Beethoven won over Vienna's musically-inclined nobility. In van Swieten's case, in addition to his official duties he was a composer, a patron of music, and leader of a group of music-loving noblemen who styled themselves *Gesellschaft der Associierten Kavaliere*. They sponsored regular concerts in the palace of

Prince Lobkowitz and other venues. Such was Beethoven's regard for the support he received from van Swieten that he dedicated his First Symphony to him — although, as we shall relate, it subsequently proved ill-fated.

It has been estimated that at the time of Beethoven's arrival in Vienna in December 1792, there were then resident in the city three princes and princess, nineteen counts and countesses, and nine barons and baronesses — compared with the more modestly ranked sixty-four musicians. Those with whom Beethoven would in due course associate included: Count Anton Appony, Count Moritz Lichnowsky, Baron Peter Braun, Countess Josephine Deym, Count Palfy von Erdödy, Count Johann Esterhazy, Count Moritz Fries (his music collection contained sixteen-hundred volumes), Count Galitzin (later a prince), Prince Ferdinand Kinsky, Prince Karl Lichnowsky, Prince Joseph von Lobkowitz, and, as already mentioned, Baron Gottfried van Swieten.[8] By the time of his death, in 1827, Beethoven's standing had transcended *all* of Vienna's nobility such that an estimated 10,000 people are believed to have followed his funeral cortege.

Beethoven's début as an orchestral composer in Vienna took place on St. Cecilia's Day, Sunday, 22 November 1795 when he conducted his Twelve Minuets, WoO 7 and Twelve German Dances, WoO 8. The occasion was the ball of the Pension Fund of the Society of Artists for which Haydn and Mozart had composed and performed their own dance music for orchestra. These balls were a social occasion in which the participants wore masks and adopted traditional dress. The venue was the Redoutensaal at the Hofburg. Haydn, who had composed Minuets and German The composition of dances for the 1792 season was probably the reaon for getting Beethoven, then, as remarked, Haydn's pupil, the commission for 1775.[9]

Beethoven's participation on 22 November 1795, in Thayer's words, 'gives a vivid proof of the high reputation which the young man had gained as a composer now at the end of his third year in Vienna'.[10] Beethoven later arranged his dances himself for pianoforte; these were subsequently published by Artaria & Co as his WoO 13. On 8 January 1796, Haydn and Beethoven collaborated at a further concert in the Redoutensaal for the benefit of the singer Mari Bolla.

Further indication of Beethoven's acceptance into Vienna's wider musical circle is evident from a letter he received on 10 February 1797 from his former teacher Antonio Salieri and Paul Wranitzky. They were respectively Vice President and Secretary to the Viennese Tonkünstier-Sozietät — Society of Musicians. Wranitzky also held the post of Music Director to Count Johann Esterhazy. At a meeting of the Society, it was resolved

> 'those famous musicians who had afforded the Society great services, or might serve the Society in some manner in the future, should be given free entrance tickets for all future Society academies [benefit concerts] and that these should be accompanied by a polite letter *ad captandum benevolentiam* [to win over good will]'.

Beethoven was one of the Society's chosen musicians and in their letter to him they expressed the hope he would 'be so kind, in the future as in the past, to support the widows and orphans of the Society through your excellent talents'.[11]

Salieri and Wranitzky did not have to wait long for their expectations to be fulfilled. On 5 November 1797, *The Society of Plastic and Graphic Artists* (sculptors and painters) announced a forthcoming Masked Ball in aid of its pension fund. The programme promised 'the beloved Minuets and German Dances of Herr von [sic] Beethoven'.[12] This mis-representation of Beethoven's name is further evidence of the confusion of his personal social-standing.

In due course, Beethoven contributed on many charitable musical-occasions. Indeed, such was his generosity that towards the end of his life he was honoured in the form of a fulsome letter signed by twenty-four admirers of his art. They expressed their esteem of him, his works and charitable inclinations. The signatories included: Artaria & Co., (one of the composer's first music publishers); Carl Czerny (Beethoven's piano pupil and pianistic pedagogue); Anton Diabelli (composer and music publisher); and Prince Eduard and Count Moritz Lichnowsky (respectively nephew and brother of Prince Carl Lichnowsky). Beethoven's devotees remarked:

> 'Out of the wide circle of reverent admirers that surround your genius in your native city, a small number of disciples and lovers of art approach you today to express long-felt wishes.'[13]

In due course, Prince Karl Lichnowsky conferred on his protégée an annuity, in effect a stipend, of 600 florins – about sixty pounds sterling. The Prince's intention was to provide Beethoven with some financial security until he obtained a secure post. The payments continued for several years until he received a more secure annuity of 4,000 florins in 1809 from three of Vienna's most notable citizens, namely the Archduke Rudolph (Beethoven's only composition pupil), Prince Kinsky and Prince Lobkowitz. Of Lichnowsky's support, Anton Schindler remarks: 'The great love this princely family felt for Beethoven was constant and unwavering.' He adds: 'In fact, for ten to twelve years, nearly all Beethoven's works were first tried out in the music circle of Count Lichnowsky.'[14]

An article in the *Allgemeine musikalische Zeitung* for the year 1800, places the value of Beethoven's annuity in its contemporary context – and also reveals how little the average musician received for his labours. A player in an orchestra could expect to earn from 200 to 300 gulden (about 20–30 pounds sterling). In the Austro-Hungarian Empire at this time the gulden was a standard unit of currency and was the equivalent of the Austrian silver florin (about two English shillings or a half-crown, depending on currency values). Violinists were in the worst position because, as the article states, 'they are expected to play for nothing since ten dilettantes can readily be found who will do so with great pleasure'. A teacher of pianoforte could earn a decent living but 'must possess enough self-denial to serve willingly the houses that support him' and, furthermore, 'to give lessons 'morning, noon and night'. On a more positive note, the article concludes: 'But as there are exceptions ... amongst musicians, so there are worthy houses to which the above complaints do not apply.'[15] Clearly, the household of Prince Lichnowsky was one of these and Beethoven was fortunate to secure a patron who valued his gifts so highly.

Beethoven was never reduced to impecunious circumstances – 'starving in a garret'. During his early years in Vienna there is even evidence that he made attempts to overcome his sartorial deficiencies – doubtless to facilitate his acceptance into Viennese society. Entries from an account book, recording his personal income, reveal he acquired black silk stockings, boots, incurred expenses for a wig maker and a dancing master![16] With regard to the latter, his piano pupil Ferdinand Ries recalls: 'He could never learn to dance in time, and his clumsy movements lacked all charm.'[17] By means of his annuities and the income from his compositions, Beethoven was able to maintain a modest standard of living 'typical of an unmarried middle-class gentleman of the period'. Barry Cooper, whose words we have just quoted, estimates that in Vienna around 1793 the cost of living for such an artist was 775 florins per year, 900 florins by 1800, and 967 florins by 1804. Inflation, caused by the Napoleonic wars, further eroded money values and raised the cost of living.[18]

Beethoven's negotiations with his publishers give some indication of the prices he had to set in order to maintain his standard of living. For example, on 15 January 1801, he offered the Leipzig publisher Franz Anton Hoffmeister 20 ducats for the First Symphony.[19] One ducat (a gold coin) exchanged for about 4 1/2 gulden. The gulden was interchangeable with the florin. Thus, in daily cost-of-living terms, Beethoven priced his First Symphony at about 90 florins. So, to maintain his standard of living, he would have to sell ten compositions of similar value, or fewer works but priced more highly. As time passed, Beethoven did indeed gain a reputation for charging highly for his works — especially when he placed his financial affairs in the hands of his younger brother Carl (see later).

Beethoven's first lodgings — one of very many — were a small attic room in the house of a printer-bookbinder. Soon after he lived in apartments provided by Prince Lichnowsky which he occupied until May 1795. Beethoven never owned a home of his own and had few possessions or furniture. Although his powers of concentration when composing his music were supreme, in everyday domestic matters he appears to have been negligent — especially as he grew older and withdrew more from society. His rooms were invariably plain, almost poor, with no sign of anything that could suggest comfort or luxury. The poet and music critic Ludwig

Rellstab called on Beethoven in 1825 and described Beethoven's apartment in the following terms:

> 'Everything [was] mixed together, scores, shirts, socks, books ... bits of scores on all the tables and chairs ... a disorderly mess ... On the piano dirt and dust carried on a continual battle with written and printed sheets of music ... chairs were covered with items of his clothing ... books and sheets of music were strewn in all the corners.'[20]

Beethoven's disregard for social conventions sometimes caused friction with landlords and neighbours. This, combined with his restless nature, disposed him to relocate frequently. For example, after he had left Prince Lichnowsky's apartments — when he was at work on the First Symphony and several other major works — Beethoven's addresses were:

- 1795, 35 Kreuzgasse, (1st floor) now 6 Lowelstrasse, Ogylischeshaus;
- 1796–99 (May) Beethoven's addresses are unknown;
- 1799, 650 St. Petersplatz (3rd floor), now 11 Petersplatz; 800–01, Greinersches Haus 24 (3rd floor), now Tiefen Garden, No. 10;
- 1800–02 (April), Hambergischeshaus, 1275, Wasserkuntsbastei, now 15 Seilerstatte,
- 1802 (October–1803 (April), 649, now 11, Petersplatz (2nd floor).[21]

What is remarkable is that, despite his many house moves, Beethoven retained all his precious sketchbooks and manuscripts intact.

We have a description of Beethoven at the period under consideration from a remarkably gifted young pianist by the name of Elisabeth von Kissow – known in Beethoven musicology as Frau von Bernhard. When a mere twelve years old her father sent her from her native Augsburg to Vienna to study piano with Johann Andreas Streicher – celebrated for not only being a teacher of piano but an accomplished keyboard instrument maker. Elisabeth had a number of occasions to observe Beethoven and indeed to perform in his company in the salon of the composer's patron Prince Lichnowsky's. Beethoven so prized her talent that for the next few years he sent her a copy of his newest pieces, usually accompanied with a typical Beethovenian jocular note.[22] Later in life Elisabeth, as Frau von Bernhard, recalled her musical impressions of the time when she received her instruction from the composer:

> 'I still remember clearly both Haydn and Salieri sitting on a sofa on one side of the small music room, both carefully dressed in the old-fashioned way with perruque [periwig], shoes and silk hose, whereas even here Beethoven would come dressed in the informal fashion of the other side of the Rhine, almost ill-dressed.[23]

The recollections of Eleonore von Breuning are relevant here; she was the wife of Franz Gerhard Wegeler, Beethoven's close friend from his youthful days in Bonn. On 2 November 1793 he wrote Eleonore a long letter in which he remarks: 'I have been almost a whole year in this capital.' He informed her of the dedication she was to receive of his Variations for Piano and Violin, WoO 40. He did not think too highly of 'this little work' and wanted her to be the recipient of a 'work more worthy', but, he explained, 'people in Vienna have been pestering me to publish this little work'. On more sartorial matters he adds:

'I still have the waistcoat you kindly gave me ... But it is now so out of fashion that I can only keep it in my wardrobe as a very precious token from you.'[24]

Beethoven inherited a thriving symphonic tradition. In his *Chronology of Western Classical Music*, the American musicologist Charles John Hall has made a survey of what he describes as 'cultivated art music'. In this he charts the composition-origins of a range of genres of music including orchestral symphonies. Thereby, Hall's listings provide insights into contemporary music-making of the kind with which Beethoven would have been familiar – and, in some measure, with which he would have to compete on his arrival in Vienna. By way of illustration of this proposition, we have compiled the following summation of a selection of symphonic compositions, and their composers, for the period when Beethoven arrived in Vienna to 1800, by which time he had completed work on his First Symphony; the works of lesser composers have been omitted:

1792: Luigi Boccherini, Symphony in D, Op. 45; Joseph Haydn, *London Symphonies*, No. 5 (No. 97) in C, No. 6 (No. 98) in B flat.
1793: Joseph Haydn, *London Symphony*, No. 7 (No. 99) in E flat; Ignace Pleyel, Symphony in E flat.
1794: Johann Friedrich Bach, Symphony No. 20 in B flat; François Gossec, *Military Symphony*; Joseph Haydn, *London Symphonies*, No. 8 (No. 100) in G – *Military*, No. 9 (No.

101) in D – *The Clock*, No. 10 (No. 102) in B flat; Ignaz Pleyel, Symphony in B flat.

1795: Anton André, Symphony No. 4 in C, No. 5 in F, No. 6 in C; Joseph Haydn, *London Symphonies*, No. No. 11 (No. 103) in E flat – *Drum Roll*, No. 12 (No. 104) in F – *London*.

1796: Hall, from whom we are quoting, does not list any symphonic compositions for this year but worthy of mention is the Piano Concerto of Muzio Clementi – Concerto in C, and that of Daniel Steibelt – Concerto in C.

1797: Johann André, Symphony in D, Op. 7.

1798: Luigi Boccherini, Symphony in C; Georg (*Abbe*) Vogler, Symphony in C.

1799: Ignace Pleyel, Symphony in B flat.

1800: Johann André, Two Symphonies – d*'une execution facile*, Op. 11.

The German writer and traveller Baron Johann Kaspar Risbeck is remembered for his *Letters from a Traveller about Germany* (*Voyage en Allemagne dans une suite de lettres*, 1787) In this he writes:

> 'Music is the only thing in which the nobility shows good taste. Many houses have their own special band of musicians, and all public performances indicate that this form of art is held in the highest esteem here. One can assemble four to five large orchestras, all of them unequalled ... I have heard thirty to forty instruments playing together, and all of them produce a tone so true, clean and distinct that one might have thought one was listening to a single unnaturally loud

> instrument ... There are about 400 musicians here who organize themselves into regular associations and often work together undivided for many years.'[25]

Of his experience of music-making in Vienna, the German writer and music critic Johann Friedrich Reichardt remarks:

> 'The nobility were probably the most musical that has ever existed. The whole population took part in the happy art, and their lively spirit, their sensual, pleasure-loving character demanded variety and cheerful music on all occasions.'[26]

When Beethoven arrived in Vienna in 1792, there were two principal public concert locations, namely the Burgtheater and Kärntnertortheater. Both were situated near one another and in close proximity to the Imperial Palace. The Burgtheater was the creation of the Empress Marie Theresa. Three of Mozart's operas were premiered there: *Die Entführung aus dem Serail* (1782), *Le nozze di Figaro* (1786), and *Cosi fan tutte* (1790). Beethoven's First Symphony also received its premier at the Burgtheater on 2 April 1800. The theatre had an oval seating plan with no fewer than four tiers of boxes to the upper galleries. Estimates of its seating vary from 1000 to 1350. This was relatively small compared with other national theatres. For example, The *Comédie Français* in Paris had a capacity of 2,000, and the *Haymarket* Theatre in London could seat about 4,000.

Working-class theatre goers (labourers) could afford only the cheapest gallery seats of 15 Kreutzer – about a day's wage. Persons of rank were seated in the *fauteuils* at the front of the house – the parterre – immediately behind the orchestra. With the onset of deafness, we read of Beethoven standing by the orchestra rail to better capture the sound of the music — notably in performances of his Opera *Fidelio*. For the concert season 1792–93, when Beethoven had just arrived in Vienna, string players at the Burgtheater received an income of 350 florins; the leader of the orchestra (concert master) could expect a hundred more. Woodwind and tympani were less well paid at only 300 florins.

The Kärntnertortheater was known as the *Kaiserliches und Königliches Hoftheater zu Wien* (Imperial and Royal Court Theatre of Vienna). Mozart's Piano Concerto K. 503 received its premier there in 1787, as did Beethoven's *Fidelio* — in its present-day form — in 1814, and his Ninth Symphony in 1824. The Kärntnertortheater was a small theatre, even compared with the Burgtheater. It had only three galleries with seats, its upper two floors being provided with benches and space for standing. When full to capacity it may have housed an audience of about a thousand. Musicians at the Kärntnertortheater were paid less than their counterparts at the Burgtheater. String and wind players received a mere 125 florins. To place these figures in context, it has been estimated that during his years in Vienna (1781–91) Mozart's income fluctuated between 800 and 3,800 florins. He lived in relatively spacious apartments that cost him some 460 gulden — broadly interchangeable with the florin.[27]

Vienna's Augarten provided a venue for informal daytime concerts. A further venue was the University's *Festsaal* that was used by the *Gesellschaft der* Musikfreunde before they had their own hall. Vienna, as Europe's leading musical city, enjoyed a flourishing operatic tradition. So-called 'rescue' dramas were fashionable and were a source of stimulus to Beethoven in the composition of his only work for the lyric theatre *Leonora / Fidelio*. Beethoven was fortunate insofar as his most wealthy patrons, such as the

Princes Lobkowitz and Lichnowsky and Count Razumovsky, maintained high standards of chamber music in their own salons. Touring virtuosi were sought after in these venues to showcase their skills. Beethoven himself was obliged to take part on occasions in pianistic contests against such would-be rivals as Joseph Johann Baptist Wölfl (Woelfl) and Daniel Gottlieb Steibelt.[28]

We recall Beethoven had relocated to Vienna to receive formal instruction from Haydn. In due course, though, he became dissatisfied with his teacher's response to his studies. He admired the older composer who was then at the height of his powers and was in demand both in Vienna and London. Testimony to his respect is that over the years Beethoven acquired the scores of many of Haydn's works including the autograph of *The London Symphony* that came into his possession after Haydn's death in 1809.[29] It appears though that Haydn was too pre-occupied with his own compositions to give Beethoven's studies the time and attention Beethoven expected; his exercises were returned, supposedly corrected, but with numerous errors overlooked. Evidence of Haydn's pre-occupation with his own work comes indirectly from a letter that Johann Albrechtsberger (see later) wrote to Beethoven on 15 December 1796. He invited Beethoven to pay him a visit and bring along the score of one of his Trios — probably from the Op. 9 set on which he was then at work. Significantly he adds: 'Haydn was here yesterday; he is *preoccupied* [italics added] with the idea for a grand oratorio ... and hopes to have it finished soon'. This is thought to be a reference to *The Creation*.[30]

Beethoven did show respect for his elderly teacher. For example, when his Piano Sonatas Op. 2 were announced on 9 March 1796 in the *Wiener Zeitung* ('Vienna Journal') it was made public they were dedicated to Joseph Haydn — the only professional composer ever to receive such a dedication from Beethoven with the exception of Antonio Salieri. However, tension between master and pupil subsequently marred their relationship. Beethoven resented Haydn's suggestion that he should hold back publication of the third of his Piano Trios Op. 1 — the one he cherished the most. Moreover, he was given to saying that although he received instruction from Haydn 'he had learned little from him'.[31] In later years he would renounce these headstrong views and even speak of his mentor with respect and affection. There was the occasion, for example, when the composer and publisher Anton Diabelli called on Beethoven to present him with a lithograph of Haydn's rather modest birthplace — in the village of Rohrau in Lower Austria. It gave Beethoven much pleasure prompting him to remark: 'Just see the little house, and such a great man was born in it.'[32]

By way of further illustration of Beethoven's respect for his teacher, we recall the occasion when Beethoven attended a concert on 27 March 1808 held in honour of Haydn's seventy-sixth birthday — that actually fell on the 31st of the month. The principal work performed was the composer's *The Creation*. Beethoven stood at the door of the great hall of the University, where the concert took place, to greet Haydn 'with members of the high nobility'. Haydn arrived in the coach of his patron Prince Esterhazy and was received

> 'sitting in an armchair ... lifted on high, and on his entrance into the hall was received with the sound of trumpets and drums by the numerous gathering and greeted with joyous shouts of "Long Live Haydn!" '.[33]

In later years Beethoven unfailingly referred to his old master in terms of reverence, and placed him on the same level of other great composers. This is evident in a letter he wrote on 17 July 1812 to a young admirer — thought to be a young girl of only 8—10 years. Evidently — and remarkably — she had expressed her admiration for Beethoven and his music. This prompted him to respond: 'Do not rob Handel, Haydn, and Mozart of their laurel wreaths. They are entitled to theirs, but I am not yet entitled to one.' Notwithstanding her young years, Beethoven took pains to encourage her in one of his characteristic lofty utterances:

> 'Persevere, do not only practice your art, but endeavour also to fathom its inner meaning; it deserves this effort. For only art and science can raise men to the level of gods.'[34]

According to Beethoven musicology, Beethoven's study with Haydn came to the attention of the composer and music teacher Johann Baptist Schenk. He made Beethoven's acquaintance in 1792 and in his *Autobiography* he writes:

> 'I saw the composer, now so famous, for the first time and heard him play ... He offered to improvise on the pianoforte. Having struck a few chords and tossed off a few figures as if they were of no significance, the creative genius gradually unveiled his profound psychological pictures. My ear was continually charmed by the beauty of the many varied motives which he wove with wonderful clarity and loveliness into each other.'

Schenk became aware Beethoven had been studying counterpoint with Haydn for some six months and that he was apparently dissatisfied with his studies. He agreed to give Beethoven additional instruction on the grounds that his collaboration should not be made known to Haydn. He states: 'I gave him the familiar textbook of Joseph Fux, *Gradus ad Parnassum*, and asked him to look at the exercises that followed.' Schenk relates that his instruction commenced in August 1792 and lasted until May 1793. He generously exonerated Haydn's lax supervision on the grounds that when he returned to Vienna, from London,

> 'he was intent on utilizing his muse in the composition of large masterworks, and thus laudably occupied could not well devote himself to the rules of grammar'.[35]

We should remark that later biographers suggest Schenk's role in his musical education of the young Beethoven may be somewhat exaggerated.[36]

Further testimony to Beethoven's need for formal instruction is his relationship at this period with Antonio Salieri; he was no less celebrated than Haydn as a composer and teacher and was a dominant figure in Vienna's musical scene. Beethoven turned to Salieri for instruction in vocal composition and the setting of Italian texts. His debt to Salieri is reflected in his later dedication to him of his Violin Sonatas Op. 12 and the set of Variations *La stessa, la stessima* (WoO 73) derived from Salieri's opera *Falstaff*.

When Haydn departed Vienna for his second visit to London, in mid-January 1794, Beethoven turned to the greatly admired theorist and master of counterpoint Johann Georg Albrechtsberger. He was organist and *Kapellmeister* at Saint Stephan's Cathedral and was much sought after by young composers. Although Albrechtsberger was something of a dry, painstaking theorist, many of Beethoven's studies with him of the old-fashioned contrapuntal curriculum still survive — evidence of both his diligence and respect for the learned pedagogue. Beethoven authority David Wyn Jones writes:

> 'Although primarily a church composer [Albrechtsberger] had, earlier in his career, composed some eight symphonies. That said, Albrechtsberger could not, given his nature, be a direct source of influence to Beethoven the putative symphonist.'[37]

Beethoven's eminent biographer Alexander Thayer, with his wider perspective of the composer's life and work in mind, observed:

> 'It is now known that the "dry rules" of Albrechtsberger could make a strong appeal to Beethoven as appertaining to theoretical study, and that the old method of composition, to which he remained true all his life, always had a singular charm for him as a subject of study and investigation.'[38]

With regard to Beethoven's teachers, the recollections of the pianist and composer Ferdinand Ries are relevant to this part of our narrative. Sometime in late 1801, or early 1802, Ries commenced piano lessons with Beethoven and became a trusted companion to the composer; Beethoven relied upon Ries to copy out his scores and to perform various secretarial duties. Reflecting on his master's relationships with his teachers, Ries writes:

> 'I knew them all well; all three [Haydn, Albrechtsberger and Salieri] valued Beethoven highly, but

were of one mind touching his habits of study. All of them said Beethoven was so headstrong and self-sufficient that he had much to learn through harsh experience which he had refused to accept when it was presented to him as a subject of study.'

He adds:

'Beethoven found Albrechtsberger's "dry rules" irksome and was not readily disposed to Salieri's, Italianate school of dramatic composition that was then in vogue — although he did value Antonio Salieri's advice regarding the setting of Italian words.'[39]

With Beethoven established in Vienna, we direct the next part of our discussion to a selection of events bearing on his life and work during the years 1795–1800.

1795 was an auspicious year for Beethoven. It was when he made his public debut as a concert pianist. In March the annual concerts in the Burgtheater were announced for the benefit of the widows of the Tonkünstler-Gesellschaft/Societät — 'the Society of Musicians'. Two concerts were advertised for the evenings of the 29th and 30th of the month at which 'a concerto by Beethoven', then a pupil of Antonio Salieri, was promised. Whether Beethoven performed the B flat Concerto or the C major Concerto on the 29 March is somewhat open to question.[40] In response to the services Beethoven had rendered to the Society, on 10 February 1797 he received a letter styled in the following terms.

'Most esteemed Sir! — The Society for the Protection of Widows and Orphans of Musicians has the honour to pay you its respects with the accompanying free ticket to all of its future concerts. Please pardon the fact that the Society ... can show its gratitude in no way other that this for the services that you have already rendered ... through your excellent talents.'

Haydn had been similarly honoured. Significantly, the Imperial Kapellmeister Antonio Salieri was one of the signatories to the Society's letter of commendation to Beethoven.[41]

We refer next to Beethoven's two younger brothers.

Nikolaus Johann van Beethoven (1776–1848) was Beethoven's youngest brother. He was apprenticed to a pharmaceutical chemist at Bonn before moving to Vienna in 1795 where he was apprenticed to the Court pharmacist. In 1808 he acquired a business of his own at Linz and from 1809 he accumulated considerable wealth by supplying the military with medications. We encounter Johann — as he is typically referred to — in connection with Beethoven's tour of Europe as a concert pianist. On 19 February 1796 Beethoven wrote to Johann of his progress: 'I am well, very well. My art is winning me friends and renown, and what more do I want? And this time I shall make a good deal of money.'[42] Early in 1796, Beethoven journeyed to Prague in the company of his patron Prince Lichnowsky; Mozart had made a similar trip — remembered today through its association with his *Prague* Symphony, K. 504 that was premiered in the city in January 1787.

This was Beethoven's first concert tour and was a considerable success. After a brief return to Vienna he departed for Leipzig, Dresden, and Berlin where he gave further concerts. In Berlin, he met the celebrated pianist Friedrich Heinrich Hummel and played to Friedrich Wilhelm II, King of Prussia. Beethoven's playing created such an impression that it disposed the Court musician August von Schall to write to the Elector Maximilian Franz on 24 April 1796: 'The young Beethoven arrived here [Dresden] ... He is said to have improvised immensely and to compose well.'

On 6 May he wrote once more:

> 'Beethoven has delayed here for almost eight days, everyone who heard him play was enchanted. Beethoven was granted by the Elector of Saxony, a man who knows music, the favour to play in the evening all alone without accompaniment for an hour and a half. H.R.H. was well satisfied and presented him with a golden *tabitière* [snuff box].' The latter is said to have been filled with louis d'ors.[43]

Kaspar Karl van Beethoven — sometimes referred to as Caspar Carl — was the elder of Beethoven's two younger brothers; he was born in April 1774. Twenty years later he followed Beethoven to Vienna where he undertook some composing and started to give music lessons. An entry in the *Allgemeine musikalische Zeitung* of 1802 announced he played a number of instruments. From 1800 he was employed as a clerk in Vienna's Department of Finance. His duties do not appear to have been unduly onerous, enabling him to assist Beethoven in his negotiations with publishers. Beethoven appreciated Carl's efforts as is evident from a letter he wrote on 22 April 1802 to the Leipzig publishers Breitkopf and Härtel: '[You] can rely entirely on my brother — who, in general attends to all my affairs.'[44] Carl, however, soon earned a reputation for striking hard bargains with publishers. As Peter Clive remarks:

> 'To judge from the numerous letters which Kaspar Karl addressed to publishers, on Beethoven's behalf, he promoted his brother's interests with a good deal of determination, if not with a maximum of tact.'[45]

Something of the animosity felt towards Carl is evident in a letter Beethoven's pupil Ferdinand Ries sent to Nikolaus Simrock on 6 May 1803. Simrock played the horn and was familiar with Beethoven from their days together in the Electoral Court Orchestra. In Bonn, he ran a small business dealing with music publishing and instruments. Of Carl van Beethoven he writes:

> '[He] is the biggest skinflint in the world — for a single ducat he would take back 50 words of promise, and his good brother makes the greatest enemies because of him. For every note that Beethoven plays there is a corresponding base element in his brother's soul.'[46]

Carl's resolve to have his role in his brother's affairs more widely known is evident in a letter he wrote on 23 June 1802, to the *Allgemeine musikalische Zeitung* informing the journal of his new role in his brother's business affairs. He added that as a music lover himself he would be amenable to offering his services to the periodical should the management so wish.[47]

With Carl's marriage in 1806, his support for Beethoven as his part-time secretary and business manager largely ceased. In 1812 Carl contracted tuberculosis from which he died in 1815. By then Beethoven's relations with his brother had become strained. He disapproved of his wife and her alleged amorous proclivities calling her 'The Queen of the Night' — a thinly veiled reference to the formidable character in Mozart's opera *The Magic Flute*. Nevertheless, Beethoven was solicitous of Carl's wellbeing and cared for him financially to the end.

In 1796, the musicologist Johann von Schönfeld published *A Yearbook of the Music of Vienna and Prague* — a compendium of contemporary musicians and musical personalities. It provides the first published account of Beethoven's relationship with Haydn. During the 1790s, Haydn was increasingly recognised in Vienna as a popular composer both for his contributions to charitable enterprises and to such works as his large-scale Oratorios *The Creation* and *The Seasons*. Such was his celebrity that for his guidance and instruction he could demand a hundred-ducat fee from his pupils. Of Haydn's new pupil, Schönfeld writes:

> 'Beethoven, a musical genius has chosen Vienna as his residence for the past two years [Beethoven had in fact arrived in Vienna in 1792] ... He seems already to have entered into the inner sanctuary of music, distinguishing himself for his precision, feeling, and taste; consequently, his fame has risen considerably. A living proof of his true love of art lies in the fact that he has put himself in the hands of our immortal Haydn in order to be initiated into the holy secrets of the art of music.'[48]

Shortly after arriving in Vienna, Beethoven made the acquaintance of Nikolaus von Zmeskall. He was employed in the

Hungarian Court Chancellery and, as an accomplished cellist, was prominent in Vienna's musical circles. Beethoven came to rely on Zmeskall for rendering him small everyday services, usually initiated by a short note; numerous such notes occur throughout Beethoven's correspondence. The hapless Zmeskall became the butt of Beethoven's dubious humour and badinage, being addressed typically as 'Baron Muck-Driver'! Beethoven wrote such a note (undated) in 1798 to Zmeskall. Although its contents are of no inherent significance Beethoven gave expression to one of his most frequently quoted utterances that exemplifies his self-belief: '*Power is the moral principle of those who excel others, and it is also mine.*' [Beethoven's italics][49]

Another of Beethoven's friends from his early days in Vienna was Karl Amenda. By vocation a clergyman, he was an excellent violinist and music teacher to the children of Prince Lobkowitz; it was probably in the Palais Lobkowitz that Amenda first met Beethoven. The two became close friends to which Beethoven gave expression by presenting Amenda with a copy of his String Quartet Op. 18, No. 1. In the summer of 1799 Beethoven wrote to Amenda to inform him:

> 'Yesterday I was offered a trip to Poland – in September ... I can amuse myself quite well in Poland and there is money to be made there too. I have accepted the offer.' [50]

It is not clear who invited him but Beethoven clearly hoped to recreate the triumphs of his previous Leipzig-Berlin concert-tour. In the event, however, the promised Polish tour did not take place.

When Amenda departed Vienna in 1800, for his native Courland, he gave expression to his estimation of his friend in a long and touching letter. In this he writes: 'You are responsible not only to yourself ... but to the general progress of your art, which lies close to your heart as a true artist.'

Amenda reflected more generally:

> 'Outside of Vienna ... the musical public is still too backward, the so-called connoisseurs are too shallow, or too pedantic, to be able to evaluate your beautiful compositions according to their worth. You must yourself play for them, and compose for them pieces of all sorts according to their prevailing comprehension; [you] must educate them to your level, as you have done with me and others in Vienna.'[51]

According to contemporary reviews of Beethoven's recently composed works, Amanda's perception of the challenges his music posed to performers and music critics appears to have been justified. Maynard Solomon comments:

> 'Early critics were apparently more sensitive than we are to the extent of Beethoven's departures — and especially those of a harmonic nature — from tradition.'

For example, when Beethoven published his Violin Sonatas, Op. 12 — composed in 1798 with a dedication to Salieri — the music critic of the *Allgemeine musikalische Zeitung* complained of the music's 'clumsy, harsh modulations ... an aversion to conventional key relationships ... [and] a piling up of difficulty upon difficulty'.[52]

The *AmZ's* music critic likened the experience of listening to the Violin Sonatas, Op. 12 as to a man 'who expected to take a stroll through an inviting wood with a congenial friend, but who found instead only hostile entanglements, and finally emerged from the thicket exhausted and disheartened'.

The critic chastised Beethoven 'for going his own way' and pleaded:

'If Herr v. B. would only assert himself a little less, if he would only consent to the natural idiom, he would certainly, with his talent and zeal, produce much good music for an instrument which he seems to have mastered exceptionally well'.[53]

Beethoven's Piano Sonatas Op. 10 — published in September 1798 — were accorded a somewhat more friendly reception in the second volume of the *Allgemeine musikalische Zeitung*:

'It cannot be denied that Herr v. B is a man of genius, a man of originality, and above all a man of independence. He is sustained by an extraordinarily thorough grounding in the art of composition and by his own phenomenal mastery of the instrument for which he writes. He assuredly ranks as one of the foremost pianists and composers for the piano of our time.'

However, the critic had reservations:

'His superabundance of ideas ... becomes an obsession [which] ... leads too often in

Beethoven's case to a wild piling up of these ideas, or sometimes to a bizarre grouping of them, so as to produce an effect of gloomy contrivance'.

The critic charitably concluded with words of intended encouragement: 'Spare your treasures and practice thrift.'[54]

By 1800–01, Beethoven was receiving recognition as being a composer of considerable promise and, moreover, was gaining greater independence from the more restrictive forms of aristocratic patronage. On 2 April 1800, he gave his first public concert (*akademie*) with performances of his Piano Concerto, Op. 15, Septet, Op. 20, and the First Symphony, Op. 21. Significantly, these compositions were heard alongside the works of Mozart and Haydn; Beethoven had emerged, by inference, as a major creative personality of their equal standing. Shortly thereafter, his ballet *The Creatures of Prometheus* earned Beethoven wider public recognition. It was a resounding success in the 1801–02 season being performed at the Burgtheater Theatre more than twenty times.[55] Such was its popularity that Beethoven sanctioned a piano transcription of the score by his pupil Carl Czerny.

We can conclude that since his arrival in Vienna, Beethoven had emerged as a major creative personality – with publishers eager to bid for his works, 'thereby giving Beethoven a sense of his international importance and, perhaps, a glimpse of the possibilities of immortality as well'.[56]

[1] See: Beethoven-Haus, Bonn website and Barry Cooper, 1991, p. 69.
[2] Emily Anderson, editor and translator, 1961, Vol. 1, Letter No. 8, p. 12.
[3] Thayer-Forbes, 1967, p. 144 and Theodore Albrecht, translator and editor, 1996, Vol. 1 Letter No. 16, pp. 32–4. For a commentary on this extended and eloquent letter, with remarks concerning the compositions mentioned therein, see also: H. C. Robbins Landon 1959, pp. 141–2.
[4] Theodore Albrecht, editor and translator, 1996, Vol. 1 Letter No. 17, pp. 34–5.

[5] Emily Anderson editor and translator, 1961, Vol. 1, Letter No. 10, pp. 15–16 and Letter No. 12, pp. 17–13.
[6] These are the views of Beethoven's pupil Carl Czerny who was well acquainted with the Lichnowsky family. See, for example: Paul Badura-Skoda, editor, 1970, p. 8.
[7] H. C. Robbins Landon, 1992, p. 79.
[8] Tia De Nora, *Beethoven and the Construction of Genius: Musical Politics in Vienna, 1792–1803*, 1997, p. 19.
[9] As suggested by H. C. Robbins Landon, *Beethoven: A Documentary Study*, 1970, p. 49. Landon's study of the composer includes an engraving by J. Schütz, from about 1880, that conveys an impression of the of the great ballroom of the Redoutensaal; see Plate 33.
[10] Elliot Forbes editor, *Thayer's Life of Beethoven*, 1967 p. 177.
[11] For a facsimile reproduction of this letter, together with the German text, see: Beethoven House, Digital Archives, Library Document, BH 194. For a translation of the text with commentaries see: Theodore Albrecht editor and translator, 1996, Vol. 1, Letter No. 24, pp. 46–47.
[12] Theodore Albrecht editor and translator, 1996, Vol. 1, Letter No. 27, pp. 50–51.
[13] Quoted in: Theodore Albrecht, editor and translator, 1996, Vol. 3, Document No. 344, pp. 4–11.
[14] Anton Felix Schindler, edited by Donald W. MacArdle and translated by Constance S. Jolly from the German edition of 1860, 1966, p. 50.
[15] Cited in Piero Weiss and Richard Taruskin, 1984, p. 325.
[16] Elliot Forbes editor, *Thayer's Life of Beethoven*, 1967 p. 135.
[17] As recalled in: Hans Conrad Fischer and Erich Kock, 1972, pp. 29–30.
[18] Barry Cooper, 2000, p. 104.
[19] Quoted in: Theodore Albrecht, editor and translator, 1996, Vol. 3, Document No. 344, pp. 4–11.ol. 1, Letter No. 44, pp. 47–48.
[20] Hans Conrad Fischer and Erich Kock, *Ludwig van Beethoven: A Study in Text and Pictures*, 1972, pp. 113–20 and accompanying illustrations.
[21] Elliot Forbes editor, *Thayer's Life of Beethoven*, 1967 pp. 1108–09.
[22] The reminiscences of Fräulein von Kissow, as Frau von Bernhard, are told in: Oscar Sonneck, 1927 pp. 19–20.
[23] As recounted in *Vienna and its Musical Life* in: *Haydn: The Years of the Creation*, H. C. Robbins Landon, 1977, p. 25.
[24] Emily Anderson editor and translator, 1961, Vol. 1, Letter No. 7, pp. 9–11.
[25] Cited in: H. C. Robbins Landon, 1992, p. 51.
[26] *Ibid.*
[27] Mary Sue Morrow, *Concert life in Haydn's Vienna: Aspects of a Developing Musical and Social Institution*, 1989, pp. 71–81, and pp. 113–14, and p. 115. Morrow's account of Vienna's principal theatres includes seating plans and contemporary engravings of both their exteriors and interiors.
[28] For a comprehensive study of concert life in Beethoven's Vienna see Anne-Louise Coldicott, *Beethoven's Musical Environment* in: Barry Cooper, 1991, pp. 87–91.
[29] For a discussion of these circumstances see: Beethoven House, Digital Archives, Document, Sammlung H. C. Bodmer. HCB Mh 42.
[30] Theodore Albrecht editor and translator, 1996, Vol. 1, Letter No. 21, pp. 41–42.

[31] Franz Wegeler, 1838, English edition, 1988, p. 75.
[32] Gerhard von Breuning, 1874, English edition, 1992, pp. 98–9. Diabelli made the gift of the lithograph of Haydn's birthplace when Beethoven was in his last illness. Von Breuning was a frequent visitor to Beethoven at this time and helped to have the lithograph framed.
[33] Elliot Forbes editor, *Thayer's Life of Beethoven*, 1967 p.430.
[34] Emily Anderson editor and translator, 1961, Vol. 1, Letter No. 376, pp. 380–81.
[35] Johann Baptist Schenk, as recorded by Oscar George Theodore Sonneck, *Beethoven: Impressions of Contemporaries*, 1927, pp. 15–16.
[36] Peter Clive writes: 'Schenk's statements concerning his role in the musical education of the young Beethoven used to be fully accepted by the latter's biographers but they have been challenged by a modern scholar, James Webster, who argues that Schenk exaggerated whatever help he may have given to Beethoven.' Peter Clive, 2001, pp. 307–08.
[37] David Wyn Jones, 2006, pp. 156–57.
[38] Elliot Forbes, editor, 1967, *Thayer's Life of Beethoven*, 1967, pp. 149–50. See also: Philip G. Downs, 1992, pp. 559–60 and Barry Cooper, 2000, pp. 78–9.
[39] The original account is given by Ferdinand Ries as, *Impressions of Beethoven*, in: Oscar George Theodore Sonneck, 1927, p. 49.
[40] Barry Cooper suggests since the B flat Concerto was not 'entirely new' in March 1795, the evidence is in favour of Op. 15 being the work performed. Barry Copper, 2000 p. 53.
[41] Theodore Albrecht editor and translator, 1996, Vol. 1, Letter No. 24, pp. 46–47.
[42] Emily Anderson editor and translator, 1961, Vol. 1, Letter No. 16, pp. 22–23.
[43] Elliot Forbes, editor, 1967, *Thayer Life of Beethoven*, 1967, p. 184.
[44] Emily Anderson editor and translator, 1961, Vol. 1, Letter No. 58, p. 74.
[45] Peter Clive, 2001, pp. 20–22.
[46] Theodore Albrecht editor and translator, 1996, Vol. 1, Letter No. 58, pp. 100–01.
[47] Fort a facsimile reproduction of this letter, together with the original German text, see: Beethoven House, Digital Archives, Library Document, HCB Br 297.
[48] Quoted in Tia De Nora, *Beethoven and the Construction of Genius: Musical Politics in Vienna, 1792–1803*, 1997, p. 87.
[49] Emily Anderson editor and translator, 1961, Vol. 1, Letter No. 30, p. 32.
[50] *Ibid*, Vol. 1, Letter No. 32, p. 34.
[51] Theodore Albrecht editor and translator, 1996, Vol. 1, Letter No. 31, pp. 56–58.
[52] Maynard Solomon, 1977, p. 75.
[53] Quoted from *Allgemeine musikalische Zeitung*, 1, 1799 and cited in Anton Felix Schindler, edited by Donald W. MacArdle and translated by Constance S. Jolly from the German edition of 1860, 1966, pp. 76–77.
[54] *Ibid*, pp. 77–78, quoted from *Allgemeine musikalische Zeitung*, II, 1800.
[55] Writing of *Prometheus*, Thayer remarks: '[It] stood higher than ever before ...'. Elliot Forbes editor, *Thayer's Life of Beethoven*, 1967 p. 271.
[56] Maynard Solomon, 1977, p. 128.

BEETHOVEN: A CONTEMPORARY PORTRAIT

We pause here for a moment, in our consideration of Beethoven's progress with the composition of his First Symphony to provide a portrait of the composer as he appeared to certain of his contemporaries at the period of gestation of his Op. 21.

Baron Carl Friedrich Kübeck was an Austrian government official and a pianist of some ability. He kept a *Tagebücher* (Diary) for the period 1796–1801 from which the following extract is derived:

> '[Beethoven] was a small man with unkempt hair with no powder, which was unusual. He had a face deformed by pock-marks, small shining eyes, and a continuous movement in every limb in his body.'

Kübeck adds — unfavourably:

> 'Whoever sees Beethoven for the first time, and knows nothing of him, would surely take him for a malicious, ill-natured and quarrelsome drunkard who has no feeling for music.'

On hearing Beethoven play Kübeck readily set aside his prejudices and enthused:

> 'He sat down at the fortepiano and played in a masterly manner for half-an-hour to everyone's delight ... [He] who sees him for the first time surrounded by his fame and glory, will surely see musical talent in every feature of his ugly face.'[1]

One of Beethoven's women piano pupils was Countess Therese von Brunswick. She came from a noble Hungarian family and from about 1801 received instruction from Beethoven; moreover, he developed a deep affection for his pupil. Later in life she recalled her lessons to the Mozart scholar Otto Jahn. She relates how at her forth meeting she took the music from one of Beethoven's three Piano Trios, Op. 5, carrying it, 'like a schoolgirl' up the three flights of winding stairs to his apartment. She continues:

> '[Dear] immortal Louis van Beethoven was very amiable and as polite as possible ... [He] had me sit down at his piano, which was out of tune, and I at once led off by singing the violin and cello accompaniment [no mean feat], while I played quite decently.'

This so delighted Beethoven he promised at once to give her lessons. Therese further recalls:

> '[Beethoven] came assiduously, but instead of remaining for an hour, from 12 o'clock on, he would often stay until 4 or 5 and never wearied of holding down and bending my fingers, which I had learned to stretch up and hold flatly.'

Beethoven later conferred immortality upon Therese by dedicating to her his Piano Sonata No. 24 in F-sharp major, Op. 78.[2]

Beethoven's most precociously gifted pupil was Carl Czerny. In course of time he became the foremost authority on the art of pianoforte technique in Germany, as manifest in more than a thousand published studies — each containing numerous (hundreds) pedagogical exercises. Many celebrated pianists of the nineteenth century — including nonother than Franz Liszt — owed a debt to Czerny and could trace their pedagogical ancestry back to him. Through his exercises he sought to provide the student with the means to acquire the art of finger dexterity and expression in even the most challenging of keyboard music — including his teacher's piano sonatas.

A child prodigy, he made his public début in 1800 playing Mozart's C minor Concerto, K 491. Czerny describes the day (sometime in 1801) when, just ten years old, he was introduced to Beethoven to be considered as a potential pupil:

> 'With what joy and trembling I looked forward to the day when I was to see the great man ... We [Czerny's father and the mandolin player Wenzel

Krumpholz] mounted five or six stories high to Beethoven's apartment ... In a very desolate room, with papers and articles of dress strewn in all directions, bare walls, a few chests, hardly a chair except a rickety one standing by the Walter piano ... Beethoven ... dressed in a jacket and trousers of long dark goat's hair which at once reminded me of the description of Robinson Crusoe I had been reading. He had a shock of jet-black hair (*cut à la* Titus) standing straight upright. A beard of several day's growth made his naturally dark face still blacker. I noticed also, with a child's quick observation, that he had cotton wool, which seemed to have been dipped in some yellow fluid, in both ears.'

On being invited to perform, Cerny began with Mozart's C major Concerto No. 25, K 503. This stirred Beethoven's immediate interest and he joined in, supplying the orchestral passages with his left hand. Czerny describes Beethoven's hands as being covered with hair 'and the fingers very broad, especially at the tips'. Beethoven's evident satisfaction with the young Czerny's interpretation emboldened him to play the recently composed *Pathétique* Piano Sonata, prompting Beethoven to exclaim 'the boy has talent, [an understatement!] I will take him as my pupil'.

In due course, Beethoven established a close relationship with Czerny inviting him, for example, to première his *Emperor* Piano Concerto in 1812 — by which time Beethoven, through his loss of hearing, was unable to perform in public. For his part, in 1839, Czerny published the *Complete Theoretical and Practical Piano School* and in 1842 provided an autobiographical sketch *Erinnerungen aus meinem Leben* ('Memories from my Life'), both of which provide recollections of Beethoven and give insights into the performance of his keyboard music. Czerny himself learned the art of composition by copying out the parts from Beethoven's First and Second Symphonies. In 1821, Czerny, now in the role of teacher, accepted the youthful Franz Liszt as a pupil disposing him to enthuse: 'Never before had I so eager, talented, or industrious a student.'[3]

We close our selection of pen portraits of Beethoven with the reminiscences of Ignaz von Seyfried. He was variously a composer, conductor, teacher and, according to his own account, had studied piano with Mozart. He made Beethoven's acquaintance sometime in 1803 and the two became close friends. Seyfried was familiar with the composer's works and rehearsed performances of his Second, Fifth, and Sixth symphonies, the Oratorio *Christus am Ölberge*, and the Third and Fourth Piano Concertos. In 1805, Seyfried rehearsed and conducted *Fidelio* and directed its revised version in April the following year. Seyfried was living with Beethoven when he was at work on *Fidelio* and *Christus am Ölberge* and remarks: 'At that time Beethoven was bright, always ready for a joke, cheerful, brisk, and full of spirits, witty, and occasionally satirical.'

Seyfried was privileged to hear the composer's music as it came from his pen, as he recounts:

> 'He used to play over to me on the piano, as soon as it was finished, every portion of the above-named compositions ... Without giving me time to reflect, he immediately demanded my opinion, which I was able to give freely and frankly, without any fear of offending that false pride from which his nature was entirely free.'

Commenting on the years between 1800 and 1805, before Beethoven's hearing had begun to seriously fail, Seyfried describes Beethoven's manner when conducting:

> 'Our Beethoven was not one of those fastidious composers whom no orchestra could please; sometimes he was too lenient, and would not even repeat passages which went badly at the rehearsal; "It will go better next time", he would say. But he was most particular about expression, the small *nuances*, the numerous alterations of light and shade, and the frequent passages in *tempi rubato*, all of which he was, however, quite ready to discuss with anyone. When he saw that the performers entered into his ideas, played together with increasing spirit, and captivated by the magic of his music were carried away by enthusiasm, then his face would grow bright, and with pleasure beaming from every feature, and an agreeable smile, he rewarded the successful achievement with a thundering "Bravi tutti".'

Seyfried's final homage to Beethoven was to serve as a pallbearer at his funeral.[4]

In his Autobiography *Mémoires de Hector Berlioz* — published in 1879, the year after his death, the French composer expressed his opinions on composers conducting their own works — with an aside to Beethoven:

> 'It is generally supposed that every composer is a born conductor, that is to say that he knows the art of conducting without having to learn it. Beethoven was an illustrious example of the

fallacy of this opinion, and one might name a host of other masters whose compositions are held in general esteem, but who, the moment they take up the baton, neither mark time nor nuance, and would indeed literally bring the musicians to grief if the latter did not quickly perceive the inexperience of their leader and make up their minds to pay no attention to his whirling arms.'[5]

From our pen-portraits of Beethoven we turn now to a consideration of the visual impressions of him taken at the period under consideration.

On 21 May 1801, the Leipzig music publisher Gottfried Christoph Härtel wrote to Beethoven in encouraging terms regarding business matters. He stated how pleased his publishing house would be 'to do everything that circumstances allow' to further his compositions, especially 'piano sonatas without accompaniment, or with accompaniment of violin, or of violin and violincello'. Härtel adds a touch of flattery, doubtless to secure the composer's commissions: 'The fame of your talents is established firmly enough.' Härtel concludes by requesting where Beethoven's portrait may be seen so that a likeness could be taken for its publication alongside his series of 'the most prominent composers'.[6]

In response, an engraving of Beethoven duly appeared in Volume 6 of the *Allgemeine musikalische Zeitung* (October 1803 – September 1804). Johann Neidl created this from a drawing by the artist Gandolph von Stainhauser, made sometime in 1800, and later reproduced by the Viennese music publisher Giovanni Cappi (who subsequently published the composer's three Piano Sonatas, Op. 26 and the two Piano Sonatas, Op. 27). The artist C. F. Riedl also made an engraving from Stainhauser's drawing that was published by Anton Hoffmeister at the *Bureau de Musique*, Leipzig. These, near identical studies, are the first of Beethoven's portraits since the early likeness of him taken in his Bonn days — see our previous account of the silhouette portrait of the youthful composer made by Joseph Neesen in 1796.

Beethoven appears to have been satisfied by his new portrait since he mentioned it in a letter of 16 November 1801 to his Bonn friend Franz Gerhard Wegeler — although the subject proper of this poignant letter was his encroaching deafness (see later). The Stainhauser-Neidl-Riedl likeness depicts Beethoven well-dressed and elegant, as he might have appeared as a lion of the keyboard in the glittering salons of the Viennese aristocracy, and, indeed, how he may have appeared before the public on the occasion when he premiered his C minor Concerto. The likeness in question also serves to remind us that Beethoven, 'the colossus', was in fact a relatively slight figure of about 1.62 m. — much the same as Mozart and Schubert.[7]

From 1803, we have a miniature portrait of the composer, set on ivory, created by the Danish artist Christian Horneman. This depicts Beethoven elegantly attired with fashionable stylish sideburns. Beethoven gave the miniature as a keepsake to his friend Stephan von Breuning, with whose descendants it remained for a hundred years before eventually finding a home in the Beethoven House in Bonn — via the famous collector of Beethoven memorabilia Dr H. C. Bodmer. A facsimile reproduction can be seen, with a later portrait of the composer, in the Beethoven House Digital Archives (Library Documents B 7 and HCB Bi 1). A copy of the portrait hangs in the New York Public Library. For his portrait Beethoven wore a blue tailcoat and white neckerchief, then both fashionable. His short hairstyle, created after the model of antique standards, also corresponds to the fashion of the time.

> 'It can be assumed that this is a good painting of Beethoven's physiognomy and expression, and that the painter has captured a lot of Beethoven's character while he was young and expressed it very well through this vivid expression and the concentrated look.'[8]

A measure of Beethoven's growing fame at this period is further indicated by the circumstance of him being persuaded to have his portrait painted by Joseph Mähler — a personal friend of the composer. In Mähler's study, Beethoven is portrayed in an Arcadian setting striking a lyre, in the background is a temple of Apollo. Although this portrait situates Beethoven in a somewhat idealised pastoral setting, the artist is not considered to have sacrificed his appearance in striving for romantic effect.[9]

After Beethoven's death, as the nineteenth century progressed, he became deified and was represented in visual imagery with exaggerated striving for visual effect.[10] Writing of this, the composer's biographer Alexander Thayer comments:

> 'Sculptor and painter, in turn, has idealized the work of his predecessor, until the composer stands before us like a Homeric god — until those who knew him personally, could they return to earth, would never suspect that the grand form and noble features of the more pretentious portraits are intended to represent the short muscular figure and pock-pitted face of their old friend.'[11]

Although our subject is Beethoven the emerging symphonist,

at the period in his life that we are considering he was celebrated as a virtuoso pianist. To add, therefore, to our 'portrait of Beethoven' we consider how his contemporaries responded to his pianism and prowess at the keyboard.

As a young man new to Vienna, one of the challenges Beethoven had to accept, and confront, was to take part in pianistic contests. These were nothing less than duals at the keyboard in which virtuosi, visiting Europe's musical capital, were expected to take part. The venues for such pianistic rivalry were the music salons of the nobility. One of Beethoven's contemporary 'lions of the keyboard' was Daniel Steibelt. He was a German-born pianist and composer who toured as an accomplished exponent of keyboard technique. It was in this capacity when he arrived in Vienna in 1800 on a concert tour from Paris. His prowess at the keyboard had earned for him, with the public at large, the reputation for being a formidable virtuoso — although professional musicians were inclined to dismiss him for being something of a showy charlatan.

Beethoven and Steibelt met at the house of Count Moritz Fries for a pre-arranged pianistic contest. Fries was a wealthy banker, a patron of the arts and a founder member of the famed *Gesellschaft der Musikfreunde*. For his later generosity to Beethoven, he was rewarded with the dedication of his Seventh Symphony. On the evening in question, Steibelt performed a carefully prepared *improvisation*, having provocatively chosen a theme used by Beethoven in his then recently published Trio in B-flat major, Op. 11. Ferdinand Ries, although not present himself, relates how this 'outraged Beethoven's admirers as well as Beethoven himself'. It was then Beethoven's turn to improvise. He went to the piano, turned upside down the copy of Steibelt's music — a quintet of his own composition — and 'hammered out a theme from the first few bars with one finger' and 'improvised in such a manner that Steibelt left the room before Beethoven had finished'. He shunned Beethoven's company ever after.[12]

Ferdinand Ries, to whom we have referred, heard Beethoven play on many occasions. Of his teacher's powers of extemporising he recalls:

> 'His improvising was ... the most extraordinary thing one could ever hear, especially when he was in a good mood or irritated. All the artists I ever heard improvise did not come anywhere near the heights reached by Beethoven in this discipline. The wealth of ideas which poured forth, the moods to which he surrendered himself, the variety of interpretation, the complicated challenges which evolved or which he introduced were inexhaustible.'[13]

The Czech composer and pianist Joseph Gelinek was renowned for his prowess at improvisation; it had impressed even Mozart and, later in his career, Carl Maria von Weber was so taken by Gelinek's playing that he wrote an epigram in celebration of his powers. On being invited to take part in a pianistic contest with Beethoven, Gelinek rashly boasted: 'We are going to thrash him soundly! I'll work him over!' A few days later, quite dejected, he bemoaned: 'That young man is possessed of the devil. Never have I heard such playing! He will play me and all of us to death! And how he improvised!' Beethoven had apparently improvised on a theme of Gelinek's choosing and then performed compositions of his own (unspecified) that Gelinek regarded as 'wonderful and grandiose to the highest degree'. He adds how Beethoven achieved effects 'such as we have never even dreamed of'.[14] Gelinek appears to have swallowed his pride since he went on to create a piano arrangement of

Beethoven's First Symphony and later composed a set of variations on the *Allegretto* of the Seventh Symphony.

Wenzel Tomaschek was another Czech composer and pianist who considered Beethoven to be 'the giant among pianoforte players'. He heard Beethoven perform during his concert tour of Prague — probably in October 1798 —when he played his First Piano Concerto and two movements from his Piano Sonata Op. 2, No. 1. However, it was Beethoven's improvising on a theme from Mozart's Opera *La Clemenza di Tito* that captivated him most and held him in thrall to his powers of improvisation. Writing later of these he states:

> 'Beethoven's magnificent playing, and particularly his daring flights in his improvisation, stirred me strangely to the depths of my soul; indeed, I found myself so profoundly bowed down that I did not touch my pianoforte for several days.'

Sometime later Tomaschek heard Beethoven play once more but qualified his admiration of Beethoven's playing saying:

> 'This time I listened to Beethoven's artistic work with more composure. I admired his powerful and brilliant playing, but his frequent daring deviations from one motive to another, whereby the organic connection, the gradual development of ideas was put aside, did not escape me.'

Reflecting more generally on Beethoven's keyboard music he added:

> 'It is not seldom that the unbiased listener is

> rudely awakened from his transport. The singular and original seemed to be his chief aim in composition.'[15]

Johann Aloys Schlosser was a partner in a publishing firm in Prague who may have first learned of Beethoven's fame and celebrity from the composer's concert tours in his hometown in 1796 and 1798. His study of the composer — *Ludwig van Beethoven: Eine Biographie* — appeared in Prague a few months after the composer's death. Barry Cooper has edited a modern-day edition of Schlosser's study of the composer and remarks: 'The principal significance of Schlosser's *Biography* is that it was the very first on Beethoven to be published...'. It is dated 1828 but it may have actually appeared in the year of Beethoven's death. In this pioneering study of the composer, his powers of improvisation at the keyboard were considered to be worthy of mention. Schlosser informs:

> 'People marvelled at the facility with which he executed difficult passages. His playing may not always have been delicate, and at times may have lacked clarity, but it was extremely brilliant. He excelled at free improvisation. Here it was really quite extraordinary with what ease, and yet soundness of execution of ideas he would improvise on any theme given to him, not just varying the theme in his fingers but really developing it. In this he resembled Mozart more than any other modern artist.'

As a consequence of his powers, Schlosser adds: 'Everyone vied to have Beethoven attend their social events.'[16]

Carl Czerny compared Beethoven's playing with that of Mozart's followers:

> 'Mozart's school [is] clear and a markedly brilliant [style of] playing, based more on staccato than legato; a witty and lively execution. The pedal rarely used. Beethoven's manner [has] characteristic and passionate strength, alternating with all the charms of smooth *cantabile*, [this] is its outstanding feature.'

Writing of Beethoven performing, he adds:

> 'Beethoven ...drew entirely new and daring passages from the fortepiano by the use of the pedal, by an exceptionally characteristic way of playing, particularly distinguished by a strict legato of the chords and thus created a new type of singing tone and many hitherto unimagined effects. His playing did not possess that clean and brilliant elegance of certain other pianists. On the other hand, it was spirited, grandiose and, especially in adagio, very full of feeling and romantic. His performance, like his compositions, was a tone-painting of a very high order and conceived only for a tonal effect.'[17]

The German-born, London-based composer, pianist and publisher Johann Baptist Cramer was resident in Vienna in the winter of 1799–1800. According to Carl Czerny: 'He caused a great stir by his playing three sonatas dedicated to Haydn [*Trois Grandes Sonates pour le Pianoforte*].'[18] It is perhaps no coincidence that the first of these is in the key of A-flat major — that chosen by Beethoven for his own Piano

Sonata Op. 26. Although at times pianistic rivals, a measure of mutual admiration appears to have existed between Cramer and Beethoven. Cramer considered Beethoven to be 'the supreme improviser' and, according to Beethoven's pupil Ferdinand Ries: 'Cramer was the only pianist whom Beethoven had praised as being truly excellent.'[19]

The Viennese music cognoscenti were captivated not only by Cramer's playing of his own works but also by those of his teacher Muzio Clementi. As a consequence, it has been suggested

> 'Beethoven felt the need to compete with this virtuosity and thereby wrote a number of works that began to break away from the more classically oriented sonatas, of the 1790s, towards his mature second-period style'.[20]

Thayer suggests when Beethoven was writing his Piano Sonata in A flat, Op. 26, 'there is purposely a reminder of ... Clementi-Cramer passage work in the finale'.[21] Later in life, Beethoven admired Cramer's *Instructions for the Pianoforte* (*Grosse Pianoforteschule*), published in 1815 that are still in use today.[22]

With Beethoven at the height of his powers as a virtuoso concert pianist, it is necessary to close our portrait of him by alluding to circumstances that would oblige him to set aside his career as a virtuoso and would, in effect, transform his life forever.

In June 1801, Beethoven had occasion to write to Franz Gerhard Wegeler, his close friend from schooldays in Bonn; it is one of Beethoven's longest and most moving letters. The first part is full of optimism. He tells his friend about his benefactor Prince Karl Lichnowsky who, as we have seen, the year previously had settled upon him an annual sum of 600 gulden 'on which', he writes, 'I can draw until I obtain a suitable appointment'.[23] He adds: 'My compositions bring me in a good deal, and I may say that I am offered more commissions than it is possible for me to carry out.' Moreover, Beethoven's standing with Vienna's music publishers was high as he further explains:

> '[For] every composition I can count on six or seven publishers, and even more, if I want them; people no longer come to arrangement with me, I state the price and they pay. So, you see how pleasantly situated I am.'

However, towards the end of the letter Beethoven discloses his inner feelings to Wegeler regarding his health:

> '[That] jealous demon, my wretched health, has put a spoke in my wheel ... for the last three years my hearing has become weaker and weaker ... Heaven alone knows what is to become of me.'[24]

On 1 July 1801, Beethoven wrote to Karl Amenda to whom we have made reference; his opening salutation is indicative of the affection he felt for him: 'My Dear Amenda, My Kind Amenda, My Warm-Hearted Friend!' He continues:

> 'How often would I like to have you here with me, for your B[eethoven] is leading a very unhappy life and is at variance with Nature and his Creator. Many times already I have cursed Him for exposing His creatures to the slightest hazard, so that the most beautiful blossom is thereby often crushed and destroyed.'

Beethoven explained the reason for his mortification:

> 'Let me tell you that my most prized possession, *my hearing*, has greatly deteriorated. When you were still with me, I already felt the symptoms; but said nothing about them. Now they have become very much worse. We must wait and see whether my hearing can be restored. The symptoms are said to be caused by the condition of my abdomen. So far as the latter is concerned, I am almost quite cured. But that my hearing too will improve, I must hope, it is true, but I hardly think it possible, for diseases of that kind are the most difficult to cure. You will realize what a sad life I must now lead.'

Beethoven reflected further on his adversity:

> 'Oh how happy should I be now if I had perfect hearing ... But in my present condition I must withdraw from everything; and my best years will rapidly pass away without my being able to achieve all that my talent and my strength have commanded me to do.'

He urged Amenda to be circumspect:

> '*I beg you to treat what I have told you about my hearing as a great secret to be entrusted to no one, whoever he may be.*' [Beethoven's emphasis][25]

On 16 November, Beethoven wrote again to Wegeler asking if he considered if galvanism might benefit his hearing. Only ten years previously (1791) Luigi Galvani had published his treatise on what he termed 'biological electricity' with sensational claims of its alleged powers to animate the muscles of dead limbs – including those of human beings (derived from the corpses of criminals). The reader will recall this innovation was the genesis of Mary Shelly's *Frankenstein*. It is a measure of Beethoven's desperation concerning his hearing that he was prepared to contemplate such new and untested procedures. His letter to Wegeler, however, reveals how love and his indomitability of spirit were helping him to conquer his *jealous demon*. He tells Wegeler he is 'leading a slightly more pleasant life' and mixing more with his 'fellow creatures'. Hitherto, he explains, how his poor hearing had haunted him everywhere 'like a ghost' and had made him seem to be 'a misanthrope' which he insists he is 'far from being'. This more positive transformation in his life, and outlook, had been brought about by 'a dear charming girl who loves me and whom I love'. Beethoven even contemplated marriage in the hope it might bring him further happiness. He recognized, however, this was impossible since he was obliged to concede 'unfortunately [the lady in question] is not of my class'. In any event, Beethoven concluded, he could not marry at the present moment on the grounds: 'For me there is no greater pleasure than to practice and exercise my art.'[26]

The 'dear charming girl', to whom Beethoven makes reference, was Countess Gillette Guicciadi. She would eventually receive the dedication of the second of the Piano Sonatas Op. 27 – the *Moonlight*. Beethoven's hopes of marriage, however, were not fulfilled and in 1803 Gillette married Count Wenzel Gallenberg.[27]

Other composers have suffered from a loss of hearing and what they have to say serves to further illustrate Beethoven's misfortune.

In his later years, the Czech composer, pianist and conductor Bedřich Smetana suffered from both deafness and tinnitus — incessant ringing in the ears. As his condition worsened he was given to saying: 'If my disease is incurable, then I should prefer to be liberated from this life' — sentiments that closely approximate to those expressed by Beethoven in his despairing *Heiligenstadt Testament* that he addressed to his brothers Carl and Johann on 6 October 1802.

Around 1905, Gabriel Fauré realized he was losing his hearing. At first, like Beethoven, he tried to conceal it, and only his wife knew of the torment he was enduring. He wrote to her when away in Switzerland:

> 'I am overwhelmed by the affliction that has struck me in what is most important I should preserve intact ... I am constantly weighed down by a frightful cloak of misery and discouragement.'[28]

In our own time, the English composer and broadcaster on music Michael Berkeley — Baron Berkeley — has expressed his personal anguish at the loss of his hearing. He gave expression to his feelings in *The Guardian* newspaper — in what was, in effect, his own *Heiligenstadt Testament*. He confides:

> 'I have now looked ... into that abyss ... Sudden pain ... accompanied by frenetic gurgling, bubbling and popping ... [Beethoven's] reported descriptions of distortion and frequency loss now sound horribly familiar to me ... Contemplating afresh Beethoven's sheer willpower and sublime creativity as his hearing deserted him, and listening again to the defiant *Grosse Fuge* and the haunting *Cavatina* from the Opus 130 Quartet that he himself did not live to witness in its final form, I find myself reconsidering Beethoven's extraordinary achieve-

ment. It brings tears to the eyes – eyes, which for Beethoven, became his ears.'[29]

Other musicians and musicologists have reflected on the consequences to Beethoven occasioned by his loss of hearing. From the very many of these writings, we close our 'personal portrait' of the composer with just two of these.

The American music scholar William Kinderman reflects

> 'The crisis of [Beethoven's] deafness forced him to reconsider the most fundamental assumptions about his life and art. For, as Beethoven put it to Amenda, [see above] he was consumed by doubts not only about his social life but about his "being able to achieve all that [his] talent and strength demanded [him] to do". One of his worst fears may have been that his deafness would stifle the realization of his artistic potential.'

Kinderman continues: 'Despite his initial fears [resulting] from a lack of hearing, his art actually became richer and deeper as his hearing declined.'

In this positive context, Kinderman quotes Maynard Solomon:

> ' "[One] begins to suspect that Beethoven's crisis and his extraordinary creativity were somehow related. And even that the former may have been the necessary precondition of the latter." '[30]

In her discussion of sound and hearing, the American writer and biographer Electra Yourke adopts the memorable phrase: 'The gate of music is the ear.' She elucidates: 'Our faculties of musical perception, and the ability to perform music, depend upon the perfection of our auditory apparatus.'

With regard to Beethoven, she remarks:

> 'It is amazing, therefore, that Beethoven was able to write great music when, if not totally deaf, then certainly so hard of hearing he had to rely on a notebook in which his collocutors wrote their remarks.'

She asks: 'How could Beethoven compose if he could not hear sounds?'

She responds:

> 'The answer is that his creative imagination had already built a *dome of sound* [italics added] and he no longer needed external stimuli to organize these sounds into melodies and harmonies.'[31]

---

[1] Derived from: *The Diaries of Carl Friedrich Kübeck*, cited in H. C. Robbins Landon, 1992, pp. 67–68. See also Peter Clive, 2001, pp. 197–98.
[2] As recalled in Oscar George Theodore Sonneck, *Beethoven: Impressions of Contemporaries*, 1927, pp. 33–35.
[3] Carl Czerny as recounted in: Ludwig Nohl, *Beethoven depicted by his Contemporaries, 1880*, pp. 36–48. See also: Paul Badura-Skoda, Carl Czerny, *On the Proper Performance of all Beethoven's Works for the Piano*, 1970; Charles K. Moss, *Carl Czerny, Teacher and Composer*, 2005, website article; and Oscar George Theodore Sonneck, 1927, pp. 23–31.
[4] Ignaz von Seyfried, as recounted in: Ludwig Nohl, *Beethoven depicted by his Contemporaries*, 1880, pp. 49–56 and Oscar George Theodore Sonneck, *Beethoven: Impressions of Contemporaries*, 1927, pp. 35–46. See also Elliot Forbes editor, *Thayer's Life of Beethoven*, 1967 p. 371.
[5] Quoted in Sam Morgenstern, editor, 1956, pp. 117–18.
[6] Theodore Albrecht, 1996, Vol. 1, Letter No. 34, pp. 63–4.
[7] For reproductions of the Neidl and Riedl studies of Beethoven see: H. C. Robbins Landon, 1992, plates 3 and 4.
[8] Derived from the text to, Beethoven House Library Document HCB Bi 1. See also H. C. Robbins Landon, 1970, text to plate 5.

[9] Beethoven House Digital Archives, *Beethoven Gallery* and Library Document B 2388. See also: H. C. Robbins Landon, 1992, plate 6.
[10] See Beethoven House Archive for illustrations of numerous portrayals of Beethoven by sculptors and artists.
[11] Elliot Forbes editor, *Thayer's Life of Beethoven*, 1967 p. 238.
[12] Ferdinand Ries as recorded in: Franz Wegeler, 1838, English edition, 1988, p. 71. For a more extended account of Beethoven's pianistic confrontation with Steibelt, see: Thayer-Forbes, 1967, p. 257.
[13] Ferdinand Ries in: Franz Wegeler, 1838, English edition, 1988, pp. 87–88.
[14] From the recollections of Carl Czerny, see: Paul Badura-Skoda, editor, 1970, p. 4. Czerny conveyed his father's recollections of Gelineck to Beethoven's early biographer Otto Jahn. For a brief account of Joseph Gelinek and his relationship with Beethoven see: Peter Clive, 2001, pp. 124–5.
[15] Oscar George Theodore Sonneck, 1927, pp. 21–23.
[16] Johann Schlosser, *Beethoven: The First Biography*, 1827, edited by Barry Cooper. 1996, pp. 9–10 and pp. 79–80.
[17] Carl Czerny, *Pianoforte Schule* Part III, Chapter 15, Op. 500, 1839 (available in modern-day editions). See also: H. C. Robbins Landon, 1970, p. 44.
[18] From the recollections of Carl Czerny, see: Paul Badura-Skoda, editor, 1970, p. 9.
[19] Peter Clive, 2001, pp. 77-8. Clive's citation of the views of Ferdinand Ries is derived from Ries's study *Beethoven Biographische Notizen*, p. 87.
[20] Matthew Rye, BBC Radio Three, *Beethoven Experience*, 3 June 2005.
[21] Thayer-Forbes, 1967, p. 296.
[22] Related biographical information, and a portrait of Cramer, can be seen on the Beethoven House Website, Beethoven House Bonn, Digital Archives, Library Document B. 1254.
[23] In Vienna, at the turn of the century, the gulden was the equivalent of the Austrian florin. The practical value of Beethoven's annuity can be estimated from the following: The *Wiener Zeitung* of 28 January 1792 recorded the appointment of Salieri's pupil, Joseph Weigl, as 'Kapellmeister and Composer to the Royal Imperial National Court Theatre with a salary of 1,000 florins'. Allowing for inflation, Beethoven's 600 florins was the equivalent of about two-thirds of the annual salary of a professional musician. Derived from Thayer-Forbes 1967, p. 150.
[24] Beethoven's letter to Wegeler is translated in Emily Anderson, 1961, Vol. 1, Letter No. 51, pp. 57-62. A facsimile of the original document can be viewed on the Beethoven House Website: Beethoven House Bonn, Digital Archives, Library Document Sammlung Wegeler, W. 17.
[25] Emily Anderson editor and translator, 1961, Vol. 1, Letter No. 53, pp. 63–65. For a facsimile reproduction of this letter see: Beethoven House, Digital Archives, Library Document, Audio Letter HCB BBR 1.
[26] Emily Anderson, 1961, Vol. 1 Letter No. 54, pp. 66–8. For facsimile reproduction of this letter, together with the original German text, see: Beethoven House, Digital Archives, Library Document, W 18.
[27] A measure of the affection Beethoven felt for Gillette Guicciadi is that he treasured a miniature portrait of her all his life. It was found among his possessions after his death.
[28] As quoted in: Madeleine Goss, 1945, p. 51.

[29] Michael Berkeley, *My Beethoven Moment*, *The Guardian*, 7 September, 2010. The words quoted are derived from a much longer article.
[30] William Kinderman, *Beethoven*, 1997, p. 61. The reference to Maynard Solomon is derived from his *Beethoven*, 1977, p. 115.
[31] Electra Yourke, 2003–5, Vol. 4, p. 150.

BEETHOVEN: A NEW PATH

The years 1798–1802 were significant for Beethoven; we see him striving for mastery of the Viennese high classical style and achieving mastery within its major instrumental genres. Alongside work on the First Symphony, he had composed several major works including: String Trio, Op. 9 (1798); String Quartets, Op. 18 (1799–1800); String Quintet, Op. 29 (1801); Piano Concerto No. 3, Op. 37 (1800); and Piano Sonatas, Opp. 22 and 28 (1800–01). Contemplating these, Maynard Solomon contends:

> 'Beethoven had gained the high ground of the Viennese tradition; he was now faced with the choice of endless repetition of his conquests or casting out in an uncharted direction ... Beethoven was now well launched upon his "new

path" — a qualitative change in his style which would become a turning point in the history of music itself.'[1]

In this part of our discourse, we consider Beethoven's progress along his 'new path' with particular regard to the orchestra and orchestral composition. First, the expression 'new path' requires a few words of explanation.

Shortly after completing his D major Piano Sonata Op. 28 (published in 1801), Beethoven expressed dissatisfaction over his piano writing to date. He confided this to his close friend, the mandolin and violin player Wenzel Krumpholz; he was an accomplished performer and a member of Prince Nikolaus Esterhazy's orchestra. We learn of Beethoven's feelings concerning his piano music through an interesting chain of events that are as follows. Krumpholz conveyed Beethoven's expression of dissatisfaction with his work to Carl Czerny — who was also an intimate friend of Krumpholz. Years later (1842) Czerny left an account of Beethoven's remarks in a short autobiography he made of his life that was later deposited in the archives of the *Gesellschaft der Musikfreunde* at Vienna.

Czerny's account only came to light in 1870 when the keeper of the archives published it in his *Annual Report* to coincide with the celebrations planned for that year — Beethoven's Birth Centenary. In 1880, Czerny's account of Beethoven's conversation with Krumpholz was eventually published by the musicologist Ludwig Nohl — to whom, amongst other things, posterity owes a debt for discovering the lost autograph of one of Beethoven's most cherished miniature compositions, his Bagatelle *Für Elise.* Back in1803, Beethoven had apparently exclaimed to Krumpholz: 'God knows why my piano music still makes the worst impression on me.'[2]

With characteristic resolution, he confided to his sketchbook how he 'intended to make a fresh start' — his first steps along his 'new path'.

Beethoven faced a number of challenges when contemplating composing works for the orchestra. These embraced such considerations as: the size of the orchestra to be used; the instruments available to him, a number of which were undergoing transformation — such as the horn for which valves were becoming available; performance-practice, with regard to such musicological considerations as ornamentation, articulation and, significantly, tempo — in an attempt to regulate which Beethoven was an early advocate of the metronome; and the evolving role of the direction of the orchestra as it transitioned from the hands of the leader to that of the conductor.[3]

Writing of Beethoven's orchestration, the German musicologist Paul Mies makes reference to what he describes as Beethoven's preference for 'deep colours' and orchestral sounds 'more opaque' than those of Mozart's or Haydn's. He suggests the oboe was for Beethoven 'a gay instrument' and how well-suited are the sharp sounds of the piccolo to the concluding bars of the Overtire *Egmont* and the finale of the Fifth Symphony. He also cites the manner in which Beethoven occasionally employs additional instruments for special effects, for example, cymbals, triangle and drum to characterize Turkish music that was so popular in his day — as, for example, in the incidental music to *Die Ruinen von Athen* and his *Turkish* March, Op. 113.

In his overview of Beethoven's orchestral writing, Paul Mies cites Beethoven's characteristic use of two each of flutes, oboes, clarinets, bassoons, trumpets, horns, and timpani. Beethoven modified these orchestral resources in a number of ways, for example: Symphony No. 1, *Andante* without second flute; Symphony No. 2, *Larghetto* without trumpet,

Symphony No. 3, third horn added; Symphony No. 4, one flute; Symphony No 5, three trombones (first use of), piccolo, and double bassoon; Symphony No. 6, trombones and piccolo in the *storm*, and solo cellos in the *Andante*; *Battle Symphony*, piccolo, triangle, cymbals, bass drum, three trombones and — off stage — two great drums, two rattles, four trumpets, and military drums; Symphony No. 7, a reversion to the 'standard' orchestra; Symphony No. 8, second movement without timpani and trumpets; Symphony No. 9, four horns, three trombones, double bassoon, piccolo, triangle, cymbals, bass drum, with four solo voices and chorus.[4]

Musicologist Anne-Louise Coldicott comments in similar manner to Paul Mies regarding the changing size and nature of the orchestras available to Beethoven. In an earlier part of our account we have remarked on Vienna's major concert venues. From Coldicott we learn:

'In 1808 the orchestra in the Theater an der Wien consisted of 12 violins, 4 violas, 3 cellos, 3 bases, 2 each of flutes, oboes, clarinets, horns and trumpets and timpani. But in 1815, in the Redoutensaal, the strings comprised 36 violins, 14 violas, 12 cellos and 17 double bases.'

Concerning the performance of Beethoven's early symphonies, she adds:

'[In] the 1807–08 season Beethoven's first four symphonies were performed in the University Hall by a much larger compliment of strings — 13, 12, 7, 6, 4 — but still single wind ... As the time went on, large orchestras became increasingly normal: in 1817 the *Tonkünstler-Societät* performed *Christus am Oelberg* with 20, 20, 8, 7, 6, 4 [strings] —

and woodwind doubled or trebled, and in 1824 the Ninth Symphony was performed by 24 violins, 10 violas, 12 cellos and 12 bases.'[5]

We may ask here, 'What did a Beethoven orchestra sound like?' To quote Coldicott once more:

'The sound and balance of the orchestra were different from today. Overall the wind were louder and more piercing than the strings; oboes were louder and more penetrative, bassoons produced a more vital sound, and only the flutes, made of wood, were softer than present-day instruments. The strings were softer due to their gut strings and their different manner of articulation dictated by contemporary bows.'[6]

Leon Botstein pays tribute to Beethoven's adoption of the orchestral resources that would have been available to Haydn and Mozart. He enthuses:

'A remarkable aspect of Beethoven's use of the orchestra is the shear variety and extreme range of colour, texture, and sound that he achieved without adding substantially to the forces used by Haydn and Mozart. Only Symphonies 3, 5, 6, and 9 use more instruments than can be found in Haydn and Mozart: double winds (flute, oboe, clarinet, bassoon), double brass (two horns, two trumpets,) tympani and strings.'

He cites the epochal *Eroica* Symphony when Beethoven used an additional French horn to supplement the traditional complement of two horns and his no-less pioneering use, in symphonic writing, of three trombones in the Fifth Symphony; Mozart, we recall had used the trombone to dramatic effect in his late works such as *The Magic Flute*, and the *Requiem*.[7] In later compositions, Beethoven would expand the sonority of the orchestra. In the Ninth Symphony in which he makes use of four horns and likewise in the Overtures *King Stephen*, the three *Leonora* Overtures, *Fidelio*, and *The Consecration of the House*. Beethoven was inventive in the use of the tympani. To quote Botstein once more: 'The last movement of the First Symphony ... contains an early example ... in which the tympani assume a leading role in establishing the texture of the music.' To this observation we may add Beethoven's prominent use of the tympani in the Violin Concerto — notably in the Piano Transcription — and at the close of the *Emperor* Piano Concerto. Botstein summarizes Beethoven's achievement in the genre of orchestral writing in the following terms:

> 'The creation of sounds coming from the entire orchestra, the roles given to the solo wind instruments, the varied demands made on the different constituents of the orchestra, and the mode of integration and combination of the elements of the orchestra were part and parcel of Beethoven's originality and novelty — particularly his role for the Romantic movement as the champion of inner subjectivity.'[8]

Early Romantic writers, such as the German composer and music theorist Gottfried Wilhelm Fink, identified with 'the overpowering effect of Beethoven's orchestral sound [and] his novel sense of integration and unity'. Fink found in Beethoven's orchestral music

> 'an organic approach to compositional development which successfully reconciled individuality and subjectivity with an overarching sense of totality'.[9]

The contemporaneous classical scholar and musician Ferdinand Gotthelf Hand expressed similar thoughts in his *Asthetik der Tonkunst* – translated into English by W.E. Lawson as *Aesthetics of Musical Art, or The Beautiful in Music* (1880). To Hand, the dramatic dimension in Beethoven's orchestral writing suggested 'gravity and profundity that moved the concerns of humankind'.[10]

In his study of Beethoven's Symphonies (1896), Sir George Grove writes of Beethoven's orchestration in the First Symphony, recognizing that he learned his craft through a study of Haydn's symphonies and the operas of Mozart. Of his Op. 21, he reflects:

> 'The ease with which he handles the orchestra, in his first large work, is somewhat remarkable. His only orchestral practice before it would seem to have been his two Cantatas, written in 1790 on the death of Joseph II and the accession of Leopold II, the first movement of the Violin Concerto, and his first two Piano Concertos.'[11]

In his *L'orchestra* (1920) the Italian composer and musicologist Gian Francesco Malipiero expressed his thoughts on the question of *sonority* in orchestral music, making particular reference to Beethoven's symphonies: He maintained:

> 'The sonority of an orchestral work infallibly reveals as much of its composer's individuality as the harmonic and thematic content ... Beethoven,

for instance, without the continuous doubling indispensable to Anton Bruckner and without the harmonic support favoured by Wagner, attains to an orchestral intensity to that of these two composers.'

Malipiero considered:

> 'Nothing could be added to the orchestra of Beethoven and nothing subtracted from that of Bruckner or Wagner without causing, respectively, heaviness or emptiness.'

Regarding contemporary performance-practice, though, Malipiero recognized that changes had come about occasioned, notably, by the increase in the size of the modern-day concert hall. In the more extreme cases of changes to Beethoven's orchestration he speculates if Beethoven would even recognise his own work! More restrainedly he accepted:

> 'Today, the body of violins, violas, violincellos, and double basses is more than twice as numerous in relation to the proportion desired by the composer. And yet ... no unbalanced combination ever occurs.'[12]

Wilhelm Furtwängler is closely associated with the interpretation of Beethoven's symphonies. Concerning the composer's orchestration, he wrote in an essay:

> 'There are *fortissimi* which, though scored for ridiculously few instruments, have an inner-drive and power which completely overshadow the

explosive outbursts of a modern symphony orchestra.'

Furtwängler maintained:

> 'Confronted with the inner-stresses and tensions of this music, all our genteel, refined striving after artistry and euphony proves useless. Beethoven lies beyond the limits of what people call *Beauty*. The smouldering heat within his works consumes all who perform it, singers and instrumentalists alike. To change the metaphor — every work has to be wrenched from the consciousness of whoever performs it.'[13]

The British musicologist Clive Brown is an authority on authentic, classical-performance and historical violin playing. He reminds us how significantly different performances of Beethoven's symphonies are today than in his own time:

> 'This is strikingly true of the sounds of the individual instruments and their effects in combination: brass instruments were valve-less, woodwind had fewer keys and were more sharply differentiated from one another in tone-quality than their modern counterparts, while the skin-covered timpani made a particularly distinctive sound.'

Regarding his own instrument Brown states:

> 'Members of the violin family, though they were rapidly approaching modern instruments in the thickness of the bass bar, angle of neck and length

of fingerboard, continued to be strung with gut until the end of the nineteenth century, giving a clearer articulation and brighter sound.'

He adds:

'Pitch was about a semitone lower than today ... furthermore the balance of the orchestra was weighted much more heavily in favour of the wind instruments. Instead of the usual eight to ten desks of the first violins in a modern symphony orchestra, most early nineteenth-century German orchestras had only three or four desks, and where string numbers were substantially increased (as for festive performances such as the premiere of the Eighth Symphony in 1814) it was usual to double the wind instruments.'

Making reference to Beethoven, Brown comments:

'In its final form the First Symphony was scored for an orchestra of pairs of flutes, oboes, clarinets, bassoons, horns, trumpets, and strings, but there is evidence to suggest that, as with Mozart's G minor Symphony K 550, the clarinets may have been an afterthought.' He believes they may have been added after the first performance and the publication of the orchestral parts in 1801.[14]

The British conductor Sir Roger Norrington is known for his historically informed performances of Classical and Romantic music. Writing of this he apprises:

'Every single instrument was subtly different from

today's equivalent, and each was perfectly adapted to the world of Classical music. The strings, cleaner but more plaintive, articulate easily and expressively. The woodwind each has an individual colour, creating character and clarity of ensemble within the section. The horns' hand-stopped notes give a vivid, dramatic variety to their playing, while the tympani, small and beaten with hard sticks, sound as if they have come straight from the field of Waterloo. This sheer variety of sound is essential to Beethoven, who was using a full orchestra that had recently matured under the hands of Haydn and Mozart.'[15]

We give the last words on the subject of 'authentic' performance to the German-born orchestral conductor and composer Otto Klemperer. In 1961 he contributed an essay to accompany his complete recordings of Beethoven's symphonies that was published in 1964 as his *Minor Recollections*. We quote the following extract:

'Much has been said about the instrumental retouching of Beethoven and the conflict between fidelity to the original and the reverse. Both schools of thought are at once right and wrong. Mahler once said at a rehearsal of his own Eighth Symphony that, after his death, anyone would be welcome to alter anything in his work which sounded wrong. Both Richard Wagner and Mahler subjected Beethoven to extensive retouching. Today we feel this to be unnecessary. Besides: "Let each man see to his own, where he stands and, when he stands, see that he does not fall".' [Quoted from Goethe's *Beherzigung*][16]

*

In Vienna in the early 1800s, performances of large-scale works, such as symphonies, overtures, and concertos, were directed by the violinist-leader of the orchestra. In this context, two such figures were pre-eminent in Beethoven's day, namely, Ignaz Schuppanzigh and Franz Clement. Schuppanzigh was the leader of a string quartet that bore his name. For a period, he gave Beethoven instruction in violin-playing and towards the end of the composer's life his Quartet was active in the promotion of his late string quartets. From 1798–99, Schuppanzigh took charge of the concerts held in the Augarten, at which he would occasionally beat the time with his bow when some steadying of the orchestra was required – he was also known to beat time with his feet! Ignaz von Seyfried described Schuppanzigh as 'a natural-born and really energetic leader of the orchestra'.[17]

Franz Clement was Viennese by birth and was a gifted child-prodigy violinist. In 1804 he was appointed leader of the orchestra of the Theater an der Wien, becoming *Musikdirektor* the following year. Beethoven became acquainted with Clement in 1794 and so respected his playing he wrote his Violin Concerto expressly with him in mind. In his *The Orchestra from Beethoven to Berlioz*, Adam Carse writes:

> 'This "conducting" was obviously only a sort of general supervision, the actual control of the orchestra would then be in the hands of the violinist-leader.'[18]

Worthy of additional remark Is that Beethoven's first six symphonies were published initially in parts only without the full score. This placed even greater reliance on the leader of the violins to direct the music from a reading of his own part.

Writing of the origins of the orchestral conductor, Norman Del Mar states:

> 'The necessity for such a figure arose during the days of Beethoven and Berlioz, principally owing to the rapid increase in the size and complexity of concerted and ensemble music which soon reached the point where it could no longer be controlled by one of the actual instrumentalists as had hitherto been the case with the composer or kapellmeister.'[19]

Beethoven never held the appointment of *kapellmeister*, either at Bonn or at Vienna. He did occasionally direct performances of his works (see later), but had no regular experience as a conductor. His biographer Anton Schindler explains:

> 'At the time when his hearing was yet perfect, he had not often occasion to come in contact with the orchestra, and especially to acquire practice in the conducting department at the theatre, which is the best school for that purpose.'[20]

With the advent of Johann Nepomuk Maelzel's metronome (1816–17), Beethoven seized upon its potential as a means of securing reliable tempi for the performance of his works. A report in the *Wiener Vaterländische Blätter* (*Vienna Patriotic Periodical*) stated:

> 'Herr Beethoven looks upon this invention as a welcome means with which to secure the per-

formance of his brilliant compositions in all places in the tempos conceived by him, which to his regret have so often been misunderstood.'[21]

To this end, Beethoven had a pamphlet printed by the publisher Sigmund Anton Steiner that gave his suggested metronome markings for his first eight symphonies.[22] A measure of Beethoven's wish to have his orchestral works performed, at what he considered to be the 'correct' tempi, is evident in a letter he wrote to the Mainz publisher Bernhard Schotts: 'We can scarcely have *tempi ordinari* any longer, since one must fall into line with the ideas of unfettered genius.'[23]

Beethoven's metronome markings are today generally considered to be too fast. It has been suggested the reason for this is that, confined by deafness to an inner world of *imagined* sound, he ascribed quicker markings to his music than he would have had if he had the benefit of experiencing his music *in performance*. We cite Roger Norrington once more:

> 'Beethoven inherited a whole series of traditional speeds, including an *allegro* which was not very fast and an *andante* which was by no means slow. He was most insistent on the importance of using a metronome (partly, no doubt, because his deafness prevented him from directing performances). In virtually every case his metronome marks tally with an eighteenth-century understanding of tempo indications.'[24]

Today we take it for granted that orchestral conductors adopt a baton in order to better emphasize and communicate their musical thoughts and feelings to the players. That it was not always so is aptly told in the recollections of Louis Spohr — a pioneer of baton-technique; In his *Autobiography* he describes his experience of introducing the use of the baton with the players of the orchestra of the newly formed Philharmonic Society of London. This was the period when Beethoven's pupil Ferdinand Rise was one of the Society's Directors. It was also the era when the orchestra was directed by the leader of the first violins and who, as remarked, should the tempo falter, beat the time with his bow.

Spohr observed with a large number of players, spread over a spacious platform, unanimity of expression would frequently falter. He resolved to remedy this by the use of the baton. He relates how at a morning rehearsal:

> 'I produced from my pocket my baton and taking my stand at a desk in front of the orchestra gave the signal to begin ... I could not only give the tempi but indicate the entries of the horns and wood instruments which much-increased the confidence of the performers. I also took the liberty to stop when the execution did not please me and make polite but earnest comments [in German] which Mr. [Ferdinand] Ries translated.'

Spohr describes the players' response:

> 'The novelty roused their attention and, helped by seeing the time beaten out so clearly, the players performed with a spirit and correctness unknown before.'

As to the actual performance of the work being rehearsed, Spohr enthuses:

> 'In the evening the result was still more brilliant
> ... the orchestra performed ... with unusual power
> and precision, there was long and loud applause.
> The baton had triumphed.'[25]

The Vienna-born artist Joseph Wielder, a younger contemporary of Beethoven, was renowned for his portraits and watercolours. He made a study of the composer that, with a little imagination, suggests how he might have appeared when standing before an orchestra. Wielder has depicted Beethoven in a pose characteristic of a conductor, although he appears to be wielding a club not a baton; Beethoven could be demanding in the performance of his orchestral music, but he never resorted to cowing the players into submission with a club![26]

Descriptions of Beethoven conducting have been left by several of Beethoven's musician-contemporaries. These are found, for example, in the recollections of Carl Czerny, Ignaz Moscheles, Johann Friedrich Reichardt, Ferdinand Ries, Ignaz von Seyfried, and Louis Spohr. They describe Beethoven standing before the orchestra in animated fashion, making gestures with his arms and body by way of conveying the dynamics of the music. Before turning our attention to the creation origins of the First Symphony, we take leave of Beethoven, the conductor, as two of these contemporaries recall him.

Moscheles relates how when Beethoven was conducting, in order to indicate the *tempi* and required sonority, in the *piano* passages he would stoop down more and more until he almost disappeared, then, with the music gradually rising up at the *crescendo*, he would stand on tiptoe and bound up at the *fortissimo*.[27]

In his *Autobiography* (English translation 1865), Louis

Spohr describes an account he received from Ignaz von Seyfried that relates to the 1803 concert series in Vienna. Spohr relates:

> '*Beethoven* was playing a new Pianoforte-Concerto of his, but forgot at the first *tutti*, that he was a solo player and, springing up, began to direct in his usual way. At the first *sforzando* he threw out his arms so wide asunder, that he knocked both the lights off the piano upon the ground. The audience laughed, and *Beethoven* was so incensed at this disturbance, that he made the orchestra cease playing and begin anew.'

Seyfried intervened and requested two chorus boys, from the Oratorio *Christus am Ölberge*, that was to be sung, to place themselves on either side of *Beethoven* to hold the lights in their hands. However, such was Beethoven's loss of composure, it is alleged that at the first chords of the solo he pounded the keys so vehemently that several strings broke – and the boys, holding the candles, had to keep clear to prevent them from knocked out of their hands.[28]

With Beethoven set upon his new path we now consider the creation origins of his First Symphony, Op. 21.

---

[1] Maynard Solomon, 1977, p. 107.
[2] Derived in part from: Ludwig Nohl, 1880, p. 48; Peter Clive, 2001, p. 197; and Denis Matthews, 1997, p. 2.
[3] With acknowledgement to Barry Cooper, 1991, pp. 280–09.
[4] Paul Mies, with adaptations, *Beethoven's Orchestral Works* in: *The Age of Beethoven, The New Oxford History of Music, Vol. VIII*, Gerald Abraham, editor, 1988, pp. 122–23.
[5] Anne-Louise Coldicott *Performance Practice in Beethoven's day* in: Barry Cooper, *The Beethoven Compendium: A Guide to Beethoven's Life and Music,* 1991, pp. 283–84.
[6] *Ibid.*
[7] Leon Botstein, *Sound and Structure in Beethoven's Orchestral* Music in: Glenn Stanley, editor, *The Cambridge Companion to Beethoven,* 2000, pp. 172–81.

8 Leon Botstein, *ibid*, p. 171. The following text makes a fitting companion to Botstein's observations: 'Above all, [Beethoven's orchestral] works distinguish themselves from those of any prior composer through his creation of large, extended, architectonic structures, characterized by the extensive *development* of musical material, themes and motifs, usually by means of modulations or key changes ... Beethoven's innovation was the ability to rapidly establish a solidity in juxtaposing different keys and unexpected notes to join them. This expanded harmonic realm creates a sense of a vast musical and experiential space through which the music moves, and the development of musical material creates a sense of unfolding drama in space.' Anonymous, Wikipedia article *Beethoven's Musical Style and Innovations*, March 2007.
9 Leon Botstein – see above citations.
10 *Ibid.*
11 George Grove, *Beethoven and his Nine Symphonies*, 1896, p. 3.
12 Gian Francesco Malipiero, originally published in *L'Orchestra*, 1920 and quoted in: John L. Holmes, *Composers on Composers*, 1990, pp. 432–33.
13 Wilhelm Furtwängler, originally published in, *Vermächtnis Nachgelassene Schriften* and quoted in: Robert Taylor, editor, *Furtwängler on Music: Essays and Addresses*, 1991, p. 35.
14 Clive Brown, Introduction to, *Beethoven, Symphonies*, The Academy of Ancient Music conducted by Christopher Hogwood, DDD Music.
15 (Sir) Roger Norrington, Liner notes *Beethoven, Symphonies 1 & 6*, The London Classical Players, EMI CDC 7497462, 1988.
16 Martin Anderson editor, *Klemperer on Music: Shavings from a Musician's Workbench*. 1986, pp. 97–99.
17 Elliot Forbes editor, *Thayer's Life of Beethoven*, 1967 p. 229.
18 Source: Adam Carse, *The Orchestra from Beethoven to Berlioz: A History of the Orchestra in the First Half of the 19th century, and of the Development of Orchestral Baton-Conducting*, 1948, pp. 306–07, and pp. 365–66.
19 Norman Del Mar, *Modern Music and the Conductor* in: Rollo H. Myers, editor, *Twentieth-Century Music*, 1960, p. 85.
20 Anton Felix Schindler, edited by Donald W. MacArdle and translated by Constance S. Jolly from the German edition of 1860, 1966. The quotation is derived from the 1845 edition of Schindler's biography, p. 112.
21 Elliot Forbes, editor, *Thayer's Life of Beethoven*, 1967, p. 544.
22 Anne-Louise Coldicott, *Performance Practice in Beethoven's Day* in: Barry Cooper, 1991, pp. 280–09.
23 Emily Anderson editor and translator, 1961, Vol. 3, Letter No. 1545, p. 1325.
24 (Sir) Roger Norrington, Liner notes *Beethoven, Symphonies 1 & 6*, The London Classical Players, EMI CDC 7497462, 1988.
25 Louis Spohr, *Autobiography*, Longmans 1864, quoted in: Ferruccio Bonavia, *Musicians on Music*, 1956, pp. 126–27.
26 For a facsimile reproduction of Wielder's portrait see: Beethoven House, Digital Archives, Library Document, HCB Bi 3. Wielder's study is also reproduced as Plate 22 in H. C. Robbins Landon, 1992.
27 Adapted from: A. D. Coleridige, *Life of Moscheles, with Selections from his Diaries and Correspondence by his Wife*, 1873, pp. 139–40.

[28] The original source is: Louis Spohr's *Autobiography*, translated from the German, 1805, and recalled in Oscar George Theodore Sonneck, *Beethoven: Impressions of Contemporaries,* 1927, pp. 97–98.

CREATION ORIGINS

Beethoven's first venture into the genre of symphonic composition dates from his adolescent years in his hometown of Bonn. Sketch sources for a projected symphony in C minor are found in the so-called Kafka Miscellany, SV 185, f. 70 and Kerman, Miscellany, ii, pp. 175–76, both of which are preserved today in the British Library.[1] We make further reference to Beethoven's sketches sources and sketchbooks later in connection with the origins of the C major Symphony. The sketch of a first movement, intended for the C minor Symphony, is more fully realized in one of Beethoven's youthful keyboard Quartets WoO 36 (1785), 'the composer's most potent and earliest C minor *appassionata* statement'.[2] In this context, Paul Mies remarks how, from his earliest works on, 'Beethoven's rhythms are sharply profiled, often irregular, with a predilection for syncopations and accents'.[3]

The sketches for the C minor symphony are fragmentary

but have been reconstructed by the Swiss composer and Beethoven musicologist Willy Hesse. With added conjectural orchestration they can be heard as Hesse 298. Commenting on his reconstruction of Beethoven's youthful sketches, Hesse considers, if Beethoven had completed the symphony, it would have counted, together with the Cantata on the death of Emperor Joseph II, WoO 87, as one of the most important compositions from the composer's Bonn period. Hesse maintains the Cantata already points to the Beethoven 'we know and love' and the symphony sketch perhaps even more so:

> 'It is fascinating to see the youth of a mere 20 or 22 years, already writing music that is so close to the *Eroica* and Fifth Symphony. Sketched when Robespierre's reign of terror in France was rapidly reaching its bloody climax, one is inclined to say that this is the French Revolution in music.'

In his commentary to his reconstruction of the sketches to Beethoven's putative C minor Symphony, Hesse further remarks:

> 'As is clear from the state in which Beethoven has left the sketch, it is impossible to complete this movement without the addition of extra material. A completion can therefore never claim to be authentic. It should be stressed that the aim of such a completion is to merely provide a framework which places the notes as written by Beethoven in an appropriate context, so that they can be judged and enjoyed as real music. Although not authentic by definition, one can,

and should, demand of a completion that it be within Beethoven's style, using only compositional techniques known by him, and intellectually up to his standard.'[4]

We have remarked on the challenges Beethoven had to confront when he resolved to compose his first symphony. We reaffirm this in the words of Barry Cooper:

'[The] symphony ... had become a grand, public display of compositional craft in which motivic development and continuity on a large-scale were prime elements. Thus, a serious composer such as Beethoven could not approach the genre without due preparation in the hope to succeed at the highest artistic level rather than produce mere works of entertainment. Here, it was a question of inheriting Haydn's spirit more than Mozart's.'[5]

Cooper may be considered to be recalling, in inverted form, Count Waldstein's words of encouragement to Beethoven — on his departure from Bonn — 'Through uninterrupted diligence, you shall receive *Mozart's spirit from Haydn's hands'.*

Having set aside his work on a symphonic movement in C minor, Beethoven returned once more to the task of writing a symphony during the period 1795–96. This time he projected a work in the key of C major, which was to be the key of his eventual Op. 21. Beethoven's study with Haydn may have disposed him to want to compose a symphony that he would then take back with him to Bonn — to where it was assumed he was going to return. In addition, his teacher's own achievements must have been a further source of encouragement. We can assume he was aware of Haydn working on his Symphonies Nos. 99–101 that were destined to be performed in London. Moreover, Beethoven would have most certainly attended Haydn's benefit concert that took place on 15 March 1793 in the Redoutensaal and at which three Haydn symphonies were performed. Additionally, in December 1793, Beethoven had a further opportunity to hear more renderings of his teacher's symphonies.[6]

Of particular significance is that in 1792, Haydn had just completed the fifth of his so-called London Symphonies that is also in the key of C major. It has been suggested this may have given added impetus to Beethoven to write such a work of his own and, moreover, one that would serve him as a compositional model.[7]

Beethoven had other composers of symphonies with whom he had to contend. These include such prolific composers as: Paul Wranitzky, whose output comprises some 44 symphonies; Mozart's contemporary Joseph Leopold Eybler; and the Polish-Austrian violinist-conductor Antonio Casimir Cartellieri. Although their works have made no lasting impression, in their time they featured regularly in Vienna's concert programmes. It is not surprising, therefore, that Beethoven, mindful that these works were in the current repertoire, should approach the composition of his first symphony with some caution.[8]

Writing of Beethoven's first attempts to write a symphony, his early biographer Alexander Thayer suggests he had the composition of a symphony in mind when studying with Johann Albrechtsberger. Drawing on the pioneering researches of the musicologist Gustav Nottebohm, he makes reference to symphonic sketches in the Kafka Notirungsbuch (see later). These are believed to have been intended for a symphonic first movement which later found expression in the final movement of Op. 21.[9]

Commenting on Nottebohm's researches, the German musicologist Wilhelm Altmann elucidates:

'Beethoven had already conceived the plan of a symphony in his early Bonn period. Gustav Nottebohm (*Zweite Beethoveniana*, 1887, p. 567) prints from sketches the opening of a C minor movement labelled "Sinfonia" that corresponds to the beginning of the first Allegro of the Second Quartet [Op. 18, No. 2], composed in 1785. The same scholar (p. 228) also found sketches for a Symphony in C major on which Beethoven must have been working in 1794 and early 1795, but never completed. These sketches, which Nottebohm (*Beethoveniana*, p. 202) at first erroneously connected with the Symphony published as No. 1, have no relation to the Symphony in C major published by Fritz Stein in 1911 from old parts of the Akademisches Konzert in Jena, founded in 1780 [see below].'[10]

Modern-day study has established the extent of Beethoven's sketches for a projected Symphony in C major. We quote the researches of the American musicologist Alfred Peter Brown:

'Covering some fifteen pages, they contain at least nine drafts for a slow introduction, six drafts for an exposition, and two drafts for an extended coda. The last are indicative of the more mature Beethoven ... In addition, there are sketches for the last three movements: an adagio in A, a minuet with trio, and a finale in 6/8.'

Brown believes the sketches reveal the influence of the late symphonies of Haydn (Nos. 95 and 97) and Mozart (K. 425 and K551) – and the challenges Beethoven faced with regard to his ability to absorb these influences without over reliance upon them.[11]

Commenting on Beethoven's early studies, David Wyn Jones suggests they reveal the composer finding his way cautiously in the genre of symphonic writing. He cites the manner in which he first placed the slow movement in the key of E major before raising the key a semitone to F, 'a more conventional key for a slow movement of a symphony in C.' He elaborates:

> 'Beethoven's first thoughts for the opening of the symphony are similarly cautious, a slow introduction of eight bars rather similar in scope to the earliest symphonies of Paul Wranitzky. Later sketches yield a longer introduction with an arresting motif of tonic, median to subdominant, coincidentally also used by Wranitzky at the beginning of a C major symphony, (the one performed in Frankfurt in 1792) and, before that, by Mozart in the *Linz* Symphony (K. 425).[12]

A sketch leaf from 1795 reveals Beethoven exploring further ideas for a symphony in C major, preserved today in the Archives of the Beethoven House in Bonn. The commentary to this states:

> 'Beethoven had already worked on a symphony in C major in 1795 and 1796 – numerous drafts and jottings bear witness to this. These are the most extensive working materials from his first creative period. With one exception, Beethoven

did not use any of the material from these first attempts in his later First Symphony. The composer only "recycled" the opening of the rondo theme in the last movement of Op. 21 from his earlier sketches.'[13]

The American musicologist Douglas Johnson suggests it was Beethoven's professional aspirations that disposed him to work on a C major symphony, during his tour of Prague and Berlin; a symphonic composition he maintains would have formed a fitting centrepiece to one of his concerts. Such an opportunity, however, was not forthcoming and the work was subsequently abandoned sometime after his return to Vienna. Nonetheless, the sketches reveal drafts for an *andante* inscribed '*zur Sinfonie*', a minuet and trio, and a few thematic ideas for the finale.[14]

Citing Johnson's studies, the American music scholar William Kinderman avers:

'Beethoven's sketches for a Symphony in C major occupied him in Vienna in 1795 and again during his concert tour to Prague and Berlin the next year. Douglas Johnson has also speculated that Beethoven may have expected a performance [of a symphony] at Berlin that did not materialize. Johnson convincingly places the piece in the context of Beethoven's frustrated ambition to match Haydn's towering symphonic achievements, and points as well to parallels between Beethoven's fragment and Haydn's Symphony No. 97 in the same key.'

Kinderman adds:

> 'Characteristically, some thematic material from the abandoned work came to light five years later in the Finale of Beethoven's First Symphony in C major, Op. 21, a piece that owes little to the fragment but still falls short of Haydn's lofty standard.'[15]

Barry Cooper reflects in similar manner to the foregoing and speculates:

> 'Why Beethoven abandoned the [C major symphony] after so much effort is unclear: perhaps it was intended for use on his tour to Prague and Berlin in 1796 and was simply not finished in time; or, perhaps, he became dissatisfied with some of the basic ideas and eventually had better ones for a new symphony in the same key.'[16]

Cooper further suggests Beethoven's work on this symphony was in order to fulfil a personal ambition — perhaps to emulate his teacher? — and not simply to satisfy the obligations of a commission.

By December Beethoven had drafts of a slow introduction, the development, most of the coda, a minuet, and ideas for the finale — some of which were developed in full score. Most significant for the First Symphony, were his sketches for the main theme of an allegro, in rapid scale, which, was eventually used in the finale of Op. 21. More generally Cooper elucidates, in the same spirit as Hesse whose words we have quoted:

> 'Although the symphony remained unfinished in this form, it was one of his most significant

creations of the 1790s in terms of his development as a composer.'[17]

When working on his orchestral scores, Beethoven made use of oblong (landscape) format sheets, pre-ruled with sixteen staves. On the first sheet he typically identified the instruments in descending order: first and second violins, flutes, oboes, clarinets, bassoons, horns, trumpets, tympani, cellos, and basses.

To follow Beethoven working on a symphonic composition, musicologist Alan Tyson invites us to imagine the composer seated at his writing desk — preserved today in the Beethoven House in Bonn — with a gathering of pre-ruled, blank sheets before him alongside his compositional sketches. Tyson proposes:

> 'Beethoven set out to draft his score from start to finish, proceeding from the first bar and 'maintaining the melody ... for about a page at a time. He would next consider the basic accompaniment, usually filling in the bass-line and strings on their appropriate staves. Beethoven's score-sketches reveal him changing his mind, correcting errors and squeezing as many bars as possible to a page. If emendations became too numerous he would cross out the rejected sections and even substitute overworked pages for new ones.'[18]

Of Beethoven's abandoned C major sketches, Peter Brown remarks:

> '[These] C major efforts were not for naught; they helped to work out Beethoven's problem with the music of Haydn and Mozart and provided

the basic material for the finale of Symphony No. 1 in C major, Op. 21.'[19]

Of related interest are sketches for a projected symphony in E on which Beethoven is believed to have worked whilst on his Prague concert tour; they are written out on paper deriving from this time. About seventy measure have been identified. They are set out in a melodic line with indications for orchestral accompaniment. Authorities consider the main melody has a Mozartian character that seems to point forward to the composer's Piano Sonata No. 27 in E minor, Op. 90 of 1814.[20]

For the moment, we set aside discussion of Beethoven's progress with the composition of his First Symphony to consider an occurrence of related interest. In 1909 the international musical community was stirred with the discovery of a symphony that was considered to come from the hand of the youthful Beethoven. We refere to these events insofar as they bear, albeit somewhat obliquely, on Beethoven's early progress with symphonic writing.

The musicologist Fritz Stein, of Jena University, had occasion to search the archives of the town's *Collegium Musicum*. In so doing, he discovered a set of orchestral parts of a four-movement symphony in C minor, certain passages of which he believed bore some Beethoven stylistic similarities. Stein's conviction that the music was of Beethoven's authorship was strengthened by his awareness that the composer had embarked on the composition of such a symphony in C minor. More tellingly, the second violin parts bore the inscription 'par Louis von [sic] Beethoven' and the cello part 'Symphonie von Beethoven'. Professor Stein reconstructed the parts to create a performing edition that was published in 1911 by Breitkopf & Härtel. This was announced as a hitherto unknown symphony by Beethoven and became colloquially known as the *Jena* Symphony.

Publication of the composition by Breitkopf & Härtel — the oldest publishing house in the world — added credibility to Stein's conviction that the work was indeed by Beethoven. This was further enhanced when he published his views in the *Sammelbände der Internationalen Musikgesellschaft,* Vol. 13, 1911.[21] For sometime thereafter the *Jena* symphony was performed in several concert halls, regarded as being the possible 'missing link' that connected with Beethoven's earlier attempts at symphonic writing. However, it soon fell into neglect; from the outset doubts had been cast upon its authenticity.

It was not until the 1950s when the Haydn scholar H. C. Robbins Landon established the true authenticity of the *Jena* Symphony. In 1957 his researches led him to the archives of the Benedictine monastery at Göttweig, about forty miles west of Vienna. It was here Landon discovered manuscripts of the music by the cellist-composer Friedrich Witt — a close contemporary of Beethoven (1770-1837) — who also composed nine symphonies. These included an authentic copy of the *Jena* Symphony, bearing Witt's name, and, thereby its true author.

With the benefit of hindsight, and with a more secure understanding of Beethoven musicology than was available over a century ago, it now seems unbelievable that the symphony could ever have thought to have been from Beethoven — even in his youth. The English violinist Ralph Homes dismissed it as being little more than 'a piece of plagiarism, put together almost with scissors and paste from reminiscences of Haydn'.[22]

Having considered Beethoven's youthful attempts to compose a C minor symphony, followed by his more mature pre-occupation with a C major symphony, we now direct our attention to the origins of his First Symphony proper, his Op. 21. We first make reference to Beethoven's working method and the importance to him of committing his initial thoughts to paper in sketch form.

Musicologist Nicholas Cook comments on the 'enormous repertoire of compositional sketches and other materials' Beethoven has bequeathed to musicologists as a consequence of his working method — putting his thoughts down in sketch form as distinct from working directly at the piano. This process he suggests was Beethoven's way of 'using paper to improvise'. Beethoven would write something down, perhaps when out on one of his walks in the country — which he found so stimulating to his personal wellbeing and creativity — and then, back at his writing desk, he would, in Cook's memorable phrase, 'let the paper speak back to him'.[23]

The assembly of the many sketches — usually only after much effort — finally resolved in the finished composition. Alfred Brendel, in the guise of musicologist, compares Beethoven with Mozart regarding the construction of their music:

> 'I see both Mozart and Beethoven as architects. But how differently they built! From the beginning of a piece, Beethoven places stone upon stone, constructing and justifying his edifice in accordance with the laws of statics. Mozart, on the other hand, prefers to join together the most wonderful melodic ideas as prefabricated components ... Whereas Beethoven draws one element from another, in what might be called a procedural manner, Mozart arranges one element after another as though it could be otherwise.'[24]

As cultural artifacts, Beethoven's sketches have long been the object of veneration; from the time of the auction of his effects following his death they have been sought by collectors. Musicologists have valued them — even more so — as providing insights into Beethoven's creative process. In this context we are indebted to Paul Lang who has drawn our attention to the imagery of William Wordsworth in his verses *The Prelude*, and their bearing on the sometimes arcane-appearance of the composer's sketches:

> 'There is a dark
> Inscrutable workmanship that reconciles
> Discordant elements, making them cling together.'[25]

From his earliest days, Beethoven was given to jotting down ideas for potential compositions on any available piece of manuscript paper — what he self-disparagingly referred to as his 'bad habit'. About two hundred loose sheets of sketches date back to Beethoven's days in Bonn, from about 1790 or even earlier.

> 'The sketches are private notes, meant only for the composer's eyes ... They have different functions within the creative process and range from short first ideas and longer passages to score-like elaborations ... Sketches and drafts are found on single leaves and in notebooks made up for the purpose. They can also be found in clean copies of autographs, copies made by copyists, or scattered in [so-called] conversation books.'[26]

Up to 1798 Beethoven made his sketches on single sheets. From the autumn of 1798 onwards, he began to work with bound sketchbooks. He used small pocket sketchbooks for composing outdoors in the countryside. These were written in pencil with some of the jottings being inked over later. Beethoven used oblong (bifolia) desk sketchbooks when working at his writing desk. In the last years of his life he also used so-called 'score sketches' – particularly in the composition of the late string quartets. Score sketches were a step closer to the final finished score.

Amongst the Beethoven House Archives of the composer's sketches, from the period 1790–92, a sketch leaf survives that exemplifies Beethoven's exacting manner of exploring ideas for various compositions – procedures he would retain and adapt all his life. Of particular interest is the care he took with his handwriting (more correctly his musical notation) at this stage in his career. This is clear, legible and could readily be used as copy from which to perform the music being explored. This is in marked contrast to the composer's sketches of later years that can pose a challenge of decipherment to even the most accomplished musicologist-detective.

The sketches of Beethoven's Bonn period reveal notes that are carefully placed on the stave bearing neat rounded heads. Also evident is Beethoven's characteristic tendency to work on ideas for several compositions simultaneously. In the case of the sketch leaf in question, the manuscript shows ides for various orchestral compositions with titles for movements designated *allegro, presto sinfonia,* and *menuett presto* – indicative of Beethoven turning his mind to symphonic composition.[27]

Beethoven's early sketches have been assembled into two large gatherings, the larger of which is now preserved in the British Library and is known as the 'Kafka Sketchbook' (more correctly 'miscellany') – taking its name from its one-time owner Johann Nepomuk Kafaka. Beethoven later systematised his sketching procedure by binding together bundles of pocket-sized sheets that he could take with him on his much-loved strolls in the country; later still he made use of ready-bound sketchbooks.[28]

Gustav Nottebohm, a pioneer in the study and decipherment of Beethoven's sketchbooks, has this to say:

> '[In] spite of this unsystematic procedure it is evident that as a rule Beethoven was clear about his objectives from the start; he remained true to his original conceptions, and once an idea was grasped, he carried it through to the end ... We may seek [in the sketchbooks] the artist himself, in the unity of his whole character and spirit, and in the harmony of his inner powers.'

Nottebohm offered three reasons for the study of Beethoven's sketch-sources:

> (1) the determination of the date of a composition
> (2) the disclosure of works started but not finished
> (3) the insights they offer into Beethoven's creative process — adapting, and rejecting, one idea after another.'[29]

Nottebohm considered Beethoven's sketches suggest he may have started work on as many as fifty symphonies (!), but seldom progressing beyond the first few bars.[30]

Beethoven himself was given to saying:

> 'I make many changes, and reject and try again until I am satisfied. Then, the working-out in breadth, length, height, and depth begins in my head, and since I am conscious of what I want, the underlying idea never deserts me.'

In his scholarly commentary to Beethoven's sketchbooks, Alan Tyson suggests they may have 'performed a special function for him in maintaining his morale as well as in facilitating his creative processes'. They did, indeed, become indispensable to him and at times, when his working method came up in conversation, Beethoven was given to quoting from Schiller's *Joan of Arc*: 'Without my banner I dare not come.'[31]

As remarked, Beethoven would set down ideas for a new piece, starting on a fresh page, frequently noting ideas for different movements alongside each other. As his powers of invention took hold, he would insert further thoughts cramming them into any available space or even going back to make use of pages previously left blank. As a consequence, sketches for different compositions co-exist side-by-side, many to be discarded but others to be fully worked into the compositions that we now know and cherish. In his lecture 'Questions about music' Roger Sessions, in his role as Charles Eliot Norton Professor, remarked:

'Beethoven could have made a great deal out of any one of the earlier versions [of his sketches] ... Obviously it would have been a different piece, and since that piece is not in existence, we can never know what it would have been like.'[32]

Commenting on, and defending, Beethoven's method of working, Donald Tovey states:

'No artist has left more authoritative documentary evidence as to the steps of his development than Beethoven ... and thereby he has, perhaps, misled some critics into overemphasizing the contrast between his "tentative" self-critical methods and the quasi-extempore outpourings of Mozart ... The number and triviality of Beethoven's sketches should not, then, be taken as evidence of a timid or vacillating spirit.'[33]

*

Writing about Beethoven, and his tireless pursuit to achieve his compositional goals, Wilhelm Furtwängler avers:

> '[Held] in the grip of raging passion, he retains his steely control, his singularity of purpose, his unshakable determination to shape and master his material down to the very last detail with a self-discipline unparalleled in the history of art. Never has an artist, driven by an irresistible creative force, felt so intensely the "law" that underlies artistic creation, and submitted to it with such humility.'[34]

Beethoven finally found time to work on his C major Symphony during the autumn of 1799 through to the spring of 1800, adapting, in part, his earlier sketches. No additional sketches have survived from this period. Mention has been made of the Kafka miscellany. Beethoven's next surviving sketchbook for the period 1798–99 is the so-called Grasnick sketchbook, but this revels no evidence of the composer at work on the C major Symphony. It is assumed, therefore, that the sketchbook Beethoven would have used has been lost.

An incentive to make progress with the composition of his First Symphony was Beethoven's hope of securing a performance in the spring of 1800, at a benefit concert in Vienna's Burgtheater or Kärntnerthor Theater. However, such concerts were strictly allocated by the Director of the two Court Theatres, namely Baron Peter von Braun, with whom Beethoven had a testy relationship; in his correspondence he complains of the restraining grip of the theatre manager.[35] To secure the hoped-for performance of the First Symphony Beethoven may, as Cooper suggests, have resorted to some tact insofar as he dedicated his Piano Sonatas Op. 14 to the Baron's wife Josephine — perhaps, thereby, disposing the Baron to eventually granting Beethoven access to the Burgtheater for Wednesday 2 April 1800.[36] Beethoven had first, however, to complete his negotiations with publishers. It is to these that we direct the next part of our narrative.

[1] See: Barry Coper, 2000, p. 23.
[2] Alfred Peter Brown, *The Symphonic Repertoire, Vol. 2: The First Golden Age of the Viennese Symphony: Haydn, Mozart, Beethoven, and Schubert*, 2002, p. 441.
[3] Paul Mies, *Beethoven's Orchestral Works in: The Age of Beethoven, The New Oxford History of Music, Vol. VIII*, Gerald Abraham, editor, 1988, pp. 120–21.
[4] Website text, *The Unheard Beethoven, Symphony in C minor, Hess 298*, orchestrated and completed by Wilhelm Altman.
[5] Barry Cooper, 1990, p. 78.
[6] For an account of early symphonic performances in Vienna see: David Wyn Jones, 2006, p. 156.
[7] Nicholas Marston, [*The*] *Symphonies* in: Barry Cooper, 1991, p. 214.
[8] With acknowledgment to Maynard Solomon, 1997, p. 103.
[9] Elliot Forbes editor, *Thayer's Life of Beethoven*, 1967 pp. 216–17. For a discussion of the Beethoven's sketchbooks for the period see: J. S. Shedlock, *Beethoven's Sketch Books, The Musical Times*, Vol. 33, 1892, pp. 591–92.
[10] Wilhelm Altmann, *Beethoven: Symphony No. 1 in C major*, Introduction to Score, Dover Publications, 1976 (reprint). See also: Paul Mies, *Beethoven's Orchestral Works in: The Age of Beethoven, The New Oxford Dictionary of Music, Vol. VIII*, Gerald Abraham, editor, 1968, pp. 120–21.
[11] Alfred Peter Brown, 2002, p. 441.
[12] David Wyn Jones, 2006, p. 159.
[13] Beethoven House, Digital Archives, Library Document, NE 96.
[14] Douglas Johnson, *Music for Prague and Berlin: Beethoven's Concert Tour of 1796*, in: Robert Winter editor, *Beethoven, Performers, and Critics*, the International Beethoven Congress, Detroit, 1977, 1980, p. 33 and p. 38.
[15] Kinderman, William. 1997, pp. 43–44.
[16] Barry Cooper, 1991, p. 276.
[17] Barry Cooper, 1990, p. 32, p. 61, and pp. 67–68.
[18] Alan Tyson, *Sketches and Autographs*, in: Denis Arnold, and Nigel Fortune editors, *The Beethoven Companion*, 1973, pp. 452–54.
[19] Alfred Peter Brown, *The Symphonic Repertoire, Vol. 2: The First Golden Age of the Viennese Symphony: Haydn, Mozart, Beethoven, and Schubert*, 2002, p. 441.
[20] Website article, *The Unheard Beethoven, Symphony in E, Slow Movement*, GV 1. The sketches have been realized for piano and in an orchestral version by Wilhelm Altman.

[21] Wilhelm Altmann, *Beethoven: Symphony No. 1 in C major, Introduction to Score*, Dover Publications, 1976 (reprint).
[22] The Jena Symphony is discussed in the following sources: H.C. Robbins Landon, *The Jena Symphony, Music Review*, 1957; reprinted in: *Essays on the Viennese Classical Style*, 1970; Joseph Braunstein, *Musica Aeterna, Program Notes for 1971–197*, New York: *Musica Aeterna*, 1978, pp. 28–29; and Alfred Peter Brown, *The Symphonic Repertoire. Vol. 2, The First Golden Age of the Viennese Symphony: Haydn, Mozart, Beethoven, and Schubert*, 2002, p. 436.
[23] Nickolas Cook, *How does the Mind Compose?* In: Michael Oliver, editor, *Settling the Score: A Journey through the Music of the Twentieth Century*, 1999, pp. 224–25.
[24] Alfred Brendel, 2001, pp. 2–3.
[25] Quoted in: Wilfrid Mellers, 1957, p. 56.
[26] Beethoven House source, Archive Document 'Draft Research'.
[27] Beethoven House, Digital Archives, Library Document, BH 117. Of related interest is a preserved sketch leaf in the form of a bifolium – a large double-format sheet – folded about the middle to fit into the composer's coat pocket. It reveals traces of pencil annotations, marked in when he was out of doors, some of which have later been inked over. Beethoven sometimes collated several such sheets to form a homemade sketchbook. For a facsimile illustration of a typical two-page bifolium, of the kind Beethoven carried around with him, see: Beethoven House, Digital Archives, Library Document, Sammlung H. C. Bodmer, HCB BSK 16/24.
[28] The artist Donna Dralle has created an imaginary study in pencil and watercolour titled *Beethoven Stitching a Notebook*.See:http/www.graphixnow.com/fine_art/images/fine_art_pgs/lvb sew.jpg
[29] Gustav Nottebohm, *Zweite Beethoveniana*, 1887, quoted in: John V. Cockshoot, 1959, p. 200. See also Gustav Nottebohm, 1979 (reprint), pp. 4–7.
[30] As remarked by Barry Cooper, *The Compositional Act: Sketches and Autographs* in: Glenn Stanley, editor, *The Cambridge Companion to Beethoven*, 2000, p. 32.
[31] Cited by Alan Tyson, *Sketches and Autographs*, in: Denis Arnold, and Nigel Fortune editors, *The Beethoven Companion*, 1973, p. 443–58.
[32] Edward T. Cone, editor, *Roger Sessions on Music: Collected Essays*, 1979, p. 45.
[33] Michael Tilmouth, editor, *Donald Francis Tovey: The Classics of Music: Talks, Essays, and other Writings Previously Uncollected*, 2001.
[34] Wilhelm Furtwängler, originally published in, *Vermächtnis Nachgelassene Schriften* and quoted in: Robert Taylor editor, *Furtwängler on Music: Essays and Addresses*, 1991, p. 33.
[35] For example, on 22 April 1802, Kaspar Karl wrote on Beethoven's behalf to the publisher Breitkopf & Härtell in the following terms: '[The] Theater Director Baron von Braun ... has refused him the Theater for his concert ...'. Theodore Albrecht editor and translator, 1996, Vol. 1, Letter No. 38, pp. 70–71.
[36] Barry Cooper, 2000, p. 99.

PUBLISHERS AND PUBLICATION

The growing interest in Beethoven on the part of music publishers has been mentioned. In the autumn of 1800 Beethoven received a request for his publications from the music publisher and composer Franz Anton Hoffmeister. His name is known to Mozartians through association with the *Hoffmeister Quartet* (K. 499). In 1800 Hoffmeister had established a publishing house in Leipzig with his colleague Ambros (Ambrosius) Kühnel, an organist in the employ at the Electoral Saxon Court Chapel. The two transacted business under the name *Bureau de Musique*, in Leipzig, and as *Hoffmeister and Kühnel* in Vienna. Beethoven already had dealings with Hoffmeister; the year previously — he had published the composer's celebrated *Sonate Pathétique*. It is not surprising therefore that Hoffmeister, having published the works of Albrechtsberger, Dittersdorf, Mozart, and Pleyel, should want to establish a relationship with Beethoven — a rising star in Vienna's musical firmament. Thayer writes, in his characteristically fulsome manner:

> 'Knowing Beethoven personally and so intimately, it is alike creditable to the talents of the one and the taste and appreciation of the other that Hoffmeister, immediately upon organising his new publishing house, should have asked [Beethoven] for manuscripts.[1]

On 15 December 1800, Beethoven replied to Hoffmeister, opening his letter in characteristically florid terms — 'MOST BELOVED AND WORTHY BROTHER' [Beethoven's capitals]; he typically adopted this style of salutation in his negotiations with publishers, fellow musicians, and others whom he considered devoted their lives to the promotion of music. He apologised to Hoffmeister:

> 'Many times have I intended to reply to your enquiries. But I am dreadfully lazy about writing letters and it takes me a long time to write down instead of notes some dry letters of the alphabet.'

We pause here to observe Beethoven frequently expressed his dislike of the business-side of his negotiations with publishes. He was, nevertheless, astute and conscientious in his dealings with the financial side of his affairs. His letters and notes amount to three volumes containing the texts to some 1,570 letters and short notes[2] and another three volumes of such letters to Beethoven, and his close associates, account for a further 492 documents.[3]

Beethoven offered Hoffmeister his First Symphony, Op.

21 together with his Second Piano Concerto, Op. 20 as well as the Piano Sonata, Op. 22. He expressed regret that he could not offer his recently composed six String Quartets, Op. 18 since they had already been offered to the publisher T. Mollo in Vienna. Beethoven suggested Hoffmeister should set the prices to be paid for the various compositions concluding, 'no doubt we shall come to an agreement'.[4]

Beethoven wrote to Hoffmeister's once more on 15 January 1801 — or thereabouts; Beethoven did not always date his correspondence with due care. He expressed in fulsome terms his wish to contribute to the endeavours of his 'fellow brothers in art' and trusted that their works would profit 'the lot of the true and genuine artists'. Turning to business matters, it appears he had decided himself the prices he wanted for his compositions. He offered Hoffmeister the following works: Septet Op. 20 (20 ducats) — Beethoven also suggested this could be arranged for piano 'with a view to its wider distribution and to our greater profit'; Symphony No. 1, Op. 21 (20 ducats); Piano Concerto No. 2, Op. 19 (10 ducats); and Piano Sonata Op. 22 (20 ducats). Beethoven described the latter as 'a first-rate composition'. In the following passage he explains his estimation of the relative value of the works in question:

> 'I make no distinction between Sonata, Septet and Symphony. The reason is that I find a septet or a symphony does not sell as well as a sonata. That is the reason why I do this, although a symphony should undoubtedly be worth more.'

With reference to the B-flat Concerto he adds: 'I am valuing the Concerto at only 10 ducats because, as I have already told you, I do not consider it to be one of my best concertos.' More generally he explains: 'I have endeavoured to make the prices as moderate for you as possible.' Acknowledging his limitations in business matters, he states:

> 'The only currency I can cope with is Viennese ducats. How much that sum amounts to in your thalers and gulden does not concern me, because I am really an incompetent business man who is bad at arithmetic.'

Beethoven closes his letter to Hoffmeister: 'Well that tiresome business has now been settled', by which he means the complex, and time-consuming, procedures he had to transact with Hoffmeister to see his works in print. Beethoven calls it 'tiresome' because, as he remarks, 'he should like such matters to be differently ordered in this world'. He goes on to say:

> 'There ought to be in the world *a market for art* [Beethoven's italics] where the artist would only have to bring his works and take as much money as he needed.'

He laments how he has to be both an artist and 'to be to a certain extent a business man as well'. He concluded by exclaiming 'how can he manage to be that — Good Heavens!'.

Worthy of note is that Beethoven's gifted contemporary Franz Schubert, in the years of his maturity, gave expression to just such frustrated sentiments as those expressed by Beethoven in his letter to Hoffmeister.

Beethoven briefly mentions the reviews of his works by the Leipzig critics of the *Allgemeine musikalische Zeitung* — to which he had taken exception. He states he does not take them seriously but they had clearly annoyed him. He protested: 'Just let them talk, they will never be immortal nor would they be able to take immortality away from anyone upon whom Apollo had bestowed it.' Beethoven clearly considered himself to be one so favoured by the gods.[5]

Beethoven resumed his correspondence with Hoffmeister on 22 April 1801. He explained that illness had prevented him from making an earlier response and also how busy he had been. To assist Hoffmeister with the publication of the works upon which they had reached agreement, he provided him with the requisite opus numbers: Piano Concerto, Op. 19; Septet, Op. 20; First Symphony, Op.21; and Piano Sonata, Op. 22. The Septet was proving so popular, Beethoven suggested:

> 'It would be very nice if my dear brother, besides publishing the Septet as it stands, were [you] to arrange it too for a flute, for instance, and perhaps as a quintet. This would satisfy the *lovers of the flute* who have already entreated me to do this; and they would swarm around it and feed on it like insects.'[6]

On 21 June 1801, Beethoven wrote once more to Hoffmeister to confirm his firm Hoffmeister & Kühnel had the exclusive rights to publish the First Symphony; there had been a misunderstanding and he was anxious to reassure the Leipzig publishers of their priority. With publication in mind, he provided Hoffmeister with the Symphony's dedicatee and the wording he wanted to appear on the Title Page:

> 'Grande Simphonie avec deux violons viole violoncelle et contre-basse, deux flute, deux oboes, deux cors, deux fagots, deux clarines, et

tymbales. / Composée et dédiée / à son Altesse serinissime / Maximilien / François / et de Boheme / Electeur de Cologne / par / Louis van Beethoven / Oeuvre 21.'[7]

Regarding the work's dedicatee, the Elector Maximilian Franz had left Bonn in 1794 (two years after Beethoven) when the French Armies began to occupy the Rhineland. After sojourns in various towns in Germany he eventually settled at Hetzendorf near Vienna. It was there he died on 26 July 1801 — just one month after Beethoven's letter to Hoffmeister. Beethoven, thereby, had to find another worthy individual upon whom to confer the dedication. We reveal his name in due course.

In our *Portrait of Beethoven*, we made reference to the Leipzig publishers Breitkopf and Härtel. They enter our narrative once more. The head of the firm Gottfried Christof Härtel wrote to Beethoven in the spring of 1801.[8] Of relevance to our discussion is Härtel's request to publish a selection of the composer's works. Beethoven responded on 22 April in what was the first of his many exchanges of letters with this celebrated Leipzig-based publishing house; he maintained a correspondence with Gottfried Christof Härtel until 1816. Beethoven informed Härtel:

> '[Please] be so kind just to inform me what types of composition you would like to have from me, namely, symphonies, quartets, sonatas, and so forth, so that I may be guided by your wishes and, should I happen to have the works you require or desire, [and] be able to supply them.'

At the same time, Beethoven could not refrain from

chastising the hapless Härtel — the publisher of the *Allgemeine musikalische Zeitung* — in the following terms:

> 'Advise your reviewers to be more circumspect and intelligent, particularly in regard to the productions of younger composers. For many a one, who perhaps might go far, may take freight.'

Beethoven added — provocatively:

> 'As for myself, far be it from me to think that I have achieved a perfection which suffers no adverse criticism. But your reviewer's outcry against me was at first very mortifying.'

Beethoven contented himself with the assertion: 'They [the critics] don't know anything about music.'[9]

At the period under consideration, there was no effective copyright to protect composers from having their works exploited by others in the form of unauthorised pirate editions and adaptations. It was just such a circumstance that obliged Beethoven, on 18 October 1802, to instruct his brother Carl to write to Breitkopf and Härtel on his behalf. The composer requested assistance in having it made known to the public that a quintet arrangement of his C major Symphony, by Tranquillo Mollo, was not sanctioned by him; it had been published earlier in August.[10] [11] Beethoven's protest duly appeared in the *Wiener Zeitung* of 20 October:

> 'I consider that I owe it to the public and myself to state publicly that the two quintets in C major and E major, one of which (taken from one of my symphonies [No. 1]) was published by Herr Mollo in Vienna and the other (taken from the

well-known Septet of mine, Op. 20) by Herr Hoffmeister at Leipzig, are not original quintets, but merely transcriptions made by these worthy publishers.'

Beethoven then expressed his views concerning such nefarious undertakings:

'The making of transcriptions is on the whole a thing against which nowadays (in our prolific age of transcriptions) a composer would merely struggle in vain; but at least he is entitled to demand that the publishers shall mention his name on the title-page so that his honour as a composer may not be infringed nor the public deceived.'[12]

The following year on 21 May 1803 Carl van Beethoven wrote once more to Breitkopf and Härtel to offer the publisher further compositions. These included the Overture *Prometheus*, for which he requested 25 ducats, and 'a new symphony'. The latter is thought to be a reference to the Second Symphony, Op. 36 that Beethoven had recently revised following its performance earlier on 5 April. Somewhat ambiguously, he asked Härtel to offer his opinion about this — presumably taken to mean, would he like to have it published?[13] Härtel responded on 2 June in fulsome terms: 'We highly esteem your kind offer concerning the Overture and the Symphony [No. 2] as proof of the regard you have for us.'

At the same time, however, Härtel expressed a note of caution. As fervently as he wished to publish the composer's works, he was reluctant to bring out single or occasional pieces. He much preferred to publish the works of a composer in a single, uniform edition. He maintained music lovers — especially of piano pieces — preferred this to works that appeared from different publishers in varying formats and styles of engraving.[14]

On 20 September Härtel wrote to Beethoven in response to Carl's suggestion that his publishing house may wish to publish Beethoven's Piano Sonatas Op. 49 'and some other works.' Härtel declined, since he could not agree the terms that were acceptable to the composer; Carl had, characteristically, set the requested payments too high. Härtel raised once more the challenges an established publishing house had to confront in the face of unscrupulous pirates. However, he closed with words of encouragement:

> '[Should] you once again produce a piano concerto or a symphony, and be inclined to entrust it to us for publication, we ask that you let us know your terms.'[15]

We take leave of Breitkopf and Härtel by remarking on the fruitful working relationship they eventually established with Beethoven. On 14 September 1808, Härtel visited Vienna and signed a contract with the composer to publish his Opp. 67–70. Furthermore, between 1809 and 1812 Breitkopf and Härtel published first editions of more than twenty of Beethoven's works. These included: the Fifth and Sixth Symphonies, the Fifth Piano Concerto, the revised score of *Fidelio*, the Oratorio *Christus am Ölberg*, the incidental music to *Egmont*, the Choral *Fantasia* for Piano and Orchestra, and the Mass in C minor.

It is one of the misfortunes of the Second World War that the magnificent premises of Breitkopf and Härtel, together with their priceless archive of memorabilia, were reduced to ashes in the course of the Allied bombing campaign.[16]

The First Symphony was introduced to the public at one of Beethoven's benefit concerts in Vienna on 2 April 1800; it was performed again on December 15 and on 15 January 1801. As remarked, Beethoven offered it to Franz Anton Hoffmeister who published the work, in parts only, as the composer's Op. 21– the original manuscript score is lost. The *Wiener Zeitung* announced the new symphony on 16 January 1802. It is a measure of Beethoven's creativity that alongside the First Symphony other compositions for the period 1801–01 include:

> Piano Concerto in C major, Op. 15;
> Quintet for piano and wind, Op. 16;
> Sonata for Piano and Horn, Op. 17;
> String Quartets, Op. 18;
> Piano Concerto in B-flat major, Op. 19;
> Septet Op. 20, Piano Sonata Op. 22;
> Sonatas for Piano and Violin Op. 23 and 24;
> Piano Sonata Op. 26;
> Piano Sonatas Op. 27, Nos. 1 and 2;
> Piano Sonata Op. 28;
> String Quintet Op. 29;
> and the Three Sonatas for Piano and Violin Op. 30.

Commenting on these, Robbins Landon remarks:

> 'It is a formidable list containing as it does some of Beethoven's most popular works (Septet, *Moonlight* Sonata, First Symphony) and which established him, together with old Haydn, as the leading composer in Europe.'[17]

As remarked the First Symphony was published, as was

the custom of the day, in parts only. This remained the case for all of Beethoven's first six symphonies as follows: Second Symphony, parts in 1804 and score in 1808; Third Symphony, parts in 1806, and score in 1809; Fourth Symphony, parts in 1808 and score in 1823; Fifth Symphony, parts in 1809 and score in 1826; and Sixth Symphony, parts in 1809 and score in 1826. The first editions of Symphonies Nos. 7–9 were, however published concurrently in parts and full score. Regarding performance, prior to their publication in full score, the symphonies were conducted from manuscript copies of the full score – sometimes borrowed from music publishers such as Hoffmeister and Kühnel (Bureau de Musique) or Breitkopf & Härtel – or, less ideally, from the first violin parts alone.[18]

The British musicologist Alain Frogley writes:

> 'But for all the unprecedented effort Beethoven put into preparing his scores for publication, with sometimes multiple sets of proofs and lengthy letters to publishers (though he was not a good or enthusiastic proof reader), even his printed scores contain numerous ambiguities and inconsistencies in their performance indications.'

The composer's strenuous efforts to have the errors in his scores corrected sometimes disposed him to reproach his publishers; on one such occasion, he rebuked the poor fellow in question: 'Errors! You, yourself are an error!' Frogley further observes:

> 'One senses here an inevitable clash between Beethoven the composer-for-posterity, trying to fix a work once and for all, and Beethoven the

> spontaneous performer, ever sensitive to the
> multiple possibilities inherent in his material.'[19]

Beethoven was particularly concerned with tempi and, as we have earlier remarked, he was a pioneering enthusiast for the metronome. He saw this as a means of conveying the composer's intentions with respect to the tempo at which the music should be taken, and, thereby, of reducing the scope for its misinterpretation. The tempo indications that Beethoven set for his compositions have subsequently proved contentious to many musicians. Notwithstanding, Alain Frogley maintains:

> '[The] consensus of modern scholarship, and the fruits of the historical-performance movement, all suggest that Beethoven's markings must be taken very seriously indeed, even if they are not followed absolutely literally.'[20]

The American pianist and writer on music Charles Rosen said much the same thing in his own inimitable manner:

> 'It is not illegal to play a piece of music at the wrong tempo: we risk neither a jail sentence nor even a fine. A certain school of aesthetics considers it immoral to contravene the composer's intentions, but sometimes it may even be a good idea.'[21]

In its October 1813 issue the *Wiener Vatwerlänidische Blätter* published an article describing a form of chronometer — precursor of the metronome.[22] The following year the Dutchman Nikolaus Winkel produced a functioning device that Johann Maelzel soon perfected to achieve the mechanism with which musicians the world over are now familiar. Beethoven's interest was immediately aroused as we can infer from a letter he wrote, sometime in 1815, to his publisher Tobias Haslinger in which he made reference to his own metronome.[23]

Two years later Beethoven expressed his views regarding tempo indications to the Viennese conductor and writer on music Ignaz von Mosel — a founder member of the *Gesellschaft der Musikfreunde*. Beethoven first refers to the tempo indications currently in use — such expressions as *allegro* — as being vague and having arisen in what he dismisses as 'the barbarous ages of music'. He next expressed his resolve to bring about changes — the first composer of standing to do so:

> 'As for me, I have long been thinking of abandoning those absurd descriptive terms, *allegro, andante, adagio, presto*, and Maelzel's metronome affords us the best opportunity of doing so. I now give *my word* that I shall *never again* use them in any of my new compositions — But, there is another question, and that is whether by doing so we are aiming at bringing the metronome into *general use*, a thing which is necessary?'
> [Beethoven's italics][24]

Beethoven was as good as his word and the tempo metronome-indications for all of his published eight symphonies duly appeared in the December 1817 issue of the *Allgemeine musikalische Zeitung*.[25]

Given Beethoven's wish to establish authenticity in the interpretation of his music, an anecdote from the recollections of his pupil Ferdinand Ries is not without its lighter side. Ries, then living in London, endeavoured to secure a reprint of Beethoven's symphonies and wrote to Beethoven asking for the required metronome numbers. Beethoven duly sent these to Ries but the letter containing them failed to arrive. Ries, accordingly, requested Beethoven to send them once more. Beethoven obliged, metronomising the symphonies *again* and sending the numbers off to London. Meanwhile, his first letter had arrived and it turned out Beethoven had given *different* numbers each time![26]

On 13 May 1822, Nikolaus Simrock in Bonn wrote to Beethoven urging him to make progress with the completion of the *Missa Solemnis*, on which he had been working, and for which for which he had paid 100 louis d'or. In the course of his letter he adds: 'For the present I have undertaken to publish your six Symphonies [i.e. Nos. 1–6] in full score.' He gave the reason:

> '[I] wanted to dedicate to my worthy old friend a worthy monument, and I hope you will be satisfied with the edition, since I have done my utmost for it.[27]

The scores of the First and Second Symphonies appeared in 1822 followed by that of the *Eroica* Symphony a few months later and that of the Fourth Symphony in 1823. In the event, notwithstanding his expressed intentions, Simrock never published the scores of the Fifth and Sixth Symphonies. They were published later by Breitkopf & Härtel in 1826.

It will be recalled Beethoven originally dedicated his First Symphony to the Elector Maximilian Franz but who had died shortly after on 26 July 1801 at Hetzendorf. The Elector's name on the Title Page to the symphony was subsequently crossed out and replaced by that of Baron Gottfried van Swieten who, thereby, became the work's new dedicatee. Van Swieten had indirect high-born connections, being the son of the Empress Maria Theresa's personal physician. He spent many years in Berlin in the diplomatic service, combining his duties with an interest in music. He particularly admired the music of Handel and J. S. Bach and commissioned six new symphonies from C. P. E. Bach.

In Vienna van Swieten held the post of Prefect (Director) to the National Library and was widely known, and respected, for the Sunday morning recitals he held there. He also entertained musicians in his own home; Mozart had participated in these concerts. Evidence of van Swieten's close attachment to Beethoven is apparent in a letter he sent to him of 15 December 1794, 'I wish to see you at my house at 8.30 in the evening with your nightcap in your bag.' — the inference being the young composer was expected to play well into the evening. The elderly van Swieten particularly enjoyed hearing Beethoven perform Bach's fugues.[28]

Van Swieten was not only an admirer of the youthful Beethoven but was also one of his earliest patrons in Vienna, at a time when he was little known. The solicitude he showed him undoubtedly helped the young composer find acceptance into the circles of Vienna's musically-minded nobility. Writing of him Robbins Landon enthuses:

> 'Baron Gottfried van Swieten (1733–1803), [was] perhaps the most prominent propagator of musical life in late eighteenth-century Vienna. After all, it was the Baron who brought both Haydn and Mozart into contact with the North German art of J. S. Bach and Handel. In addition, he was responsible for the librettos and the commissioning of Haydn's two masterful Oratorios, *The Creation* and *The Seasons.* Van Swieten was important to Beethoven not for his personal wealth but for his connections and the respect he commanded

among the Viennese nobility in musical life and cultural manners. [Beethoven's] dedication seems to reflect the historical position of this work [the First Symphony] as belonging more to the generation of Haydn and Mozart.'[29]

Given the support Beethoven received from van Swieten, it is not surprising he should dedicate his First Symphony to him. Thereby, the amended Title Page of the First Symphony was duly announced:

'GRAND / SIMPHONIE / pour / 2 *Violins*, *Violoncelle et Bass*, / 2 *Fluites*, 2 *Oboes*, 2 *Cors*, 2 *Bassons* / 2 *Clarinettes*, 2 *Trompettes et Tymbales*, / composée et dédiée / à / *Son Excellence Monsieur le Baron* / VAN SWIETEN, / Commandeur de l'ordre roy, de St. Etienne, / Conseiller intime et BibliothecaIre de sa / Majesté Imp. Et Roy / Par / Louis van Beethoven. / Oeuvre XXI. / à Leipsic au Bureau de Musique de A. C. Kühnel.'[30]

Van Swieten did not live long enough to enjoy the immortality Beethoven had conferred upon him. By a twist of fate — we recall once more the untimely death of the original dedicatee Maximillian Franz — van Swieten also died on 29 March 1803.

It so happens that the London-based publishers Cianchettini and Sperati had issued unauthorised editions of Beethoven's first three Symphonies in score between 1808–09. The Title Page to the Cianchettini and Sperati score edition of Beethoven's First Symphony was styled as follows:

'The / Compleat Collection / of / HAYDN, MOZART / and BEETHOVEN'S / SYMPHO-NIES . In Score / *Most Respectfully Dedicated, by Permission to* / H. R. H. / THE / *Prince of Wales*, / No. XXVII] / Price to Subscribers 5s. [shillings] / Non Subscribers 8s. / Rymer & Son Sct. [engraver] / LONDON / *Printed by Cianchettini & Sperati Importers of Classical Music.* / N.o 5. Princes Street Cavendish Square. [date of issue 1809][31]

Other editions of the First Symphony duly appeared in the nineteenth century. The most significant of these was the complete edition of Beethoven's collected works brought out by Breitkopf & Härtell in twenty-four series between 1862 and 1865.

[1] Elliot Forbes editor, *Thayer's Life of Beethoven*, 1967, pp. 259–60. With acknowledgment also to Peter Clive, 2001, pp. 166–67.
[2] Emily Anderson editor and translator, 1961, *The Letters of Beethoven*, London: Macmillan, 3 vols.,1961.
[3] Theodore Albrecht editor and translator, 1996, *Letters to Beethoven and other Correspondence*, Lincoln, New England: University of Nebraska Press, 3 vols., 1996.
[4] Emily Anderson editor and translator, 1961, Vol. 1, Letter No. 41, pp. 42–43. For a facsimile reproduction of this letter see: Beethoven House, Digital Archives, Library Document NE 181.
[5] Emily Anderson, 1961, Vol. 1, Letter No. 44, pp. 47-8. For a facsimile reproduction of this letter see: Beethoven House, Digital Archives, Library Document, NE 160.
[6] Emily Anderson editor and translator, 1961, Vol. 1, Letter No. 47, pp. 50–52.
[7] *Ibid,* Vol. 1, Letter No. 50, pp. 55–56. For a commentary to this letter see: Beethoven House, Digital Archives, Library Document, Sinfonie Nr. 1 (C Dur), Op. 21.
[8] The precise date of Härtel's letter is not known since no record of it appears to have survived.
[9] Emily Anderson editor and translator, 1961, Vol. 1, Letter No.48, pp. 52–54. For a facsimile reproduction of this letter see: Beethoven House, Digital Archives, Library Document, HCB BBr 7.
[10] Theodore Albrecht editor and translator, 1996, Vol. 1, Letter No. 46, pp. 79–80. See also: Beethoven House, Digital Archives, Library Document, HCB Br 298.

[11] Tranquillo Mollo was a partner in the famous publishing house of Artaria & Co. until he founded his own publishing business — T. Mollo & Co. — in 1808. Despite Beethoven's vexation with Mollo, for publishing his unauthorised quintet-adaptation of his First Symphony, he established a good working relationship with him. The firm published first editions of his Trio, Op. 11, Piano Sonatas, Op. 14, First Piano Concerto, Op. 15, Horn Sonata, Op. 17, and the String Quartets, Op. 18.
[12] Emily Anderson editor and translator, 1961, Vol. 3, Appendix II, p. 1434.
[13] Theodore Albrecht editor and translator, 1996, Vol. 1, Letter No. 59, p. 102.
[14] *Ibid*, Vol. 1, Letter No. 61, pp. 104–05.
[15] *Ibid*, Vol. 1, Letter No. 68, pp. 116–17.
[16] Photographs of Breitkopf and Härtel's premises in Leipzig's Nürnberger Strasse, taken before and after the Allied bombing, are reproduced in Theodore Albrecht editor and translator, 1996, Vol. 1, following p, 98.
[17] H. C. Robbins Landon, 1977, p. 239.
[18] With acknowledgement to: Wayne M. Senner, Robin Wallace and William Meredith editors, 1999, Vol. 1, p. 171.
[19] Alain Frogley, *Beethoven's Music in Performance: Historical Perspectives* in: Glenn Stanley editor, *The Cambridge Companion to Beethoven*, 2000, pp. 259.
[20] Ibid, p.260.
[21] Charles Rosen, 2002, p. 43.
[22] Barry Cooper, 1991, pp. 24–5.
[23] Emily Anderson, 1961, Vol. 2, Letter No. 587, p. 542.
[24] *Ibid*, Vol. 2, Letter No. 845, pp. 727–8.
[25] Barry Cooper, 1991, p. 26.
[26] As reproduced in: Edwin Fischer, 1959, pp. 93–5. In exoneration of Beethoven, we need to bear in mind this was a period of some experimentation with the new instrument and, doubtless, the regularity of the metronome itself was still being established. It is also known Beethoven's metronome was occasionally faulty.
[27] Theodore Albrecht editor and translator, 1996, Vol. 2, Letter No. 285, pp. 203–04.
[28] Theodore Albrecht editor and translator, 1996, Vol. 1, Letter No. 18, pp. 36–37.
[29] H. C. Robbins Landon, 1977, p. 27.
[30] Wilhelm Altmann, Introduction to the Score of Beethoven's First Symphony, Dover Publication, 1976.
[31] Beethoven House, Digital Archives, Library Document, HCB C Md 44.

RECEPTION HISTORY

In this part of our commentary to Beethoven's First Symphony, Op. 21, we trace the reception history of the composition from the occasion of its first performance, through the nineteenth century, with particular reference to France, Germany, and England, and, to close, with a selection of estimations of the music from nearer to our own time. Regarding the latter, we reserve our more detailed considerations of the work's musicology to our closing text.

We recall the First Symphony was performed at Beethoven's *Akademie* Concert held on 2 April 1800 at Vienna's Burgtheater; it was his first public appearance for his own benefit in Vienna, and, so far as is known, his first public appearance since his concert tour in Prague. As was the custom of the period, Beethoven had to defray all the expenses himself. Perhaps, for this reason, the better seats were sold by him from his own apartment; others were available, in the normal fashion, at the box office.

It was no easy matter for a composer — particularly a relatively unknown one — to secure Vienna's most prestigious concert venue for a personal *Akademie*. David Wyn Jones explains:

> 'Paul Wranitzky [a prominent conductor] would ... have been a natural ally in any attempt by Beethoven to secure a benefit concert at the Burgtheater, one that would have capitalized on the younger composer's growing reputation as a performer and, more unusually, allowed him to be presented as a composer too.'

A particular obstacle was that the manager of the court theatres, Baron Braun, typically sanctioned no more than two individual benefit concerts in Lent. It was perhaps to Beethoven's benefit that Braun's wife, Josephine, was an accomplished pianist, so much so that Beethoven dedicated his Op. 14 Piano Sonatas to her when they appeared in 1799. Jones suggests this may have served as

> 'an emollient gesture that may have encouraged Braun to grant a benefit evening the following April — Beethoven's first opportunity to present a symphony'.[1]

Notice of the forthcoming concert appeared in the 26 March issue of the *Wiener Zeitung* and the *Allgemeine musikalische Zeitung*:

> 'Today, Wednesday 2 April 1800, Herr *Ludwig van Beethoven* will have the honour to give a

grand concert for his benefit in the Royal Imperial Court Theatre beside the Burg.'

The notice promised:

'A grand symphony [not identified] by Mozart; an aria from Haydn's *The Creation*; a grand Concerto for the pianoforte, played and composed by Herr Ludwig van Beethoven; a Septet most humbly and obediently dedicated to Her Majesty the Empress by Herr *Ludwig van Beethoven;* a duet from Haydn's *The Creation*; and a new grand symphony with complete orchestra [the First Symphony, Op. 21], composed by *Herr Ludwig van Beethoven'.*

The announcement also intimated: '*Herr Ludwig van Beethoven* will improvise on the pianoforte.'[2] [original italics retained]

Worthy of particular remark is that Beethoven's name had now appeared on a concert programme alongside those of Haydn and Mozart. As Jones further observes:

'Commentators have seized on this concert as a defining moment in the history of the symphony: Beethoven was finally able, after several years of preparation, to rise to the challenge of Haydn and Mozart.'[3]

The association of Beethoven's First Symphony with Mozartian precedent was to linger in the minds of some, for many years. By way of illustration we recall the views of the Russian musicologist Alexndre Oulibicheff. He is remembered today for his pioneering biography of Mozart (*Nouvelle Biographie de Mozart*, Dresden 1843) in which he referred to the symphonies of Beethoven. Despite these works having long been assimilated into the repertoire, he found merit only in the composer's First Symphony, for the reason he considered it to be in Mozart's style.[4]

The circumstances of the 2 April 1800 concert were far from favourable. Alongside the First Symphony, Beethoven had hoped to make a stir by performing his dramatic Third Piano Concerto, Op. 37 in C minor. This was not yet ready and he had to perform a revised version of his First Piano Concerto, Op. 15 in C major — that he did not consider to be among his best compositions.[5] Moreover, there was disagreement as to who should conduct. The Italian Contini, who held the post of Orchestral Director, was preferred by his fellow countrymen who made up a large portion of the orchestra. Beethoven, however, mistrusted him and preferred Paul Wranitsky, a Czech musician whose conducting skills had earned both the respect of Beethoven and his teacher Haydn.

A review of the of the April concert appeared in the October issue of the *Allgemeine musikalische Zeitung*. The reviewer reported the disaffected players did not perform well under Wranitsky's direction. He records:

> 'The orchestra of the Italian Opera showed to very poor advantage. First, quarrels regarding the conductors. Beethoven believed, and rightly, that rather than Herr Contini no one could do better to conduct than Herr Wranitzky. The gentlemen did not want to play under him. The shortcomings of this orchestra ... were therefore more evident.'

The critic elaborated:

> 'While they were accompanying [the Concerto]

> the players did not make any effort to pay attention to the soloist. As a result, there was no trace of delicacy in the accompaniment.'

In the second part of the concert, when the First Symphony was played, the players became so lax that in spite of all efforts, 'no fire could any longer be brought forth in their playing – not [even] in the wind instruments'. The reviewer concluded:

> 'With such behaviour what good is all the proficiency which most of the members of this organisation undoubtedly possess? How, under such circumstances is even the most excellent composition to be effective?'

Regarding the music itself, the critic of the *AmZ* did have some positive things to say. He regarded the Piano Concerto to have been 'written with a great deal of taste and feeling' and Beethoven's improvisation 'to be masterly'. He found in the Symphony, 'considerable art, novelty and a wealth of ideas', but considered the wind instruments were used too much 'so that there was more music for wind instruments than for a full orchestra'. Doubtless Beethoven would have been pleased, though, with the critic's final verdict – he considered the concert to be 'truly the most interesting for a long time'.[6]

Maynard Solomon remarks: '[Contemporary] critics did not by any means regard [Beethoven's] First Symphony as a timid or imitative work.'[7] Donald Tovey comments:

> 'Where the contemporary critics showed intelligent observation was in marking, though with mild censure, the fact that Beethoven's First

Symphony is written so heavily for the wind band that it seems almost more like *Harmoniemusik* than a proper orchestral piece.'[8]

Two years later, Beethoven's music appeared again before the public. On 26 March 1803 the *Wiener Zeitung* announced: 'On 4 April, Herr Ludwig van Beethoven will produce a new Oratorio set to music by him, *Christus am Ölberg*, in the Theater-an-der-Wien.' The other works performed were the First and Second Symphonies and the recently composed Piano Concerto in C minor, Op. 37. The actual date of the concert has been established as having taken place on 5 April. More significantly, this was Beethoven's first public appearance as a dramatic vocal composer. Of no less significance for Beethoven was that the concert was a financial success, yielding him 1800 florins; it appears, however, to have done little to enhance his reputation with the public as a composer. Thayer records: 'The impression made upon reading the few contemporary notices of this concert is that the new works produced were, on the whole, coldly received.' A short report in the journal *Der Freymüthige* stated:

> 'True, the two Symphonies and single passages in the Oratorio were voted very beautiful, but the work in its entirety was too long, too artificial in structure and lacking expressiveness especially in the vocal parts.'

A report in the *Zeitung für die Elegante Welt* was of the opinion:

> '[The] First Symphony was better than the later one [Op. 36] because it developed with a light-

ness and is less forced, while in the Second the striving for the new and surprising is already more apparent. However, it is obvious that both are not lacking in surprising and brilliant passages of beauty.' The correspondent of the *Allgemeine musikalische Zeitung* was mostly captivated by the Oratorio, disposing him to predict: 'It confirms my long-held opinion that Beethoven in time can effect a revolution in music like Mozart's. He is hastening towards this goal with great strides.'

The concert proved challenging for all concerned, not least for the members of the orchestra who were confronted with an array of new and challenging compositions. To help relieve the exhausted players Thayer further relates:

'Prince Karl Lichnowsky [Beethoven's patron], who attended the rehearsal from the beginning [it had commenced at eight o'clock in the morning], had sent for bread and butter, cold meat and wine, in large baskets. He pleasantly asked all to help themselves, and this was done with both hands, the result being that good nature was restored again.'[9]

On 7 April 1803 a review appeared in the Journal *Zeitung für die Elegante Welt* describing 'public concerts in Vienna' for the musically-minded citizens of Leipzig. The main work mentioned was the Cantata *Christus am Ölberge* the libretto to which was criticised, prompting the reviewer to comment: 'Herr van Beethoven showed that a composer of genius is capable of making something great from the worst material.' The reviewer considered 'the First [Symphony] had more worth than the Second [Symphony]' because 'it was performed with unforced ease', while the Second he found was marred by too visible 'a striving for novel and striking effects'. He did, however, concede: 'Moreover, it goes without saying that neither was lacking striking and brilliant qualities of beauty.' Beethoven's rendering of his C minor Piano Concerto was, however, deemed to be 'not to the satisfaction of the public'.[10] Other performances of the First Symphony soon followed.

Writing of the year 1804, Thayer remarks:

'The First Symphony had hardly left Hoffmeister's press when it was added to the repertory of the Gewandhaus Concerts at Leipzig, and during the three following years was repeatedly performed at Berlin, Breslau, Brunswick, Dresden, Frankfurt-am-Main, and Munich.'

This success, alongside that of other of the composer's works, disposed Thayer to enthuse:

'Beethoven, then, although almost unknown personally beyond the limits of a few Austrian cities — unaided by apostles to preach his gospel, owing nothing to journalist or pamphleteer ... had, in the short space of eight years, by the simple force of his genius as manifested in his published works, placed himself at the head of all writers for the pianoforte, and in public estimation had risen to the level of the two greatest of orchestral composers. The unknown student that entered Vienna in 1792, was now in 1804 a recognised member of the great triumvirate, Haydn, Mozart and Beethoven.'[11]

The Gewandhaus Orchestra, just mentioned, became a staunch supporter of Beethoven's orchestral music. It performed. Beethoven's First Symphony in 1801 with that of his Second Symphony following in 1804 and the *Eroica* in 1807. In 1809, the *Pastoral* Symphony was heard and in the same years the C minor Symphony was given from manuscript parts. The Gewandhaus Orchestra featured the *Choral* Symphony in its 1826 concert season. Ten years later, the standing of the Gewandhaus Orchestra was raised by the appointment of Felix Mendelsohn as the Orchestra's Music Director — *Gewandhauskapellmeister* — an appointment he held until his untimely death in 1847.

The composer, pianist and conductor Ferdinand Hiller — a close friend of Mendelsohn — did not consider the Leipzig Gewandhaus Orchestra to be on quite the same level as that of the Paris *Société des Concerts* — for its 'little imperfections in individual execution' — but recognised 'the spirit and life' of Mendelsohn's conducting. In his estimation, Robert Schuman, perhaps the most generous-hearted of all music critics (we recall his spontaneous response to Chopin's Variations on Mozart's *Là ci darem la mano* — "Hats off gentlemen, a genius"), considered a 'united family feeling' permeated the whole of the Leipzig Orchestra and recognised 'the complete confidence' the players showed to their conductor. He remarked:

> 'Our musicians here form a family; they see each other and practice together daily; They are always the same, so that they are able to play a Beethoven symphony without the notes [without the music].'[12]

In the 5 December issue of the *AmZ*, the reviewer reported

on a performance of the First Symphony that he had heard at a concert in Berlin on 15 November. He described the music as having been received 'with so much well-deserved applause'. He singled out for special mention the affecting playing of the oboe and bassoon and, with regard to the wind instruments more generally, he enthused 'one could not want for a more perfect orchestra'. Clearly, the writing for wind instruments, that in earlier reviews had been considered 'intrusive', was now being more fully appreciated. The review continues:

> 'The aforementioned grand symphony, this exquisite, clear, harmonious, and, nevertheless, not bizarrely composed masterpiece by B[eethoven] in the genre of the most recent grand instrumental compositions, was performed with energy and taste.'[13]

In 1805, the Berlin music season opened with a concert in which the First Symphony was performed. A review duly appeared in the *Berlinische musikalische Zeitung* (issue 1 of 1805) The *BmZ's* correspondent was fulsome in his praise:

> [The concert] commenced with Beethoven's well-known Symphony in C major. Although often heard, its originality and excellent performance were listened to with pleasure.'

The following year, the Berlin concert season opened once more with a concert that incorporated another rendering of the First Symphony — further testimony to its popularity. The reviewer of this concert was Johann Friedrich Reichardt — a composer himself and on personal terms with Beethoven. He made passing reference to a parallel concert-series given by Ernst Schick and a fellow music impresario named Bohrer

— his first name is not known. Reichardt informs: 'We [have] heard [the First Symphony] performed so often and so splendidly in the Schick and Bohrer concerts.'[14]

Beethoven did not fare so well when the music critic of the *Berlinische musikalische Zeitung* reported on a concert that had taken place the previous December in Vienna's Royal Opera House; this was for the benefit of the widows and orphans of musicians. This review is the first in which Beethoven is chastised for disregarding the traditionally accepted way of opening a symphony. In response to the start of the First Symphony, the reviewer remarked:

> 'At the moment that an eager public awaited the first powerful symphonic sound of a numerically large orchestra, the First Symphony by Beethoven began on a short upbeat with a chord of the seventh above the dominant of the principal key.'

He remonstrated:

> 'No one will censure an ingenious artist like Beethoven for such liberties and peculiarities, but such a beginning is not suitable for the opening of a grand concert in a spacious opera house.'[15]

On 28 January 1805, the First Symphony was performed at the house of the wealthy banker Herr von Würth. Although not of noble birth himself, Würth was married to a baroness and appears to have had resources sufficient to support major musical events. On this occasion, the munificence and charitable inclinations of Beethoven's patron Prince Lobkowitz once again came to the fore; he paid the musicians 5 florins each for the rehearsal and performance. The orchestra consisted of 10 violins; 3 violas; 2 each of cellos, double basses, oboes, flutes, clarinets, and trumpets; timpani; and 4 horns — curiously, one more than required for the *Eroica* Symphony which featured in the music-making.[16]

It is evident from the review of the concert that Beethoven's music had by now been well assimilated into the concert repertoire and held no terrors for the players:

> '[The] Beethoven Symphony in C major was performed with precision and ease. A magnificent artistic creation. All instruments are used exquisitely, and an uncommon wealth of beautiful ideas is magnificently and charmingly displayed in it. Nevertheless, cohesion, order, and light dominate everywhere.'

As remarked, the *Eroica* Symphony was performed later in the evening. It is of course with this work that Beethoven changed the landscape of the symphony forever. Not surprisingly, the creation failed to please:

> 'An entirely new symphony by Beethoven is written in an entirely new style. This long composition, *exceedingly difficult to perform*, is actually a very broadly, expanded, bold, and wild fantasia. It is not at all lacking in startling and beautiful passages in which the energetic and talented spirit of its creator must be recognised; however, *very often it seems to lose itself in irregularity.*'[17] [critic's italics]

In their commentary to the words just quoted, the authors add:

> 'The Würth musicians featured an orchestra of amateur musicians; although they did perform

Beethoven's First Symphony and the Third Piano Concerto in their 1804–05 season, the *Eroica* may have been too difficult.'[18]

The performance of the *Eroica* Symphony disposed the music correspondent to the Berlin journal *Der Freimüthige* to reflect on the composition in its issue of 26 April 1805; the founding principle of the journal was to inform 'serious and impartial readers'. We cite part of what he had to say insofar as his remarks reveal the extent to which Beethoven's most advanced music, of the period, divided audiences.

ADVOCATES:
'One party, Beethoven's most special friends, contend that this particular Symphony [No. 3, *Eroica*] is a masterpiece, that this is exactly the true style for music of the highest type and that if it does not please now it is because the public is not sufficiently cultivated in the arts to comprehend these higher spheres of beauty; but after a couple of hundred years its effect will not be lessened.'

OPPOSITION:
'The other party absolutely denies any artistic merit in the work. They claim it reveals symptoms of an evidently unbridled attempt at distinction and peculiarity, but that neither beauty, true sublimity nor power have anywhere been achieved either by means of unusual modulations, by violent transitions or by the juxtaposition of the most heterogenous elements.'

UNDECIDED:
'The third, very small party, stand in the middle.

> They concede that there are many beautiful things in the Symphony, but admit that the continuity often appears to be completely confused and that the endless duration of this longest and perhaps most difficult of all symphonies is tiring even for the expert; for a mere amateur it is unbearable.'

The reviewer chastised Beethoven for using three horns, regarding this as an undesirable trick, and asserted that the creation of something beautiful and sublime was the true expression of genius and not 'something merely unusual and fantastic'. He acknowledged Beethoven himself, in his own early works, had demonstrated this but he complained:

> 'One wishes that H[err] v[an] B[eethoven] would use his recognised great talent to present us with works similar to his first two Symphonies in C and D, to his spirited Septet in E flat ... and other of his early compositions which will assure B[eethoven] a place among the foremost instrumental composers.'

The reviewer recognised Beethoven's independence of mind but cautioned:

> 'One fears, however, that if Beethoven continues along this road, he and the public will make a bad journey ... Overwhelmed by a mass of disconnected ideas and by a continuing tumult of all the instruments, the listener would leave the concert hall with only an unpleasant feeling of exhaustion.'

Beethoven had conducted the performance himself and the

reviewer complained he did not even acknowledge the few members of the audience who applauded at the close of the work. Beethoven 'on the contrary', the reviewer remarked, 'did not find the applause sufficiently enthusiastic'.[19]

Of related interest to the 28 January 1805 concert is that Beethoven used the occasion to perform on his newly acquired piano, a gift from the French manufacturer Sébastien Érard. This incorporated several innovations such as foot pedals that replaced the cumbersome knee-action lever-arrangement typical of instruments of the time. Érard's pianos were sturdily constructed and offered greater sonority than most other fortepianos pianos of the day — characteristics particularly valued by Beethoven in his quest for an evermore resonant keyboard-sound. The gift was in recognition of Érard's esteem of Beethoven and of his growing reputation abroad as a pianist. Other distinguished musicians of the day, who owned an Érard piano, included Beethoven's teacher Haydn and fellow pianist Ignaz Moscheles.

In 1806, the music correspondent to the *Allgemeine musikalische Zeitung* reflected on Beethoven's First Symphony that had now become established in Vienna's concert repertoire. Moreover, the correspondent placed Beethoven, the symphonist, on the same level as his great forebears:

> 'Beethoven wrote his First Symphony in C Major, a masterpiece that does equal honour to his inventiveness and his musical knowledge. Being just as beautiful and distinguished in its design as its execution, there prevails in it such a clear and lucid order, such a flow of the most pleasant melodies, and such a rich, but at the same time never wearisome, instrumentation that this symphony can justly be placed next to Mozart's and Haydn's.'[20]

*

Anton Schindler mentions two subscription concerts that were held for the benefit of the composer at the Palace of Prince Lobkowitz in March 1807. The programmes included the first four symphonies the *Coriolanus* Overture, the G major Piano Concerto, and some arias from *Fidelio*.[21]

A series of concerts was established in Vienna in 1807–08, known as the *Liebhaber-Concerte* – 'Music-Lover's Concert'. These were promoted by Johann von Häring, a banker who was recognised for being one of Vienna's foremost amateur violinists; he had the distinction of performing chamber music with Mozart. A measure of his standing is that he possessed instruments by Amati, Guarneri, and Stradivarius. Häring made a significant contribution to Viennese musical life and was elected Director (Leader) of the orchestra when the *Liebhaber-Concerte* commenced. A number of these concerts were also directed by the celebrated violinist Franz Clement, known to Beethovenians for premiering his Violin Concerto. In the opening concert season 1807–08, Clement directed performances of Beethoven's First, Second, and Fourth Symphonies as well as his First Piano Concerto.[22] From Thayer we learn:

> 'The audiences were composed exclusively of the nobility of the town and foreigners of note, and among these classes the preference was given to the cognoscenti and amateurs ... [In] twenty meetings, symphonies, overtures, concertos, and vocal pieces were performed zealously and were received with general approval.'[23]

Häring had an excellent command of English and assisted Beethoven in his negotiations with publishers such as

George Thomson, in Scotland, and influential musical figures in England such as Sir George Smart — a founder member of the Philharmonic Society. In a long letter of 16–19 March 1815, Häring wrote on Beethoven's behalf offering for sale in England several recently composed works. These included: the then immensely popular *Battle Symphony* or *Battle of Vittoria*, in full score for 70 guineas, or as arranged for piano for 30 guineas; and the equally popular Seventh Symphony also offered for 70 guineas in full score, or as arranged for piano for 30 guineas.[24]

Mention may be made here of Beethoven's growing reputation in France where his symphonies were beginning to find acceptance. In Paris, students of the Conservatoire commenced a series of concerts — *Concerts Français* — that they modestly called *Exercises Publics*. Notwithstanding their modest status, they were assisted by François-Antoine Habeneck who, from 1804, served as their lauréat — initially as violinist-leader and, from 1806, as conductor. Habeneck joined the orchestra of the Opéra-Comique in 1804 and shortly after moved to the Opéra where he succeed Rudolphe Kreuzer — of Kreuzer Violin Sonata fame — as principal violin. From 1821 to 1824 he was Director of the Opéra. Habeneck's most lasting achievements were the introduction of Beethoven's music to France and the founding of the *Société des Concerts du Conservatoire*. Concerning the students' orchestra, it gave the first performance in Paris of Beethoven First Symphony in 1805 — Habeneck had obtained the parts of Op. 21 soon after its publication. Performance of the Second Symphony and the *Eroica* followed in 1811. Such was the precision of the students' playing that the correspondent in a contemporary issue of *The Quarterly Music Magazine* enthused: '*The Exercises* of its [the Conservatoire's] pupils are the most brilliant concert's in Paris.'[25]

Sometime in February or March of 1808, Beethoven sent an undated letter to the Austrian dramatist Heinrich von Collin — known to Beethovenians for his Overture to Collin's tragedy *Coriolan* — not to be confused with Shakespeare's *Coriolanus*. Beethoven requested Collin's support in arranging an *Akademie* — another benefit concert — to promote his works and to supplement his income. The outcome was a memorable concert that took place on 22 December later in the year. Of more general interest is that between 12 November 1807 and 27 March 1808, some twenty concerts were given in Vienna by the newly formed *Gesellschaft von Musikfreunden*. Ten of the concerts included Beethoven Symphonies: Nos. One, Two, and Three were each performed twice alongside his Piano Concerto No. 1, and the Overture *Coriolan* — also performed twice. For these performances an orchestra of 55 players assembled who included the violinist Franz Clement — already mentioned for premiering Beethoven's Violin Concert on 23 December 1806 at the Theater an der Wien.[26]

The Italian violinist Giuseppe Cambini lived in Paris for a period and from there contributed articles to the *Allgemeine musikalische Zeitung* and the *Tablettes de Polymnie*. Writing in the latter, in 1811, he remarked on the impression made on him after hearing Beethoven's first two symphonies:

> 'The composer Beethoven, often bizarre and baroque, sometimes sparkles with extraordinary beauties. Now he takes the majestic flight of the eagle, then he creeps along grotesque paths. After penetrating the soul with a sweet melancholy, he soon tears it by a mass of barbaric chords. He seems to harbour doves and crocodiles at the same time.'[27]

On 6 May 1812, the music correspondent to the *Allgemeine*

musikalische Zeitung reported on music-making in Munich. The seventh programme in the city's concert series had included a performance of the C major Symphony. It was described as being — with a sting in the tale — 'more pleasing and melodic than one expects from this artist'.[28]

On 14 January 1814, the *Zeitung für die Elegante Welt* announced the première of a performance of a four-hands piano transcription of the C major Symphony. This had been made by Karl (Carl) Zulehner who had established a reputation for making piano-reductions of melodies taken from the popular operas of the day.[29] That Zulehner should turn his attention to a work from the orchestral repertoire is further indication of the popularity of the C major Symphony. Beethoven was reluctant to make transcriptions of his own works and, when he did sanction such adaptations of his music, he placed them in the hands of his most trustworthy piano pupils, namely, Carl Czerny and Ferdinand Ries. Noteworthy transcriptions of his own making include: the String Quartet arrangement of the Piano Sonata in E major, Op. 14, No. 1; a partial piano transcription of the Seventh Symphony; and, most significant of all, his four-hand piano-arrangement of the *Grosse Fuge*. Furthermore, some authorities believe Beethoven's Twelve Ecossaises, WoO 16 are an unauthentic arrangement of part of the First Symphony.[30]

What vexed Beethoven in particular was the publication of *unauthorised* transcriptions of his works — that he usually condemned for their lack of facility. On 20 October 1802, he had a notice placed in the *Wiener Zeitung* complaining of the publication of two String Quintet arrangements derived from his First Symphony. These had been published by Breitkopf & Härtel without his knowledge. He protested:

'The making of transcriptions is on the whole a

thing against which nowadays (in our prolific age of transcriptions) a composer would merely struggle in vain.'[31]

The following year, on, 22 October 1803, Beethoven learned of a proposal that occasioned him to have a further notice displayed in the *Wiener Zeitung* stating:

'WARNING: Herr Karl Zulehner, an engraver at Mainz, has announced an edition of my complete works for the pianoforte and stringed instruments. I consider it my duty to inform all friends of mine that I have nothing whatever to do with this edition ... Furthermore, I must point out that such an edition of my works, undertaken illegally, can never be complete, inasmuch as several new ones are already to appear in Paris; and these Herr Zulehner, who is a French national, my not reprint.'[32]

Despite Beethoven's publicly-expressed words of caution, piano and chamber transcriptions of his First Symphony appeared from various presses during his lifetime. We list some of these together with their composer (where known) and publisher:

Arrangement for string quintet (2 violins, 2 violas, cello), anonymous. Pleyel, 1803;
for string quintet (2 violins, 2 violas, cello). Mollo, c. 1804;
for piano solo, by Gelinek. Cappi & Co.;
for nonet (2 violins, 2 violas, cello or double bass, 2 oboes or clarinets in C, 2 horns), by Carl Friedrich Ebers. André, 1809;

> for piano four-hands, anonymous (attributed to Czerny). Peters, c. 1814;
> for septet (2 violins, 2 flutes, 2 violas, cello and double bass or 2 cellos), anonymous. Monzani & Hill, 1815;
> for flute (or violin or cello) and piano, anonymous. Monzani & Hill, 1818;
> for string quintet (2 violins, 2 violas, cello), de Pierre-Auguste-Louis Blondeau? Pacini, c. 1825;
> for piano trio (flute, violin and piano), by Johann Nepomuk Hummel. Monzani & Hill, 1825;
> and for quartet (flute, violin, cello, piano), by Johann Nepomuk Hummel.[33]

By way of a footnote to the foregoing, we cite some words from the musicologist Glenn Stanley who quotes Paul Bekker:

> 'Even though Bekker conceded that Beethoven's orchestral music was widely known in its piano versions, he argued that its real magic could only be encountered properly in an orchestral performance in a public space; the piano reductions were to the music as reproductions in art books were to large-scale canvases.'[34]

We may add our own observation that the only true analogue for a concert performance is a concert performance — although modern-day recording and reproduction come tantalisingly close to the real thing.

We resume our chronological survey of the reception of Beethoven's First Symphony by recalling an incident that took place in 1816. Schindler records Beethoven received a visitor

— identified only as 'General Ham' — who maintained he was an emissary of the London Philharmonic Society. Allegedly, on their behalf, he requested Beethoven to compose two symphonies 'in the style of the First Symphony'. Schindler relates: 'I leave it to the reader to guess with what distaste this message was received.'[35] The inference is clear; Beethoven dismissed the request with disdain, given by how much his symphonic writing had by then advanced.

Three years later there were more noteworthy musical happenings. The Vienna concert season of 1819–20 was significant for the introduction of a new series of concerts promoted under the title of *Concerts Spirituels*. These were styled on a concert series, of the same name, that had been founded in Paris some years earlier. The aim of both series was to offer public concerts whose programmes combined sacred choral and instrumental music. The Vienna concerts owed their inception to Franz Xaver Gebauer, an organist-composer, choirmaster, music director of the city's Augustinian Church, and a committee member of the *Gesellschaft der Musikfreunde*. A notice in the *Allgemeine musikalische Zeitung* announced:

> 'On 1 October 1819, a new concert series was started, soon to be known as the *Concerts Spirituels* ... *Herr Gebauer* makes the proposal to form a special society of a moderate number to bring to performance only symphonies and choruses excluding all virtuoso music [pure display music] and bravura singing.'

The 'moderate number' refers to the performers who were all amateurs and who played largely from sight. In the eighteen concerts of the first season, Beethoven's first four symphonies were performed together with the *Pastoral*

Symphony. The second season (1820–21) consisted of ten concerts which included the Symphonies in C minor, Op. 67, A major, Op. 92, and F major, Op. 93. Since the players were performing from sight, it is not surprising that the *AmZ* reviewer, commenting on the performance at the 9 April concert, felt obliged to report to Beethoven: 'I forgot to tell you that the dilettantes scraped through your symphony [unspecified] yesterday.'[36] Beethoven responded by writing to Gebauer, sometime in April 1820, requesting tickets to judge the performances himself – insofar as his hearing would permit. He appears, though, to have made up his mind in advance referring to them as 'hole-and-corner musical performances'.[37]

Of more elevated standing were the performances of Beethoven's symphonies presented by the *Gesellschaft der Musikfreunde*. For the period in question they included the following works:

1819, Nos, 2 and 3;
1820, Nos. 3, 5, and 8;
1821, Nos. 4 and 7;
1822, Nos. 1 and 5;
1823, No. 2;
1824, No. 8;
1826, Nos. 2 and 7;
1827, Nos. 1, 6, 9 (movements 1 and 2);
1828, Nos. 5 and 8.

Other composers performed by the Society included: Mozart, K. 453, k. 550 and K. 551 (three times); Haydn received a single performance in 1824 when his Symphony No. 101 (*The Clock*) was given an airing. Most poignantly, Schubert's Symphony No. 6, D. 589, was played in December 1828, a few weeks after his premature death at the age of thirty-one.[38]

*

On 25 September 1821 the music correspondent of the Berlin *Zeitung für Theater und Musik* reported on a concert held in the German capital in the following terms:

> 'The magnificent, splendid Symphony by *L van Beethoven* — one of his older, *more comprehensible* [italics added] instrumental compositions — was performed quite splendidly; the *Rondo* in a very fast tempo but nevertheless quite successfully. Nothing but applause ... rewarded the effort of the artists.'[39]

On 13 November 1822, the *Allgemeine musikalische Zeitung* announced the first, continental, publication of the C major Symphony in full score stating:

> 'We are familiar with the beautiful Paris edition of Haydn's symphonies engraved by Pleyel in full score. Beethoven's First Symphony appears here in the same format, in the same arrangement, and engraved just as beautifully.'

The edition referred to was that by the Bonn publisher Nikolaus Simrock; we have previously remarked that a full-score edition the composer's Op. 21 had had already appeared in January-February 1809 by the London publishers Cianchettini & Sperati. The *AmZ* editors add:

> 'There is no need to discuss the work here. Since its first appearance, it has been a favourite piece for all full orchestra ... and therefore is renowned and sufficiently recommended.'

More generally the editors urged the publication of orchestral music in full score — as distinct from the composition being published in separate instrumental parts — on the grounds that such 'promotes learning and facilitates precise conducting'.[40]

Cianchettini and Sperati, to whom we have just made reference, were a small but enterprising firm of Italian origin. Consideration of their London-based activities, alongside some of their contemporary publishers, provides insights into the progress of Beethoven's compositions in England. In may 1807, under the patronage of the Prince of Wales, Cianchettini and Sperati invited subscriptions for '*A compleat collection of Haydn, Mozart, and Beethoven's Symphonies in score.*' The plan was for two numbers to appear each month. In the event, their enterprise proved short-lived with the final issues appearing in 1809. Nevertheless, Beethoven's first three symphonies were amongst their earliest score-publications, alongside those of selected works of Mozart and Haydn. It is assumed that Beethoven's scores were assembled from the parts of the first editions which had been printed in Vienna sometime before — all without Beethoven's consent.

Several other English publishers realised editions of Beethoven's works that may be described as 'authentic' insofar as they were 'in some degree published with Beethoven's knowledge and approval'. Six such publishers were concerned, five in London and one in Edinburgh. The latter, George Thomson, had an extended working-relationship with Beethoven, the important results of which were the setting of many Scottish folksongs and airs. The London publishers involved were among the most distinguished of their day. They are identified as follows, together with a selection of the works of Beethoven that they published:

> Robert Birchall (Sonata for Violin and Piano, Op. 47;
> *Battle* Symphony — piano arrangement, Op. 91, Seventh Symphony — piano Arrangement, Op. 92;
> Piano Sonata, Op. 96, and Piano Trio, Op. 97);
> Chappell & Co. with Goulding & Co. (Piano Trio, Op. 121a);
> Muzio Clementi (Piano Sonata, Op. 31, No.3, String Quartets, Op. 59, Violin Concerto, Op. 61 — and as arranged for piano as Piano Concerto, Op. 73, Variations for Piano, Op. 76, Fantasia for Piano, Op. 77, Piano Sonatas, Op 78 and 79, String Quartet, Op. 74;
> *Choral Fantasia,* Op. 80, Piano Sonata, Op. 81a, Piano Sonatas Op. 110 and Op. 111;
> and Bagatelles Op. 119);
> Joseph Dale (Bagatelles, Op. 33);
> and Regent's Harmonic Institution (Piano Sonata, Op. 106).[41]

It will be seen from the foregoing that Muzio Clementi was Beethoven's most prolific English publisher at the period under consideration. He knew Beethoven personally as he made apparent in a letter of 22 April 1807 to his partner in London William Collard: 'By a little management ... I have at last made a complete conquest of that *haughty beauty* [Clementi's italics] Beethoven ...'. Clementi asked him if he was engaged to a London publisher? On being informed 'No', Clementi undertook to bring out some of the composer's works — as evident above — for which he was prepared to pay two-hundred pounds sterling.[42]

The Leipzig philosopher and music theorist Amadeus Wendt is considered to be one of Beethoven's foremost contemporary music critics. Writing in the November 1822 issue of the *Allgemeine musikalische Zeitung* he contributed an article titled. *On the Condition of Music in Germany*. Directing his subject to orchestral music he expounded:

> 'The symphony is a tone-painting that is produced through the collaboration of orchestral instruments. The masters who have devoted themselves to this genre, and they are the greatest composers of our nation, have elevated German orchestras greatly by the demands that they made on instruments in their symphonies.'

Wendt acknowledged instruments had been improved 'by many and new inventions' — for example the French horn had been supplied with valves — and, he added, 'the expanding art of virtuosity supported these demands'. These developments, Wendt suggested, had enabled composers to engage 'the masses of sound of the orchestra' as 'a master engages the sound of a pianoforte on which he improvises in a free flight of fantasy'. In this he acknowledged Beethoven's role: '[This] happened through *Beethoven* [Wendt's italics] and others who in this regard have brought forth unexcelled original works.'

Wendt considered it was in response to such works that orchestras had 'achieved a high degree of perfection' enabling them 'to overcome difficulties now that otherwise would have been considered insurmountable'. Wendt recognised, though, that Beethoven's orchestral music still posed a challenge: 'However, the gigantic works of *Beethoven* seem to frighten off his descendants in this area'.[43]

Following Beethoven's death in 1827, piano and chamber transcriptions of his First Symphony continued to be undertaken. We list some of these with their composer (where known) and publisher:

> Arrangement for string quartet (2 violins, 2 violas, cello), by Karl Zulehner. Simrock, 1828.; for piano solo, by Franz Liszt (S. 464/1). Breitkopf & Härtel, 1865.; for 2 pianos eight-hands, by Theodor Kirchner. Peters, c. 1886; for 2 pianos four-hands, by Otto Singer II. C. F. Peters, c. 1890; for piano four-hands, by Wilhelm Meves. Litolffs, 1890; for piano four-hands, anonymous. Schirmer, 1894; for piano quartet (violin, cello, piano four-hands), by Carl Burchard, Breitkopf & Härtel, c. 1898; and an arrangement for piano solo, by Ernst Pauer. Augener, c. 1900.[44]

After completing his piano studies with Beethoven, Carl Czerny remained on friendly terms with his teacher. During the composer's lifetime he prepared a piano reduction of the second version of *Fidelio* and adapted the score of the Eighth Symphony for two pianos. After Beethoven's death, Czerny made piano-duet arrangements of all Nine Symphonies that were published by Anton Diabelli & Co. between 1827 and 1829.

Franz Liszt has passed into legend for being a formidable keyboard executant who enriched keyboard music with his numerous piano transcriptions of all manner of compositions by other composers. In this capacity, he served Beethoven in a number of ways. Particularly noteworthy are his piano transcriptions of the composer's Nine Symphonies that were written over a period of about thirty years. The complete set was published by Breitkopf & Härtel in 1865. After hearing Liszt play his arrangements of the last three movements of the *Pastoral* Symphony in Vienna, in November 1839, musicologist Heinrich Adam declared in the *Allgemeine Theaterzeitung*

> 'only an artist like Liszt, who, in addition to a limitless veneration of Beethoven, possess the rare gift of understanding the great German composer, only such an artist was able, and could venture, to undertake so hazardous an undertaking'.[45]

The present writer can interpolate a related personal experience. In the late 1950s, when still a schoolboy, he recalls hearing the BBC Third Programme presentation of Liszt's transcriptions of all Nine Beethoven Symphonies; the series had been conceived by the British pianist Dennis Matthews. A few years later, having invited Matthews to give a university lecture-recital, Matthews revealed to him the difficulty he had in finding a pianist to take on the challenge of learning Liszt's transcription of the Ninth Symphony — incorporating the final movement's passages for solo voices. Matthews confided he was resigned to not including the Ninth Symphony transcription in the series until, at the last moment, the Austrian-German pianist Friedrich Wührer — possessed of a formidable pianistic technique — accepted the challenge.[46]

We return to the nineteenth century to consider the early progress of Beethoven's symphonies in France.

In 1828 the orchestra of the *Société des Concerts* was formed and is considered to have contained the best of the younger instrumentalists of Paris, all of whom had trained at the Conservatoire, and, moreover, were imbued with an *esprit de corps* and youthful enthusiasm. Six regular concerts were given each season, a programme typically including an overture, a symphony, and a concerto. During the first ten years of the *Société des Concerts*, Beethoven's symphonies were performed on no fewer than 68 occasions — eclipsing those of Haydn's seven and Mozart's five.

During the same period, Beethoven's overtures proved to be equally popular receiving 17 performances.

Of related interest is that arrangements for orchestral strings were given of selected movements from Beethoven's string quartets. The composer's Septet, that had been so popular in his lifetime, found no less appeal with Parisian audiences and was played by all the strings, with doubled wind parts — no less than 27 times by the close of concert season of 1858. For the next ten years, Beethoven's symphonies continued to feature prominently in the programmes of the *Société des Concerts*. Between 1838 and 1847 they received 90 performances compared with 23 of Haydn and 15 of Mozart. Mendelssohn's symphonies — all relatively recent works composed between 1821 and 1832 — also started to feature in the repertoire of the *Société*.

François-Antoine Habeneck (see earlier) conducted the last concert of the *Société* on 16 April 1848, having conducted no fewer than 186 concerts of the *Société*. Under his direction, the orchestra of the *Société des Concerts* had gained a considerable reputation. Richard Wagner, not one disposed to be politely flattering, remarked: 'I received a good lesson at Paris in 1839, when I heard the Orchestra of the Conservatoire [*Société des Concerts*] rehearse the enigmatic Ninth Symphony' — reference, of course, to Beethoven's *Choral* Symphony.[47]

The French musicologist Castil-Blaze, who had studied at the Paris Conservatoire, contributed articles to the influential *Journal des débats* — as, indeed, a few years later did the ardent Beethovenian Hector Berlioz. As for Castil-Blaze, he considered Beethoven's orchestral music united melody with harmony. In 1828 he wrote:

'The symphonies of Beethoven present a union

of all musical potentialities; the severe harmony blends without effort the charms of melody. The phrases of song, conceived together with the sentiment of varied harmonies which receive those phrases, accept without repugnance all the embellishments that a wise hand puts upon them.'

Notwithstanding such expressions of support for Beethoven's music — in the early part of the nineteenth century — as musicologist Leo Schrade observes:

'They did not, however, succeed in eradicating entirely the deeply rooted idea that Beethoven overstrode the limits of music as compared with [the composers of] Italy or Haydn and Mozart.'

Schrade also remarks that by the mid-nineteenth century Beethoven's music had become absorbed into French musical culture, disposing none other than the great poet and dramatist Victor Hugo to enthuse:

'The great Pelasgian is Homer; the great Greek is Aeschylus; the great Hebrew is Isaiah; the great Roman is Juvenal; the great Italian is Dante; the great Englishman is Shakespeare; the great German is Beethoven.'[48]

Berlioz's contribution to the promotion of Beethoven's symphonies was, in part, through his ardent advocacy of them in his critical writings. Shortly after the composer's death, in 1829 he published a study of Beethoven and his music in his *Critique Musicale*. After his return from Italy in 1832 (he had secured the coveted *Prix de Rome*) he commenced a series of detailed studies prompted by the regular performances of the symphonies at the Paris Conservatoire; these were published in a number of journals especially, as remarked, in the *Journal des débats* and the *Revue et gazette musicale de Paris*. Berlioz initially wrote about the Symphonies Nos. 2–8 that were the most frequently performed, the First Symphony being initially somewhat neglected. His writings subsequently formed the basis of his *À travers chants* (1862).[49]

Before considering the progress of Beethoven's symphonies in England, we briefly recall some remarks of Brahms. It is well known he delayed the composition of his own first symphony, mindful of Beethoven's intimidating legacy. And when it did finally appear, he was not best pleased to have it described as 'Beethoven's Tenth!' Much as he admired his predecessor's music, he was no Beethoven idolater. This is evident in reservations he once expressed, concerning some of the composer's early music, to his friend the Austrian composer, music critic, and conductor Richard Heuberger:

> 'I understand very well that the new personality of Beethoven, the new outlook, which people found in his works, made him greater, more important in their view [than in Mozart's later works]. But fifty years later this judgement has been altered. The attractions of novelty must be differentiated from inner value. I admit the [Third Piano] Concerto of Beethoven is more modern, but not so important! I am able to understand, too, that Beethoven's First Symphony did impress people colossally. In fact, it was the new outlook! But the last three symphonies by Mozart are each more important! Some people are beginning to feel that now.'[50]

To direct our consideration of the reception history of Beethoven's orchestral music in England, we consider the views expressed about him in the *The Harmonicon*. This was a monthly music journal that was published in London for the period 1823 to 1833. For a time it was edited by William Ayrton, who is credited with the production to England's of the first performance of Mozart's *Don Giovanni* (1817). In the very first year of issue, *The Harmonicon* published what was in effect, a quite remarkable contemporary pen-portrait of Beethoven, outlining aspects of his personal life and the character of certain of his compositions:

> '[Beethoven] has secured a name, and reached a height of renown, to which no other author, Handel, Haydn and Mozart excepted, has attained ... Beethoven is as original and independent in his modes of thinking as he is in his musical productions. A decided enemy to flattery, and an utter stranger to everything dishonorable, he disdains to court the favour of everyone, however wealthy or exalted in rank ... [Beethoven has] that deplorable calamity, the greatest that could befall a man of his profession, his extreme deafness, which we are assured is now so great as to amount to a total privation of hearing. Those who visit him are obliged to write down what they have to communicate.'

The passage that follows is of particular interest: 'To this cause [his deafness] may be traced many of the peculiarities visible in his later compositions.'

The challenges posed by many of Beethoven's works were considered attributable in his lifetime – and long afterwards– to his deafness. *The Harmonicon* continues:

'The last account we hear of this great man is that he has just completed a new grand mass [the *Missa Solemnis*]. The dark tone of his mind is in unison with that solemn style which the services of the church demand; and the gigantic harmony he knows so well how to wield enables him to excite feelings of the awful and sublime in a manner that none living can attempt to rival.'[51]

In the notices of the Philharmonic Society's performances (see following) were published in *The Harmonicon* from 1823 to 1826, Beethoven's First Symphony is described as 'the brilliant Symphony ... the great favourite', and so on.[52]

The Philharmonic Society of London was founded in 1813. Its stated aims were 'to promote the performance, in the most perfect manner possible, of the best and most approved instrumental music', and 'to encourage an appreciation by the public in the art of music'. The founding Directors were enterprising insofar as they resolved to promote 'that species of music which called forth the efforts and displayed the genius of the greatest masters'. These included contemporary composers such as Beethoven, Cherubini, and Carl Maria von Weber. Beethoven's pupil Ferdinand Ries was elected a Director of the Society and was active in the promotion of his teacher's symphonies. Perhaps Ries's most significant contribution, in this context, was the role he played in 1822 in the Philharmonic Society's commissioning of Beethoven's *Choral* Symphony.

The following is a record of the number of occasions the Philharmonic Society performed Beethoven's symphonies from the period of its inception to the close of the nineteenth century:

Symphony No. 1, (19);
Symphony No. 2, (39);
Symphony No. 3, (52);
Symphony No. 4, (54);
Symphony No. 5; (77);
Symphony No. 6; (69);
Symphony No. 7, (65);
Symphony No. 8, (47);
Symphony No. 9, (73).

The Society gave its first concert in the Argyll Rooms, Regent Street, London on Monday 8 March 1813. The impresario Johann Salomon was the Leader and Muzio Clementi directed at the piano. Symphony No. 1 first appeared in the concert programmes of the Society on 10 May 1819 but was probably performed earlier under the anonymous designation 'Symphony'. Symphony No. 2 was given on 13 April 1818 but was also probably performed earlier under the anonymous designation 'Symphony'; The *Eroica* Symphony made its first appearance at a concert of the Philharmonic Society on Monday 28 February 1814. This was not the first English performance. The Symphony had been premiered on 26 March 1807 at the Covent Garden Theatre and overseas in Boston on 17 April 1810 by the newly founded Boston Philharmonic Society. Symphony No. 4 first appeared in the concert programmes of the Society on 12 March 1821 but once more was probably performed earlier under the anonymous designation 'Symphony'.

The 1815 Philharmonic music season was significant insofar as the Society purchased from Beethoven, for the considerable sum of £200, the performing rights for three Overtures. These were, incorporating Beethoven's sub-titles:

King Stephen – 'To Hungary's first benefactor'; *The Ruins of Athens*, and *Overture in C – The Consecration of the House* – 'Written for the opening of the Josephstädter Theater'.

The Society performed the Fifth Symphony on Monday 29 April 1816. The notes accompanying the programme enthused:

> 'It is scarcely necessary to enlarge upon this important production, for it is so well known, and likely to become even more so as the Symphony in which Beethoven revealed himself and his own rugged strength, having discarded the formalism which restricted his earlier works.'

Regarding its construction, the Society's music correspondent noted: 'It is orchestrally interesting as first employing trombones and double-bassoon in a symphony.' The pianist-composer Cipriani Potter received a mention in the Society's notices for 1816. He was acquainted with Beethoven who once remarked to Ries: 'Potter visited me several times; he seems to be a good man and has a talent for composition.'

The 1817 music season was noteworthy for the Society's first performance of the Seventh Symphony on 26 May, with the *Pastoral* Symphony having been presented earlier at a concert on 24 March. The Directors of the Society, through the offices of Ferdinand Ries, invited Beethoven to compose and direct two symphonies for the sum of three-hundred guineas. His response was to request four-hundred and fifty guineas which the Directors declined; the outcome was Beethoven never visited England as he had intended. The 1821 season was noteworthy for the performance of no fewer than six Beethoven symphonies, namely, Nos. 1, 2, 4, 5, 6, and 7.

In the second decade of the Society's programmes, it became usual for six or seven Beethoven symphonies to be performed each year. 1825 was memorable in the history of the Society for realizing, on 21 March, the first performance in England of the *Choral* Symphony. It was described as a 'New Grand Characteristic Sinfonia with Vocal Finale ... [composed expressly for the Society]'. On the Title Page of the MS copy of the score that Beethoven sent to the Society, he inscribed the words 'Geschrieben für die Philharmonische Gesellschaft, London'.

In 1827, the Directors were informed by Ignaz Moscheles that Beethoven was ill and was in need of financial assistance. The Society undertook to give a concert for his benefit and to send him the sum of one hundred pounds. Beethoven later expressed his thanks:

> 'May Heaven soon restore me to health, and I will then prove to the generous English how much I appreciate the sympathy which they have shown for my condition.'

He undertook to write a new symphony for the Society — that he described as 'already sketched in outline'; his death on 26 March precluded its completion.

We are indebted to the British musicologist Barry Cooper for creating a performing version of the Tenth Symphony from the composer's fragmentary sketches. This was first realised in 1988 under the auspices of the Royal Philharmonic Society for whom, as we have seen, it was originally intended. At the time of writing (2021) an alternative version of the Tenth Symphony has been completed using an artificial intelligence program. This combines Beethoven's own intended music with passages of symphonic music derived from selected works of his contemporaries.

1829 was a significant year in the annals of the Philharmonic Society since it heralded the appearance of Felix Mendelsohn for the first time in its concert programmes. He would in due course exert a considerable influence on English musical taste and become a favourite of Queen Victoria and Prince Albert. On 6 February 1830 the Society's premises in the Argyll Rooms were destroyed by fire but the contents of the Library were saved — including precious Beethoven memorabilia. The Society relocated to the King's Theatre but the accommodation proved unsatisfactory. A later move in 1833, to premises in Hanover Square, offered better facilities and was the home of the Society until 1869.

The 1844 season was memorable insofar as the *thirteen*-year old boy-violinist Joseph Joachim performed Beethoven's Violin Concerto from memory — then something of an innovation — also supplying his own cadenzas. Beethoven's Overture *Leonora* No.1 was performed for the first time disposing the Society's music correspondent to enthuse, 'its large proportions and grand style almost gave it the importance of a symphony'.

During his stay in London, in 1856, Richard Wagner conducted the Philharmonic Society Orchestra and complimented it for being a '*strong esprit de corps*' possessed of 'superb tone' and 'the finest instruments'. He complained though of the length of the programmes that typically did not finish until after 11.00 p.m.! In 1873 the eminent interpreter of Beethoven Hans von Bülow made his debut on 28 April with a performance of Beethoven's *Emperor* Piano Concerto and would earn fame later in his capacity as an orchestral conductor — for both of which endeavours he received the Philharmonic Society's coveted Beethoven Gold Medal.

In 1885 the Society appointed Sir Arthur Sullivan as its resident conductor, a position he held for the next three years; his failing health deprived him of remaining in office for longer than he wished.

The Philharmonic Society's Centenary Year of 1912–13 provided the opportunity for a reflection of its achievements. The contributor to the records enthused:

> 'If the reader has the patience to wade through the pages of this long history, a history unique in the annals of musical institutions of this kind ... he will see what efforts were made to keep pace with all the changes in musical progress; what numbers of works, since acknowledged everywhere as masterpieces, first made their appeal to English audiences at the Philharmonic Concerts, and what crowds of singers and players, since acclaimed great, first sang and played there.'

Beethoven's connection with the Society was honoured with a performance of the *Choral* Symphony.[53]

On 14 December 1895 an Anniversary Concert was held at the Chrystal Palace to celebrate the 125th Anniversary of Beethoven's Birth. His memory was honoured with a full Beethoven programme that consisted of: Overture *Prometheus*; slow movement of First Symphony; *Emperor* Piano Concerto – the piano being supplied by Blüthner & Co.; Grand Scena 'Ah! Perfido'; *Eroica* Symphony; a selection of Beethoven songs; and to close the Overture *Leonora* No. 3. The authorities responsible for concert-programming certainly gave ticket-holders value for their money! The Secretary at the time was Sir George Grove – of *Grove's Dictionary* fame. The conductor for the concert was the German-born British conductor Sir August Mains who contributed to music-making at the Chrystal Palace for many years. Among his many noteworthy achievements, he had the honour of premiering Schubert's *Great* C major Symphony.⁵⁴

The German conductor and composer Wilhelm Furtwängler wrote at length on Wagner's views about the music of Beethoven, of which he was an ardent admirer and champion. What Furtwängler had to say about Wagner, although not specifically concerned with Beethoven's symphonic writing, makes a convenient bridge between the mid-late nineteenth century and our own time. Furtwängler first acknowledged the pioneering nature of Wagner's writings, of which he remarks: 'Some of these may strike us as overly rhetorical in parts, but we must not overlook the sense of necessity that he felt to communicate his knowledge.' Quoting Wagner: "One cannot discuss the essence of Beethoven's music other than in a mood of ecstasy." Furtwängler considered one achievement will always remain to Wagner's credit:

> '[Through] his writings, and even more through his performances, he was the first [to] invest his whole passionate nature, to reveal what Beethoven really is. He demonstrated that a merely "correct", that is, mediocre performance — the kind no less the norm than it is today — is a bad performance, the more so in the case of Beethoven than any other composer, because it ignores what lies between the lines — and it is precisely there that the essence of the music resides.'

Furtwängler believed Wagner should be credited with being the first to draw attention to 'the organic experience of the structure of Beethoven's works'. He contended:

Foremost among them is the use of rubato, that almost imperceptible yet constant variation of tempo which turns a piece of music into what it really is — an experience of conception and growth, of a living organic process.'

In the essay from which we have been quoting, Furtwängler contributed his own opinions on Beethoven's orchestration:

'The music owes far less than that of other composers to specific sensory qualities — that is to say, when working out his ideas, Beethoven does not proceed primarily from the nature of the instruments or the voices through which he conveys these ideas ... He captures the fundamental ethos of a symphony or a quartet but rarely exploits the acoustic potential of the medium in question — the wealth of timbres achievable by the orchestra, for instance. He adapts himself to the instruments he uses but never surrenders to their power. They are vehicles for ideas that go far beyond the realm of sense perception.'[55]

Sir Herbert Hamilton Harty was an Irish composer, conductor, and pianist. Notwithstanding his gifts as a pianist, when he established a career as a conductor *The Musical Times* (April 1920) described Harty as 'the prince of accompanists'. In this role he conducted the London Symphony Orchestra, the Liverpool Philharmonic Orchestra, and later was appointed the permanent conductor to the Hallé Orchestra. He earned the approval of Samuel Langford, the respected music critic of *The Manchester Guardian*. On hearing a performance of his, and comparing Harty with others who had conducted the Hallé Orchestra, he wrote (March 1919): 'Mr. Harty has latterly achieved far more immediate control over the orchestra, and his spirit, judgement, and control were ... equally admirable.' Perhaps Harty is best remembered today for his orchestral arrangements of Handel's *Water Music* and *Music for the Royal Fireworks*.

To take our discussion of the estimation and reception of Beethoven's orchestral music into the twentieth century, we quote some of Harty's writings about the composer. In 1927 *The Musical Times* invited Harty to contribute to its *Special Issue*, published to commemorate Beethoven's Death Centenary. He did so in an article titled *Beethoven's Orchestra: A Conductor's Reflections*. Harty makes the following general remarks concerning Beethoven's orchestration:

> 'Beethoven's general habit and manner in orchestration is fully exemplified in his symphonies, and it is not necessary to go further afield, even if, in other works, he makes use of some instrument which does not appear in his scores. If we take the nine symphonies and regard them from a merely technical point of view, they reveal, to an impartial eye, that the strings are always used with the greatest fullness and resource, the bassoons and drums with a special originality. And the flutes, oboes, clarinets, horns, trumpets, and trombones in a way we might expect (and that we get) from any well-equipped typical musician of those days. There are obscurities and miscalculations in certain places, some of which appear to be due to the impatience and brusqueness which were part of the composer's character, others which are undoubtedly the result of simple errors in questions of balance. Instances of both will occur to the minds of those familiar with the scores.'

Harty next considered the changes some orchestral instruments had undergone since Beethoven's time — and their modern-day consequences:

> '[Nowadays] we use a very much larger body of strings than was the general custom in Beethoven's lifetime [and] there is no doubt that many of the wind instruments have undergone since then a considerable change, and have gained in ease of manipulation at the expense of beauty of tone. The flute, for instance, must have frequently possessed a much sweeter and more characteristic tone before it was furnished with the ingenious mechanism in use today, and there is no doubt that the horn has also suffered in this respect by the addition of valves, and the trumpet, probably for the same reason. The oboe and bassoon, on the other hand, were rougher and coarser in quality, and the timpani less accurate and shallower in tone. It is likely that the trombone is the only wind instrument which has not altered in timbre, for there has been no change in its mechanism. Keeping these considerations in mind, it is interesting to imagine how Beethoven's symphonies may have sounded to his audiences, and, at the same time, it may give some justification for the readjustments it is felt necessary to make in modern performances.'

Harty suggested modern-day alterations to Beethoven's orchestration should take into consideration the inherent character of the music. [We recall he was writing in the late 1920s] He then, as others have done, grouped Beethoven's according to what he considered to be their inherent character:

> 'The symphonies seem to fall into two main categories. In one we might place the more idyllic works — the First, Second, Fourth, Sixth, and Eighth; in the other, those immense dramatic conceptions — the Third, Fifth, Seventh, and Ninth, in which Beethoven breaks completely with former tradition and enters his own absolute kingdom. It is in these that the technical problems of readjustment become more acute. The other symphonies (with the exception, perhaps, of part of the Sixth — the *Pastoral*) require, certainly, a carefully balanced performance in order to make their full effect, but in the main the orchestration can be left untouched and unstrengthened.'

Harty was adamant that no 'real' musician would ever contemplate touching the orchestral details of Beethoven's 'mighty works' unless he were convinced some revision would help to fulfil the composer's intentions. Reflecting on the recent past, Harty acknowledged composer-musicians, of the standing of Wagner, had given thought to such considerations as, indeed, Harty believed every conductor should. With this in mind he cited as being worthy of study — though circumspectly — Felix Weingartner's treatise *On the Performance of Beethoven's Symphonies.* Regarding Beethoven's 'grandest manner', Harty averred, 'are not power and urgency the dominant characteristics?' and therefore call for 'force and passion' rather than for 'grace and sensuous beauty of tone'. He elaborated: 'Refinement and delicacy are not the essential features of Beethoven that they are in composers like Mozart, and even in his softer moments it is unwise to overemphasise them.'

Harty considered Beethoven's slow movements and scherzi were the most deserving of individual expression. He was even prepared to sanction the use of additional instruments on occasions:

> 'Without some radical change, either by reduction of the strings or by an increase of wind instruments, it is impossible to give performances which are really satisfactory.'

He suggested, for example, the Funeral March in the *Eroica* Symphony could be 'reinforced' by the incorporation of wind instruments. That said, he cautioned:

> 'It is impossible to lay down hard and fast rules where everything must be left to individual taste and conviction, but occasionally one sees "improvements" suggested which show an entire misconception of the questions at issue.'

Certain 'improvements' to Beethoven's scoring earned Harty's censure:

> 'It is no improvement, but a horrible atrocity, to introduce trombones into scores of Beethoven where they do not already exist, or to add extra passages for the timpani merely because modern tuning is possible.'

He maintained:

> 'It should never be a question of introducing a new colour, but merely the deepening or restoration of one now faded, and the process is not that of

adding fresh tints to a picture but of allowing some which are obscured to be more clearly seen.'

Harty concluded his essay:

'It is worthwhile to consider whether over-caution is in the best interest of these bold and unconventional masterpieces, or whether, in reality, it does not cripple freedom and candour of interpretation. What Beethoven would have said to our modern methods of preforming his works it is impossible to tell. Wagner was not above taking the advice of Richter, nor Brahms of a Joachim, and, on the whole, it seems probable that Beethoven, great autocrat as he was, would not have rejected, without consideration, any suggestions made to him by a qualified craftsman who revered his music, and who disclaimed any wish or intention to interfere with essentials ... In the end, this is all that anyone entitled to the name of good musician has ever proposed, or ever will propose in connection with the music of Beethoven – "To amend the letter so that the spirit may shine forth more brightly".'[56]

In 1961 the German-born orchestral conductor Otto Klemperer contributed an essay to accompany his complete recordings of Beethoven's symphonies. This was later published in 1964 as his *Minor Recollections*. He writes how he had often conducted cycles of the Beethoven symphonies in such concert venues as Los Angeles (1933), Milan (1935), Strasbourg (1936), Budapest (1947), Amsterdam (1949), London (1957 and 1959), and Vienna (1960). As a consequence, he declared: 'The result was that, as time went by, I found myself wearing a sort of dog-collar marked

"Beethoven Specialist".' He protested: 'I am neither a Beethoven specialist nor a "modern conductor". My aim has always been to conduct competently in all musical styles.' Of Beethoven's symphonies he states:

> 'Beethoven was a revolutionary, and nothing could be more erroneous than to imagine that the great revolutionary arrived on the German scene like some well-behaved and docile lapdog. His symphonies are four-handed affairs, to say the least. Few people are familiar with Beethoven's metronome markings, though they sometimes appear to be very fast and provide only a rough indication of the tempo at which his music should be played.'

Klemperer adds:

> 'Most people think of Beethoven as a melancholy, tragic, gloomy character, but this is a crude distinction. He was, particularly in his youthful years, a happy-natured, cheerful person. The language of the First and Second Symphonies is unmistakable, and even the Fourth conveys a mood of exaltation ... It was not until the Sixth Symphony that the clouds began to gather. His hearing deteriorated progressively, but he put up a stout fight: "I shall seize Fate by the throat. It will never humble me".'[57]

We take leave of our compilation of the estimations of Beethoven's symphonies with the words of the American musicologist Leon Botstein:

'By the early twentieth century the Beethoven symphonies had achieved unique status as emblems of modernity's finest aesthetic achievements as well its worst dilemma: such heights would never again be reached. They were the yardstick against which all subsequent orchestral music had to be measured. The symphonies represented the culmination of Classicism and the model of Romanticism.'[58]

[1] David Wyn Jones, 2006, pp. 160–61.
[2] Elliot Forbes editor, *Thayer's Life of Beethoven*, 1967 p.p. 265–66. The Septet won great popularity and was frequently transcribed. Hoffmeister made an arrangement for string quintet in 1802. Later, Beethoven transcribed the work as a pianoforte trio with violin or clarinet as his Op. 38. This was in part a tribute to his physician, Dr. Johann Schmidt who played the violin; his daughter was an accomplished pianist.
[3] David Wyn Jones, 2006, pp. 160–61.
[4] Cited in Anton Felix Schindler, edited by Donald W. MacArdle and Translated by Constance S. Jolly from the German edition of 1860, 1966, p. 504.
[5] Early Beethoven biographers, such as Anton Schindler, debated whether the concerto in question was Op.15 or even Op. 19 – although by then too established in the repertoire to fit the description 'a new concerto' – as originally advertised. Modern-day musicology favours the C major Piano Concerto as the likely candidate, particularly in view of the fact that Beethoven had revised the work and amended the score – just as he would have with performance in mind. See, for example: Barry Cooper, 1991, p. 15 and 2000, pp. 89-90; Leon Plantinga, 1999, pp. 113–134; Hans-Werner Küthen, *Beethoven, Klavierkonzert, No. 3, Op. 37*, c. 1984; and William Kinderman, 1997, p. 109.
[6] Wayne M. Senner, Robin Wallace and William Meredith, editors. 1999. Vol. 1, pp. 163–64. For a more accessible review of the 2 April 1800 concert see: H. C. Robbins Landon, 1977, p. 546 and Clive Brown, Introduction to, *Beethoven, Symphonies*, The Academy of Ancient Music conducted by Christopher Hogwood, DDD Music.
[7] Maynard Solomon, 1977, p. 103.
[8] Donald Francis Tovey, *Essays in Musical Analysis*, Vol.1, 1935, p. 21.
[9] Elliot Forbes editor, *Thayer's Life of Beethoven*, 1967 pp. 328–30.
[10] Wayne M. Senner, Robin Wallace and William Meredith, editors. 1999. Vol. 1, pp. 163–64.
[11] Elliot Forbes editor, *Thayer's Life of Beethoven*, 1967 pp. 361–62
[12] Adam Carse, 1948, pp. 138–39.
[13] Wayne M. Senner, Robin Wallace and William Meredith, editors. 1999. Vol. 1, pp. 165–66.
[14] *Ibid*, pp. 168–9.
[15] *Ibid*.

[16] Theodore Albrecht editor and translator, 1996, Vol. 1, Letter No. 95, Vol. 1, p. 154.
[17] Elliot Forbes editor, *Thayer's Life of Beethoven*, 1967
[18] Wayne M. Senner, Robin Wallace and William Meredith, editors. 1999. Vol. 1, pp. 168–69.
[19] Quoted, with adaptations from: H. C. Robbins Landon, 1970, p. 92 and Barry Cooper, 2000, p. 148.
[20] Wayne M. Senner, Robin Wallace and William Meredith, editors. 1999. Vol. 1, pp. 168–69
[21] Anton Felix Schindler, edited by Donald W. MacArdle and translated by Constance S. Jolly from the German edition of 1860, 1966, p. 136 and note 95, p. 193.
[22] Peter Clive, 2001, p. 73 and pp. 149–50.
[23] Elliot Forbes editor, *Thayer's Life of Beethoven*, 1967 p. 428.
[24] Emily Anderson editor and translator, 1961, Vol. 2, Letter No. 534, pp. 502–04.
[25] Adam Carse, 1948, p. 90.
[26] Theodore Albrecht editor and translator, 1996, Vol. 1, Letter No. 128, pp. 197–99.
[27] Leo Schrade, 1942, pp. 3–6, and p. 29, p, 31, and p. 38.
[28] Wayne M. Senner, Robin Wallace and William Meredith, editors. 1999. Vol. 1, p.170.
[29] *Ibid*, pp. 170–71.
[30] See for example: Barry Cooper, 1991, p. 224.
[31] Emily Anderson editor and translator, 1961, Vol. 3, Appendix II, p. 1434.
[32] *Ibid*, p. 1435.
[33] With acknowledgment, and with adaptations, to: *Cultural Activities Department Juan March Foundation.*
[34] Paul Bekker quoted in: Glenn Stanley, editor. *The Cambridge Companion to Beethoven*, 2000, p. 167.
[35] Anton Felix Schindler, edited by Donald W. MacArdle and Translated by Constance S. Jolly from the German edition of 1860, 1966, p. 504 and endnote 408.
[36] Elliot Forbes editor, *Thayer's Life of Beethoven*, 1967 pp. 770–71.
[37] Emily Anderson editor and translator, 1961, Vol. 2, Letter No. 1066, p. 935. In his letter, Beethoven referred to Gebauer's concert as *Winkelmusik* – a pejorative term suggesting 'incompetence'.
[38] Adapted from David Wyn Jones, 2006, p. 185.
[39] Wayne M. Senner, Robin Wallace and William Meredith, editors. 1999. Vol. 1, p. 171.
[40] *Ibid*, pp. 171–72
[41] Quoted, with adaptations from: Pamela J. Willetts, *Beethoven and England: An Account of Sources in the British Museum,* 1970, pp. 26–31.
[42] Theodore Albrecht editor and translator, 1996, Vol. 1, Letter No. 119, pp. 186–88.
[43] Wayne M. Senner, Robin Wallace and William Meredith, editors, 1999, Vol. pp. 55–56.
[44] With acknowledgment – and with adaptations – to: *Cultural Activities Department Juan March Foundation.*
[45] Quoted by Peter Clive, 2001, pp. 210–11.
[46] The present writer was, at the time, a member of the Music Committee of the University of Sheffield with shared responsibility for the arrangement of

lecture-recitals. In the course of his lecture-recital, Dennis Matthews played the first movement of Liszt's transcription of Beethoven's *Pastoral Symphony*.

[47] Adam Carse, W. Heffer, 1948, pp. 92–94.

[48] Leo Schrade, 1942, pp. 3–6, and p. 29, p, 31, and p. 38. See also: Leo Schrade, Cited in: *Tragedy in the Art of Music*, 1964, p. 38.

[49] Michel Austin, translator, *Berlioz, Predecessors and Contemporaries, The Hector Berlioz website*. Originally published in: Hector Berlioz, *The Art of Music and other Essays (A travers chants)*.

[50] Originally published in Richard Heuberger, *Erinnerungen an Johannes Brahms*, 1970 and quoted in: John L. Holmes, *Composers on Composers*, 1990, p. 11.

[51] Cited in: Piero Weiss and Richard Taruskin, *Music in the Western World: A History in Documents*, 1984, pp. 329–31.

[52] Quoted by (Sir) George Grove, 1896, p. 15.

[53] Cyril Ehrlich, *First Philharmonic: A History of the Royal Philharmonic Society*, Oxford, Clarendon Press, 1995.

[54] For a full account of the concert see: Michael Musgrave, *The Musical Life of the Crystal Palace*, 1995.

[55] Wilhelm Furtwängler, originally published in, *Vermächtnis Nachgelassene Schriften* and quoted in: Robert Taylor editor, *Furtwängler on Music: Essays and Addresses*, 1991, p. 35 and p. 37.

[56] Hamilton Harty, *Beethoven's Orchestra: A Conductor's Reflections* in: *Beethoven*: London, Special Number, *Music & Letters*, 1927, pp. 172–77.

[57] Martin Anderson editor, *Klemperer on Music: Shavings from a Musician's Workbench*, 1986, pp. 97–99.

[58] Leon Botstein, *Sound and Structure in Beethoven's Orchestral Music* in: Glenn Stanley, editor, *The Cambridge Companion to Beethoven*, 2000, pp. 168–69.

MUSICOLOGY: SELECTED WRITINGS

We draw our discussion of Beethoven's First Symphony in C major to a close in the form of a documentary-style collection of texts. These are derived from the writings of musicologists and performing artists bearing on the musicology of the composer's Symphony, Op. 21. They are presented in the chronological sequence of their publication. Thereby, they convey the evolving estimation felt for this pioneering composition from the period of its first appearance to the present time.

FIRST MOVEMENT
ADAGIO MOLTO — ALLEGRO CON BRIO

'It may be said that Beethoven was and remained a composer of sonatas, for, in far the greater number and the best of his instrumental compositions, the outline of the sonata form was the veil-like tissue through which he gazed into the realm of sound; or, through which, emerging from that realm, he made himself intelligible ... He never altered any of the extant forms of instrumental music on principle; the same structure can be traced in his last sonatas, quartets, symphonies, etc., as unmistakably as in his first ... But compare these works with one another: place the Eighth Symphony in F major beside the Second in D, and wonder at the entirely new world, almost in precisely the same form! ... *The* feature in Beethoven's musical productions which is so particularly momentous for the history of art is ... every technical detail, by mean of which for clearness' sake the artist places himself in a conventional relationship to the external world, is raised to the highest significance of a spontaneous effusion.'

Richard Wagner, *Beethoven: With [a] Supplement from the Philosophical Works of A. Schopenhauer*, translated by E. Dannreuther. London: Reeves, 1893, p. 36, p. 42 and p. 45.

'The work commences with a very short introductory movement, *Adagio molto*. In his Second, Fourth, and Seventh Symphonies, Beethoven has shown how extended and independent such introductions can be made; but the present one, like many of Haydn's, is only twelve bars in length, of no special form and merely serving as a prelude to the work. Though short it is by no means without points of historical interest. The opening may not seem novel or original to us, but at that date it was audacious, and simply sufficient to justify the unfavourable notice of the day from such established critics of the day as [Joseph] Preindl, the Abbé Stadler, and Dionys Weber.' [Another critic described the work as 'a caricature of Haydn pushed to absurdity']

Sir George Grove, *Beethoven and his Nine Symphonies*. London: Novello, Ewer, 1896, pp. 3–4.

'At the very beginning of the First Symphony he avoids the conventional form of opening chord. Beethoven scorns to enter by the well-worn portal of the tonic. His C major Symphony opens with a chord of the dominant seventh of F major, a harmonic audacity which struck strangely upon the ears of contemporaries, although it had already been used by Bach.'

Paul Bekker, *Beethoven*. London: J. M. Dent & Sons, 1925, pp. 148–49.

'I am delighted to find myself anticipated by Mr. Vaclav Talich [Czech conductor, violinist and pedagogue] in the view that the opening is mysterious and groping, and that the first grand note of triumph is sounded when the dominant is reached ... The first theme of the *Allegro con brio* is a quietly energetic, business-like proposition, moving in sequences from tonic to dominant.'

Donald Francis Tovey, *Essays in Musical Analysis*. London: Oxford University Press, H. Milford, Vol.1, 1935, p. 22.

'By 1800 the [First] Symphony was complete, and had its first performance on 2 April being thus about a year ahead of *Prometheus*. Sir George Grove notes resemblances between the first movement of the one and the Overture of the other. Both start on a discord leading out of the key to arouse attention by tonal ambiguity before settling down to the main key — a device Beethoven developed with consummate art in some of his later works. Still, the Symphony was bold enough for a very young man, and brought him censure from pedants.'

Marion M. Scott, *Beethoven: The Master Musicians*. London: Dent, 1940, pp. 156–57.

'There is a broad opening *Adagio*, whose first chord sounds like a dominant seventh in F; the second bar seems to be in A minor, and the third in G. But in reality, this is only an original and forceful way of establishing the key of C, and it is less obscure than in many a passage in Mozart. The rest of the *Adagio* is in the usual vein of somewhat exalted (and somewhat trite) generalization expected of music that was held to be a copy of the emotions, but was hardly expected to copy any particular emotion ... The development begins with a series of modulating dominant-tonic progressions in which each new tonic, as it arrives, becomes another dominant by the simple addition of a seventh to the chord.'

Donald Nivison Ferguson, *Masterworks of the Orchestral*

Repertoire: A Guide for Listeners. Minneapolis: University of Minnesota Press, 1954, pp. 38–39.

> 'The prefatory *adagio molto* opens with a 4-measure passage as bold and confident as any to be found among Beethoven's earlier works: three chordal pairs suggest, in consecutive resolutions, the key of F, C, and G major. But the implication of G vanishes immediately when F natural appears in the violin lines of measure 4, and the remaining 8 measures of the *Adagio* confirm C major as the principal key of the movement.'

Louise Elvira Cuyler, *The Symphony.* New York: Harcourt Brace Jovanovich, 1973, p. 52.

> 'The first movement ... contains the first example of the composer's concept of a lyric slow introduction to a symphony's first movement. The exposition of the opening movement goes through the same multiple sectioning in each of its three thematic groups as would be seen in some of the mature Haydn and Mozart symphonies. Only the more clearly defined motivic structure of each subgroup differentiates this new style from that of the other two composers.'

Preston Stedman, *The Symphony.* Englewood Cliffs, New Jersey; London: Prentice-Hall, 1979, p.65.

> 'Following a precept set on so many previous occasions by Haydn and his contemporaries, Beethoven begins this symphony with a slow introduction. Although the opening bars may seem

undramatic to a modern ear, they are sufficiently unorthodox to have elicited a great deal of comment over the years. It should be understood that the standard way of beginning any major work, whether symphony, concerto, sonata or quartet, was to spell out a sequence of notes or harmonies that would establish a "home" key, or tonal base ... At the very start of this symphony, Beethoven leads the listener astray by suggesting other "homes" than the *proper one* [italics added] of C major so that when the music does break into a quick tempo we sense a twofold release. Not only is the sustained tension of the Introduction resolved, but also the enigma of uncertain tonality ... The so-called development section, the central part of any movement ... begins with three reminders of the first main theme divided one from the other by restless syncopations that give an air of insecurity. Furthermore, the "home" key of C major is deserted in favour of new tonal centres which shift so rapidly that not one is established with any prominence.'

Antony Hopkins, *The Concertgoer's Companion*. London: J.M. Dent & Sons Ltd., 1984, pp. 61–62.

'The first movement of Op. 21 is symphonic in character, but in a conservative, deliberate, almost self-conscious way ... Almost the entire movement consists of phrases that establish strong accents and elide with the next phrase – material that fits precisely the Classical descriptions of the symphony style,'

Michael Broyles, *Beethoven: The Emergence and Evolution of Beethoven's Heroic Style*. New York: Excelsior Music Publishing Co., 1987, p. 64.

> 'The adagio introduction to the first movement of this Symphony is especially noteworthy. The key of the Symphony is C, but the introduction begins in F, modulates to G at the fourth measure, and avoids a definitive cadence in C for the next eight measures, that is, until the first chord of the *Allegro* itself ...'.

Donald Jay Grout, and Claude V. Palisca editors. *A History of Western Music*. London: J. M. Dent, 1988, pp. 634.–35.

> 'Beethoven here succeeded in writing an innovative slow introduction to the first movement of a symphony, even after Haydn had created a wealth of creative solutions to the problem. One of the functions of the slow introduction was always architectural to provide an impressive entry into the work, comparable to the grandiose gateway to the park of an eighteenth-century mansion ... Here, the composer imposes a kind of determination on the dimension of the entire movement, i.e. the length of time taken to establish the tonic during the introduction gives the listener a sense that the structure to follow will be big and impressive.'

Philip G. Downs, *Classical Music: The Era of Haydn, Mozart, and Beethoven*. New York: W.W. Norton, 1992, p. 592.

> 'In the event, Beethoven chose to begin his career

as a symphonist with a surprise as rude as it is representative. Though advertised as being in C major, the First Symphony begins with a wind pizzicato string chord (nightmarish to co-ordinate) on the dominant seventh of the key of F major. By the fourth bar of the Symphony, G major has been reached, though whether this is a further act of usurpation or merely the dominant of the advertised key of C is something different ears hear differently. Such niceties apart, the overall effect is startling from almost every point of view. Certainly, it is difficult to imagine a shrewder start to a great symphonic career.'

'With the arrival of the *Allegro* (Beethoven's *con brio* marking is perhaps an act of supererogation of the circumstances) we meet the composer in characteristic guise, purposeful and alert. We also meet the man who sees further and notices more than most of those around him. After four bars of thrustful C major, two whole bars of sustained harmony intervene, the music stayed for seven whole beats until the little propulsive downward semiquaver (a rich source of ideas later on in the symphony) relaunches the principal theme, this time screwed up a tone, from C to D. There is nothing genteel or static about such music; its centre of gravity appears to be rising all the time ... The first movement of the First Symphony by Beethoven is indeed surprising and beautiful in almost equal measure, its beauty residing not so much in the second subject, exquisitely songful on oboe and flute, as in the music's glorious sense of proportion and the sense of power beneficially used.'

Richard Osborne, *Beethoven* in: Robert Layton editor. *A Guide to the Symphony.* Oxford: Oxford University Press, 1995, p. 83.

> 'Woodwind and horns, accented by plucked strings, slowly play a question-and-answer pair of chords. This is a formula that ought to end a piece, and using it to begin one is a good Haydn joke. Haydn had in fact used it a couple of times in string quartets: it is an example of what Beethoven could learn from Haydn's scores, but something one cannot imagine Haydn teaching in a lesson ... Beethoven keeps the music exploring and moving forward with great skill until he reaches the main, quick tempo. Critics objected to Beethoven beginning on a dissonance, which does not mean "discord"; it is simply a technical term for a chord that wants resolution to another, more stable chord. He did not care and began his next orchestral piece, the Overture to the ballet *The Creatures of Prometheus*, with a more pungent version of the same harmonic ploy.'

Michael Steinberg, *The Symphony: A Listener's Guide.* Oxford; New York: Oxford University Press, 1995, p. 5.

> '[From] the very opening chord, which is not in the expected key, to the concluding march-like theme, which bore a marked resemblance to a German drinking song, Beethoven coloured an established musical genre with his own wry wit ... Carl Maria von Weber lauded it as the "splendid, clear, fire-streaming Symphony in C".'

Elizabeth Schwarm Glesner, website text, *Classical Music Pages, Ludwig van Beethoven, Symphony No. 1, Op. 21*, 1996.

'The introduction's harmonic structure has been considered unusually daring, since it begins on the tonic. But as Siegmund Levarie [Austrian-born American musicologist and conductor] has pointed out, there was no such tradition. No remarks in contemporary reviews point to the opening chords and off-tonic beginnings; such beginnings can be found in Haydn's works as well as in pieces by J.S. and C.P.E. Bach. The idea of the "audacious" beginning was first developed by Anton Schindler, a less than trustworthy witness, and exploited by Sir George Grove. In fact, that critical reaction seems to have been directed at Beethoven's *Prometheus* Overture.'

Alfred Peter Brown, *The Symphonic Repertoire*. Vol. 2, *The First Golden Age of the Viennese Symphony: Haydn, Mozart, Beethoven, and Schubert*. Bloomington, Indiana: Indiana University Press, 2002, p. 445.

'Both Mozart and Haydn's symphonic models are evident in Beethoven's First Symphony but it was nevertheless innovative for its time and showed Beethoven as a composer with his own developing ideas. One of the most striking features is the strange opening. A dominant seventh on F leads to three cadences which "resolve" to a chord of G major, working through tonal developments until the *Allegro con brio* in C major. This immediately indicates Beethoven's intentions for the rest of the Symphony and indeed for all his music — to use keys and tonal development to achieve high drama and intensity in music.'

Coriander Stuttard, *Beethoven: Symphony No. 1 in C major, Op. 21, Notes to the BBC Radio Three Beethoven Experience*, Sunday 5 June 2005, www.bbc.co.uk/radio3/Beethoven

SECOND MOVEMENT
ANDANTE CANTABILE CON MOTO

'Here ... we have occasionally, passages which recall the strict contrapuntal school of Albrechtsberger. On the other hand, there is an elegance and beauty about it far above any school, and worth any amount of elaborate ornamentation: as well as continual sallies of fun and humour.'

Sir George Grove, *Beethoven and his Nine Symphonies*. London: Novello, Ewer, 1896, pp. 8–9.

'The *Andante*, which now follows, deepens the impression of earnest activity, conveyed in the first movement, to pensive contemplation. A simple lyrical theme is heard, touched with the spirit of resignation. The second violins enter softly and the gradual addition of the various parts reminds one of the similar opening of the *Andante* of Mozart's G minor Symphony. In Beethoven's *Andante* the parts are introduced in a kind of *fugato* and are further developed in alternating moods of gravity.'

Paul Bekker, *Beethoven*. London: J. M. Dent & Sons, 1925, p. 149.

'The slow movement begins, like its more enterprising twin-brother, the andante of the C minor String Quartet, Op. 18, No. 4, with a kittenish theme treated like a fugue.'

Donald Francis Tovey, *Essays in Musical Analysis*. London: Oxford University Press, H. Milford, Vol.1, 1935, p. 22.

'The slow movement, *andante, cantabile con moto*, is of the type affected by Haydn in some of his later symphonies — elegant, polished, eschewing emotions that could disturb the cultivated charm. Beethoven's fugato passages are introduced much as men of the world then introduced Latin quotations into their talk to show their good breading. The soft drum passage of dotted notes is the most Beethovenish thing in the movement.'

Marion M. Scott, *Beethoven: The Master Musicians*. London: Dent, 1940, p. 157.

'The slow movement (*Andante cantabile con moto*), in contrast to the first, deliberately sets out to be charming — and succeeds, from the first note. Instead of high generalisation on conventionally lofty platitudes, it assumes the character of a kind of slow minuet, and is almost more graceful than courtly dance.'

Donald Nivison Ferguson, *Masterworks of the Orchestral Repertoire: A Guide for Listeners*. Minneapolis: University of Minnesota Press, 1954, p. 40.

'The second movement (*Andante cantabile*)

commences in a fugal manner that calls to mind the second movement (*Andante scherzo*) of the simultaneously composed String Quartet in C minor, Op. 18, No. 4. The *Andante* of Mozart's G minor Symphony, K 550 may have suggested the imitative entry of the different string parts. Speaking of the animated and piquant passages in the *Andante*, Berlioz singles out the kettledrums with dotted rhythm to give the accompaniment a pungent quality. This passage is actually a prediction of the great things to come concerning the treatment of the kettledrum.'

Joseph Braunstein, *Musica Aeterna, Program Notes for 1971–1976.* New York: *Musica Aeterna*, 1978, p. 30.

'The second movement, an *Andante*, exposes its first theme in a quasi-fugal exposition of four entrances. The return of this subject in the recapitulation is varied by the use of a countermelody to accompany each entrance of the tune (measures 100–116).'

Preston Stedman, *The Symphony.* Englewood Cliffs, New Jersey; London: Prentice-Hall, 1979, p. 65.

'Those parts of the second movement of the First Symphony that writers have singled out most favourably are where the contrapuntal rigidity is lessened and Beethoven works more with blocks of sonority. At the beginning of the second group a new theme consists of a number of discrete motives which are distributed throughout various instruments to create an array of changing colours ... The dynamic quality of the opening movement ... is in large measure due to the rhythmic urgency of Beethoven's material.'

Michael Broyles, *Beethoven: The Emergence and Evolution of Beethoven's Heroic Style*. New York: Excelsior Music Publishing Co., 1987, p. 74 and p. 76.

'The second movement is cousin, a slightly less learned cousin, to the corresponding movement to the C minor Quartet, Op. 18, No.4, written around the same time. Beethoven clearly enjoys the fact that, unlike a string quartet, an orchestra provides drama. In that first drum passage it also gives him pleasure to accompany the 3/8 tune for flute and violins with cords in 2/8.'

Michael Steinberg, *The Symphony: A Listener's Guide*. Oxford; New York: Oxford University Press, 1995, p. 6.

'To perceive the second movement as a "slow movement" is to misrepresent it: *Andante cantabile con moto* [quaver = 120] with a signature of 3/8, suggests a lightweight as opposed to a serious piece. Its companion is to be found in the C minor String Quartet from Opus 18 and among its progeny is Op. 59, No. 2. All three movements are marked by their own brands of irony. Here, the high-spirited texture of a fugal exposition is combined with a scherzo-like character. The chamber-music quality of the first 41 measures is underlined by its orchestration; in contrast to the first movement, the winds merely enrich a basic five-part string sonority.'

Alfred Peter Brown, *The Symphonic Repertoire. Vol. 2, The First Golden Age of the Viennese Symphony: Haydn, Mozart, Beethoven, and Schubert.* Bloomington, Indiana: Indiana University Press, 2002, p. 446.

THIRD MOVEMENT
MENUETTO — ALLEGRO MOLTO E VIVACE

'The Minuet and Trio form the most original portion of the work. And they are original in every sense of the word. In the former, though, he entitles it *Minuet,* Beethoven forsook the spirit of the minuet of his predecessors, increased its speed, broke through its formal and antiquated mould, and out of a mere dance-tune produced a *scherzo*, which may need increased dimensions, but needs no increase of style or spirit to become the equal of those great movements which form such remarkable features in his later symphonies ... The *Trio*, or intermezzo between the so-called Minuet and its repetition, departs a long way from the original plan, [a reference to Beethoven's first-draft sketches] under which the *Trio* was only a second minuet. It is here a delicious dialogue between the wind and stringed instruments — a similar alternation of wind and strings will be found in the *Trio* of the Fourth Symphony, though in a more ethereal style than here.'

Sir George Grove, *Beethoven and his Nine Symphonies*. London: Novello, Ewer, 1896, pp. 10–12.

'[In] the Minuet we find a still more individual Beethoven; this section of the work is more nearly a scherzo than a minuet, and its harmonies, its development, and its scoring must have sounded very new in their day.'

Ernest Markham Lee, *The Story of the Symphony*. London: Scott Publishing Co., 1916, p. 48.

'In form, the *Andante* resembles the symphonies of the eighteenth century; but the third movement breaks new ground in symphonic music. The theme (probably derived from a collection of German tunes) rises light as a feather, the capricious dynamic plays with all kinds of paradoxical ideas, and the swaying rhythmic life of the whole gives the lie to the old-fashioned designation of *Menuetto*. A new spirit possesses the work, stripping the old minuet of its conventional restraint and making it a free dance-form.'

Paul Bekker, *Beethoven*. London: J. M. Dent & Sons, 1925, p. 150.

'Dr. Ernest Walker [Indian-born English composer, pianist, organist, and teacher] has well observed that the minuet is a really great Beethoven scherzo, larger than any in the sonatas, trios, and quartets before the opus fifties, and far more important than that of the Second Symphony ... The Trio, with its throbbing wind-band chords and mysterious violin runs, is, like so many of Beethoven's early minuets and trios, prophetic of Schuman's most intimate epigrammatic sentiments. But, as Schumann rouses himself from romantic dreams to ostentatiously prosaic aphorisms, so Beethoven rouses himself to a brilliant *forte* before returning to the so-called minuet.'

Donald Francis Tovey, *Essays in Musical Analysis*. London: Oxford University Press, H. Milford, Vol.1, 1935, p. 24.

'The minuet and trio ... have not the spirit of the old dance but of the new scherzo — modelled on, maybe, a little bit on Haydn's scherzos. Berlioz described this movement as of "a freshness, an agility, and a grace exquisite — the one veritable novelty of the Symphony".'

Marion M. Scott, *Beethoven: The Master Musicians*. London: Dent, 1940, p. 157.

'The third movement, although conventionally entitled Menuetto, is really a scherzo, taken at breakneck speed (*Allegro molto e vivace*). It doubtless sounded to Beethoven's contemporaries far more impudent than it does to us. Its theme is hardly more than an ascending scale; but the continuation, after the very short opening section, combines a floating phrase with the vigour of the last bars of the first section, and not only out of this a considerable development is generated.'

Donald Nivison Ferguson, *Masterworks of the Orchestral Repertoire: A Guide for Listeners*. Minneapolis: University of Minnesota Press, 1954, p. 41.

'After the First Symphony, Beethoven was not again to entitle a third movement "Menuetto" until the Eighth Symphony. In the present instance, the spirit and tempo already suggest the scherzo, which was to supplant the menuetto in the Second Symphony ... The Trio belongs to the wind choir, especially the horns. There is no change of key for this Trio; the extensive tonal digressions of the Menuetto made such constancy desirable. An interesting three-part tonal scheme emerges in this movement, with the principal key, C major, asserted most overtly in the centre of the design.'

Louise Elvira Cuyler, *The Symphony*. New York: Harcourt Brace Jovanovich, 1973, p. 54.

'The third movement, labelled a minuet by Beethoven, is probably unique among the four movements. Its adjusting of the minuet style to that which more clearly approximates a scherzo style is an early indication of the composer's plans for the Symphony's third movement.'

Preston Stedman, *The Symphony*. Englewood Cliffs, New Jersey; London: Prentice-Hall, 1979, p. 66.

'[The] third movement is a *tour de force*. Beethoven marks it *Menuetto*, a term that has no more validity than the genuflexion of a seditious valet. The initial tempo is searing — *Allegro moto e vivace* — and the mood uproarious: C major gamely astride a bucking bronco of a movement that is a scherzo in both pace and comic intent. What is more, the surprising and the beautiful are once more imaginatively twinned. With the Trio section opening out huge vistas.'

Richard Osborne, *Beethoven* in: Robert editor *A Guide to the Symphony.* Oxford: Oxford University Press, 1995, p. 84.

'Beethoven calls the next movement a minuet, but apart from being the third movement of a symphony and in 3/4 time, the connection with the old French court dance is nil. Following the example of the 1790s quartets — but not symphonies — of Haydn, who also kept calling such movements minuets. Beethoven is writing a really fast one-in-a-bar scherzo ...'.

Michael Steinberg, *The Symphony: A Listener's Guide.* Oxford; New York: Oxford University Press, 1995, p. 6.

'[Beethoven] entitled the third [movement] *Menuetto*, but that designation is contradicted by his indication *Allegro molto e vivace* and by the swift metronome marking, not to mention the sharp rhythmic accents of the opening section. [Beethoven inserted the metronome markings almost twenty years after he had composed the Symphony] The dynamic tension is evident from the very first phrase, in which a rising scale pattern in iambic rhythm drives a crescendo to an emphatic cadence in the dominant.'

William Kinderman, *Beethoven*. Oxford: Oxford University Press, 1997, p. 53.

'The third movement Menuetto, defies its title in both tempo (*Allegro molto e vivace*) and spirit; it is a true *scherzo* in every sense of the term. Here, the terminology comes from Haydn, who produced minuets which can withstand and even demand a fast tempo. The opening melody exudes energy by rushing through an octave and a fifth in eight short bars, by its anacrustic rhythm, and by its accelerating harmonic movement.'

Alfred Peter Brown, *The Symphonic Repertoire. Vol. 2, The First Golden Age of the Viennese Symphony: Haydn, Mozart, Beethoven, and Schubert.* Bloomington, Indiana: Indiana University Press, 2002, p. 446.

FOURTH MOVEMENT
ADAGIO – ALLEGRO MOLTO E VIVACE

'The finale is throughout as bright as bright can be, but it must be confessed that it is more in the sprightly vein of Haydn than it is of the Beethoven of later years ... Nothing can be more full of movement and spirit than the whole of this finale. It never hesitates from beginning to end ... The finish and care observable throughout the work are very great. Beethoven began with the determination, which stuck with him during his life, not only thinking good thoughts, but of expressing them with as much clearness and intelligibility as labour could effect; and this

Symphony is full of instances of such thoughtful pains.

George Grove, *Beethoven and his Nine symphonies*. London: Novello, Ewer, 1896, p. 12 and p. 15.

'The finale begins with a Haydnesque joke; the violins letting out a scale as a cat from a bag.'

Donald Francis Tovey, *Essays in Musical Analysis*. London: Oxford University Press, H. Milford, Vol.1, 1935, p. 25.

'How jolly to hear Beethoven being frivolous.'

Marion M. Scott, *Beethoven: The Master Musicians*. London: Dent, 1940, p. 158.

'The last movement sparkles with humour. There is first a six-bar *adagio*, absurdly solemn, as it turns out, for it consists of nothing but fragments of the ascending scale, each one note longer than the preceding, and elaborately provided with marks of "expression". By scampering up the completed scale such as an approach to the gay little tune that forms his main subject, Beethoven clearly reveals (but conductors do not always see) that "all this is only fun and pretence" ... The main theme, to start the recapitulation, comes in just as mischievously as does a rondo theme by Haydn. There are no material deviations from the pattern of the exposition, and the coda, quite as clearly derived, is only slightly weighted by a new phrase that appears towards the end, even though the approach hints that something more portentous may occur.'

Donald Nivison Ferguson, *Masterworks of the Orchestral Repertoire: A Guide for Listeners.* Minneapolis: University of Minnesota Press, 1954, pp. 41–42.

'Beethoven's humour is apparent in the introduction of the finale (*Adagio*), in which a scale starting in G is feeling its way upward step by step in steadily increasing segments of three, four, five, six, and seven notes until the octave (G) of the beginning allegro is reached ... When the highly respected organist and author Daniel Gottlob Türk presented the Symphony in Halle, he skipped the introduction to the finale because he was afraid of inciting the derision of the public.'

Joseph Braunstein, *Musica Aeterna, Program Notes for 1971–1976.* New York: *Musica Aeterna*, 1978, p. 30.

'The finale generally reverts to an earlier and more conservative style. This is recalled by the horn fifths in measures 30–32 and the *style galant* similarity of the materials of the first thematic group. Only the contrapuntal development-section distinguishes the movement from most classical symphonies (measures 116–55). A coda works briefly on a scale-motive drawn from the introduction of the Finale before returning to the principal theme. A new tune in the coda (measure 266) begins in the horns and oboes to the accompaniment of this scale motive.'

Preston Stedman, *The Symphony.* Englewood Cliffs, New Jersey; London: Prentice-Hall, 1979, p. 66.

> 'As for the finale, it begins with an impressive gesture that turns out to be a hoax, for, like a bevy of hesitant beginners, the first violins make no less than five abortive attempts to play a scale, progressing one note further each time. It is a characteristic example of his humour that Beethoven would have hated us to take so seriously. When at last the movement gets under way it sparkles with wit and vitality ... The final march, garlanded with scales from the woodwind, is like a children's game. There were no clouds in Beethoven's sky when he wrote this delightful symphony.'

Antony Hopkins, *The Concertgoer's Companion.* London: J.M. Dent & Sons Ltd., 1984, pp. 62–63.

> '[Critical] judgement holds [the finale] to be one of the weakest movements in all of Beethoven's symphonies. Its problems are two-fold. First, the structure, a text-book sonata form, is so regular as to border on the academic. Phrase structure is clear at all levels, the exposition falls into two groups with a clearly defined cadence, the development is essentially polyphonic calling [Karl] Nef to consider the movement more typical of Mozart than Haydn.'

Michael Broyles, *Beethoven: The Emergence and Evolution of Beethoven's Heroic Style.* New York: Excelsior Music Publishing Co., 1987, p. 76.

'The short introduction to the finale is a joke in the manner of Haydn: the theme is introduced, as Tovey says, by a process of "letting the cat out of the bag".'

Donald Jay Grout and Claude V. Palisca, editors. *A History of Western Music*. London: J. M. Dent, 1988, p. 635.

'At the start of the finale, we return to the seditious valet [see above] and to Beethoven's monomaniac desire to fashion a lot out of next to nothing. The *adagio* preface to the movement could outmanoeuvre Uriah Heep [obsequious character in Dickens' *David Copperfield*] himself in protestations about its humble origins. What is it, after all, but a repeated G "ever so 'umbly" [Heep's style of expression] co-opting all the notes of the diatonic scale? And who, in an upwardly mobile age, could reasonably object if, from this single note and its attendant scale, an entire uproarious movement was to be fashioned ... The delights of the finale are endless, largely because most of the jokes bear frequent retelling. Who has not smiled, and smiled again, as the woodwinds graciously usher in the recapitulation only to find that the bounder has already made his entrance?'

Richard Osborne, *Beethoven* in: Robert Layton editor, *A Guide to the Symphony*. Oxford: Oxford University Press, 1995, p. 84.

'Beethoven surprises — and amuses — us by setting a slow introduction at the beginning of the finale.

> In the first movement he had used a scale to make his way from the *adagio* to *allegro*. Here he does the same thing, except that now he makes a joke out of it, a simple but good one that is better heard than described ... The comic beginning nicely sets the mood for a high-spirited conclusion.'

Michael Steinberg, *The Symphony: A Listener's Guide*. Oxford; New York: Oxford University Press, 1995, pp. 6–7.

> 'The unrelenting energy of this finale overshadows Beethoven's mastery of orchestration. For example, the bass instruments — bassoons, cello, and contrabass — are separated for colouristic exploitation ... Most remarkable are the varied presentations of the upbeat theme ... These passages are remarkable not only for their colour but also for their wit and humour, which certainly attempted to challenge Haydn's preeminent reputation in this mode of discourse.'

Alfred Peter Brown, *The Symphonic Repertoire. Vol. 2, The First Golden Age of the Viennese Symphony: Haydn, Mozart, Beethoven, and Schubert.* Bloomington, Indiana: Indiana University Press, 2002, p. 450.

BIBLIOGRAPHY

The author has individually consulted all the publications listed in this bibliography and can confirm that each makes reference, in some way or other, to Beethoven and his works. It will be evident from their titles which of these are publications devoted exclusively to the composer. Others that make only passing reference to Beethoven and his compositions, nevertheless unfailingly bear testimony to his genius and humanity. The diversity of the titles listed testifies to the centrality of Beethoven to western culture and beyond; the mere survey of these should be of itself a rewarding experience for a lover of so-called classical music. The entries are confined to book publications, reflecting the scope of the author's researches. The cut-off date for this was 2007; no works after this date are listed, notwithstanding the author is mindful that Beethoven musicology, and related publication, continue to be a major field of endeavour.

Abraham, Gerald. *Beethoven's second-period quartets.* London: Oxford University Press: Humphrey Milford, 1944.

Abraham, Gerald. *Essays on Russian and East European music.* Oxford: Clarendon Press: New York: Oxford University Press, 1985.

Abraham, Gerald, Editor. *The age of Beethoven, 1790-1830.* London: Oxford University Press, 1982.

Abraham, Gerald. *The tradition of Western music.* London: Oxford University Press, 1974.

Abse, Dannie and Joan. *The Music lover's literary companion.* London: Robson Books, 1988.

Adorno, Theodor W., Translator. *Alban Berg: master of the smallest link.* Cambridge: Cambridge University Press, 1991.

Adorno, Theodor W. *Beethoven: the philosophy of music; fragments and texts.* Cambridge: Polity Press, 1998.

Albrecht, Daniel, Editor. *Modernism and music: an anthology of sources.* Chicago; London: University of Chicago Press, 2004.

Albrecht, Theodore, Translator and Editor. *Letters to Beethoven and other correspondence.* Lincoln, New England: University of Nebraska Press, 3 vols., 1996.

Allsobrook, David Ian. *Liszt: my travelling circus life.* London: Macmillan, 1991.

Anderson, Christopher, Editor and Translator. *Selected writings of Max Reger.* New York; London: Routledge, 2006.

Anderson, Emily, Editor and Translator. *The letters of Beethoven.* London: Macmillan, 3 vols.,1961.

Anderson, Martin, Editor. *Klemperer on music: shavings from a musician's workbench.* London: Toccata Press, 1986.

Antheil, George. *Bad boy of music.* London; New York: Hurst & Blackett Ltd., 1945.

Appleby, David P. *Heitor Villa-Lobos: a bio-bibliography.* New York: Greenwood Press, 1988.

Aprahamian, Felix, Editor. *Essays on music: an anthology from The Listener.* London, Cassell, 1967.

Armero, Gonzalo and Jorge de Persia. *Manuel de Falla : his life & works.* London: Omnibus Press, 1999.

Arnold, Ben, Editor. *The Liszt companion.* Westport, Connecticut; London: Greenwood Press, 2002.

Arnold, Denis and Nigel Fortune, Editors. *The Beethoven companion.* London: Faber and Faber, 1973.

Ashbrook, William. *Donizetti.* London: Cassell, 1965.

Auner, Joseph Henry. *A Schoenberg reader: documents of a life.* New Haven Connecticut; London: Yale University Press, 2003.

Avins, Styra, Editor. *Johannes Brahms: life and letters.* Oxford: Oxford University Press, 1997.

Azoury, Pierre H. *Chopin through his contemporaries: friends, lovers, and rivals.* Westport, Connecticut: Greenwood Press, 1999.

Badura-Skoda, Paul. *Carl Czerny: On the Proper Performance of all Beethoven's Works for the Piano.* Universal Edition: A. G. Wien, 1970.

Bailey, Cyril. *Hugh Percy Allen.* London: Oxford University Press, 1948.

Bailey, Kathryn. *The life of Webern.* Cambridge: Cambridge University Press, 1998.

Barenboim, Daniel. *A life in music.* London: Weidenfeld & Nicolson, 1991.

Barlow, Michael. *Whom the gods love: the life and music of George Butterworth.* London: Toccata Press, 1997.

Barrett-Ayres, Reginald. *Joseph Haydn and the string quartet.* New York: Schirmer Books, 1974.

Bartos, Frantisek. *Bedrich Smetana: Letters and reminiscences.* Prague: Artia, 1953.

Barzun, Jacques. *Pleasures of music: an anthology of writing about music and musicians.* London: Cassell, 1977.

Bauer-Lechner, Natalie. *Recollections of Gustav Mahler.* London: Faber Music, 1980.

Bazhanov, N. Nikolai. *Rakhmaninov.* Moscow: Raduga, 1983.

Beaumont, Antony, Editor. *Ferruccio Busoni: Selected letters.* London: Faber and Faber, 1987.

Beaumont, Antony, Editor. *Gustav Mahler, letters to his wife.* London: Faber and Faber, 2004.

Beecham, Thomas. *A mingled chime: an autobiography.* New York: Da Capo Press, 1976.

Bekker, Paul. *Beethoven.* London: J. M. Dent & Sons, 1925.

Bellasis, Edward. *Cherubini: memorials illustrative of his life.* London: Burns and Oates, 1874.

Bennett, James R. Sterndale. *The life of William Sterndale Bennett.* Cambridge: University Press, 1907.

Benser, Caroline Cepin. *Egon Wellesz (1885–1974): chronicle of twentieth-century musician.* New York: P. Lang, 1985.

Berlioz, Hector. *Evenings in the orchestra.* Harmondsworth: Penguin Books, 1963.

Berlioz, Hector. *The musical madhouse (Les grotesques de la musique).* Rochester, New York: University of Rochester Press, 2003.

Bernard, Jonathan W., Editor. *Elliott Carter: collected essays and lectures, 1937-1995.* Rochester, New York; Woodbridge: University of Rochester Press, 1998.

Bernstein, Leonard. *The joy of music.* New York: Simon and Schuster, 1959.

Bertensson, Sergei. *Sergei Rachmaninoff: a lifetime in music.* London: G. Allen & Unwin, 1965.

Biancolli, Louis. *The Flagstad manuscript.* New York: Putnam, 1952.

Bickley, Nora, Editor. *Letters from and to Joseph Joachim.* London: Macmillan, 1914.

Bie, Oskar. *A history of the pianoforte and pianoforte players.* New York: Da Capo Press, 1966.

Blaukopf, Herta. *Mahler's unknown letters.* London: Gollancz, 1986.

Blaukopf, Kurt and Herta. *Mahler: his life, work and world.* London: Thames and Hudson, 1991.

Bliss, Arthur. *As I remember.* London: Thames Publishing, 1989.

Block, Adrienne Fried. *Amy Beach, passionate Victorian: the life and work of an American composer, 1867–1944.* New York: Oxford University Press, 1998.

Bloch, Ernst. *Essays on the philosophy of music.* Cambridge: Cambridge University Press, 1985.

Blocker, Robert. *The Robert Shaw reader.* New Haven; London: Yale University Press, 2004.

Blom, Eric. *A musical postbag.* London: J. M. Dent, 1945.

Blom, Eric. *Beethoven's pianoforte sonatas discussed.* London: J. M. Dent, 1938.

Blom, Eric. *Classics major and minor: with some other musical ruminations.* London: J. M. Dent, 1958.

Blum, David. *The art of quartet playing: the Guarneri Quartet in conversation with David Blum.* London: Gollancz, 1986.

Blume, Friedrich. *Classic and Romantic music: a comprehensive survey.* London: Faber and Faber, 1972.

Boden, Anthony. *The Parrys of the Golden Vale: background to genius.* London: Thames Publishing, 1998.

Bonavia, Ferruccio. *Musicians on music.* London: Routledge & Kegan Paul, 1956.

Bonds, Mark Evan *After Beethoven: imperatives of originality in the symphony.* Cambridge, Massachusetts; London: Harvard University Press, 1996.

Bonis, Ferenc, Editor. *The selected writings of Zoltán Kodály.* London; New York: Boosey & Hawkes, 1974.

Bookspan, Martin. *André Previn: a biography.* London: Hamilton, 1981.

Boros, James and Richard Toop, Editors. *Brian Ferneyhough: Collected writings.* Amsterdam: Harwood Academic, 1995.

Boulez, Pierre. *Stocktakings from an apprenticeship.* Oxford: Clarendon Press, 1991.

Boult, Adrian. *Boult on music: words from a lifetime's communication.* London: Toccata Press, 1983.

Boult, Adrian. *My own trumpet.* London, Hamish Hamilton, 1973.

Boult, Adrian with Jerrold Northrop Moore. *Music and friends: seven decades of letters to Adrian Boult from Elgar, Vaughan Williams, Holst, Bruno Walter, Yehudi Menuhin and other friends.* London: Hamish Hamilton, 1979.

Bovet, Marie Anne de. *Charles Gounod: his life and his works.* London: S. Low, Marston, Searle & Rivington, Ltd., 1891.

Bowen, Catherine Drinker. *Beloved friend: the story of Tchaikowsky and Nadejda von Meck.* London: Hutchinson & Co., 1937.

Bowen, Meiron, Editor. *Gerhard on music: selected writings.* Brookfield, Vermont: Ashgate, 2000.

Bowen, Meirion. *Michael Tippett.* London: Robson Books, 1982.

Bowen, Meiron, Editor. *Music of the angels: essays and sketchbooks of Michael Tippett.* London: Eulenburg, 1980.

Bowen, Meiron, Editor. *Tippett on music.* Oxford: Clarendon Press, 1995.

Bowers, Faubion. *Scriabin: a biography.* Mineola: Dover; London: Constable, 1996.

Boyden, Matthew. *Richard Strauss.* London: Weidenfeld & Nicolson, 1999.

Bozarth, George S., Editor. *Brahms*

studies: analytical and historical perspectives; papers delivered at the International Brahms Conference, Washington, DC, 5-8 May 1983. Oxford: Clarendon Press, 1990.

Brand, Juliane, Christopher Hailey and Donald Harris, Editors. *The Berg-Schoenberg correspondence: selected letters.* Basingstoke: Macmillan, 1987.

Brandenbugh, Sieghard, Editor. *Haydn, Mozart, & Beethoven: studies in the music of the classical period: essays in honor of Alan Tyson.* Oxford: Clarendon Press, 1998.

Braunstein, Joseph. *Musica Æterna, program notes for 1961–1971.* New York: Musica Æterna, 1972.

Braunstein, Joseph. *Musica Æterna, program notes for 1971–1976.* New York: Musica Æterna, 1978.

Brendel, Alfred. *Alfred Brendel on music: collected essays.* Chicago, Illinois: A Cappella Books, 2001.

Brendel, Alfred. *The veil of order: Alfred Brendel in conversation with Martin Meyer.* London: Faber and Faber, 2002.

Breuning, Gerhard von. *Memories of Beethoven: from the house of the black-robed Spaniards.* Cambridge: Cambridge University Press, 1992.

Briscoe, James R., Editor. (Brief Description): *Debussy in performance.* New Haven: Yale University Press, 1999.

Brott, Alexander Betty Nygaard King. *Alexander Brott: my lives in music.* Oakville, Ontario; Niagara Falls, New York: Mosaic Press, 2005.

Brown, Alfred Peter. *The symphonic repertoire. Vol. 2, The first golden age of the Viennese symphony: Haydn, Mozart, Beethoven, and Schubert.* Bloomington, Indiana: Indiana University Press, 2002.

Brown, Maurice John Edwin. *Schubert: a critical biography.* London: Macmillan; New York: St. Martin's Press, 1958.

Broyles, Michael. *Beethoven: the emergence and evolution of Beethoven's heroic style.* New York: Excelsior Music Publishing Co., 1987.

Brubaker, Bruce and Jane Gottlieb, Editors. *Pianist, scholar, connoisseur: essays in honor of Jacob Lateiner.* Stuyvesant, N.Y., Pendragon Press, 2000.

Buch, Esteban. *Beethoven's Ninth: a political history.* Chicago; London: University of Chicago Press, 2003.

Burk, John N., Editor. *Letters of Richard Wagner: the Burrell collection.* London: Gollancz, 1951.

Burnham, Scott G. *Beethoven hero.* Princeton, New Jersey: Princeton University Press, 1995.

Burnham, Scott G and Michael P. Steinberg, Editors. *Beethoven and his world.* Princeton, New Jersey; Oxford: Princeton University Press, 2000.

Burton, William Westbrook, Editor. *Conversations about Bernstein.* New York; Oxford: Oxford University Press, 1995.

Busch, Fritz. *Pages from a musician's life.* London: Hogarth Press, 1953.

Busch, Hans, Editor. *Verdi's Aida: the history of an opera in letters and documents*. Minneapolis: University of Minnesota Press, 1978.

Busch, Hans, Editor. *Verdi's Falstaff in letters and contemporary reviews*. Bloomington: Indiana University Press, 1997.

Busch, Marie, Translator. *Memoirs of Eugenie Schumann*. London: W. Heinemann, 1927.

Bush, Alan Dudley. *In my eighth decade and other essays*. London: Kahn & Averill, 1980.

Busoni, Ferruccio. *Letters to his wife*. Translated by Rosamond Ley. New York: Da Capo Press, 1975.

Byron, Reginald. *Music, culture, & experience: selected papers of John Blacking*. Chicago: University of Chicago Press, 1995.

Cairns, David. *Responses: musical essays and reviews*. New York: Da Capo Press, 1980.

Cardus, Neville. *Talking of music*. London: Collins, 1957.

Carley, Lionel. *Delius: a life in letters*. London: Scolar Press in association with the Delius Trust, 1988.

Carley, Lionel. *Grieg and Delius: a chronicle of their friendship in letters*. London: Marion Boyars, 1993.

Carner, Mosco. *Major and minor*. London: Duckworth, 1980

Carner, Mosco. *Puccini: a critical biography*. London: Duckworth, 1958.

Carroll, Brendan G. *The last prodigy: a biography of Erich Wolfgang Korngold*. Portland, Oregon: Amadeus Press, 1997.

Carse, Adam von Ahn. *The life of Jullien: adventurer, showman-conductor and establisher of the Promenade Concerts in England, together with a history of those concerts up to 1895*. Cambridge England: Heffer, 1951.

Carse, Adam von Ahn. *The orchestra from Beethoven to Berlioz: a history of the orchestra in the first half of the 19th century, and of the development of orchestral baton-conducting*. Cambridge: W. Heffer, 1948.

Casals, Pablo. *Joys and sorrows: reflections by Pablo Casals as told to Albert E. Kahn*. London: Macdonald, 1970.

Casals, Pablo. *The memoirs of Pablo Casals as told to Thomas Dozier*. London: Life en Español, 1959.

Chappell, Paul. *Dr. S. S. Wesley, 1810–1876: portrait of a Victorian musician*. Great Wakering: Mayhew-McCrimmon, 1977.

Chasins, Abram. *Leopold Stokowski, a profile*. New York: Hawthorn Books, 1979.

Charlton, Davi, Editor and Martyn Clarke Translator. *E.T.A. Hoffmann's musical writings: Kreisleriana, The Poet and the Composer*. Cambridge: Cambridge University Press, 1989.

Chávez, Carlos. *Musical thought*. Cambridge: Harvard University Press, 1961.

Chesterman, Robert, Editor. *Conversations with conductors: Bruno Walter, Sir Adrian Boult, Leonard Bernstein, Ernest Ansermet, Otto Klemperer, Leopold Stokowski*. Totowa, New Jersey: Rowman and Littlefield, 1976.

Chissell, Joan. *Clara Schumann: a dedicated spirit; a study of her life and work*. London: Hamilton, 1983.

Chua, Daniel K. L. *The "Galitzin" quartets of Beethoven: Opp.127, 132, 130*. Princeton: Princeton University Press, 1995.

Citron, Marcia, Editor. *The letters of Fanny Hensel to Felix Mendelssohn*. Stuyvesant, New York: Pendragon Press, 1987.

Clark, Walter Aaron. *Enrique Granados: poet of the piano*. Oxford, England; New York, N.Y.: Oxford University Press, 2006.

Clark, Walter Aaron. *Isaac Albéniz: portrait of a romantic*. Oxford; New York: Oxford University Press, 1999.

Clive, Peter. *Beethoven and his world*. Oxford University Press, 2001.

Closson, Ernest. *History of the piano*. Translated by Delano Ames and edited by Robin Golding. London: Paul Elek, 1947.

Cockshoot, John V. *The fugue in Beethoven's piano music*. London: Routledge & Kegan Paul, 1959.

Coe, Richard N, Translator. *Life of Rossini by Stendhal*. London: Calder & Boyars, 1970.

Coleman, Alexander, Editor. *Diversions & animadversions: essays from The new criterion*. New Brunswick, New Jersey; London: Transaction Publishers, 2005.

Colerick, George. *From the Italian girl to Cabaret: musical humour, parody and burlesque*. London: Juventus, 1998.

Coleridige, A. D. *Life of Moscheles, with selections from his diaries and correspondence by his wife*. London: Hurst & Blackett, 1873.

Colles, Henry Cope. *Essays and lectures*. London: Humphrey Milford, Oxford University Press, 1945.

Cone, Edward T., Editor. *Roger Sessions on music: collected essays*. Princeton, New Jersey: Princeton University Press, 1979.

Cone, Edward T. *The composer's voice*. Berkeley; London: University of California Press, 1974.

Cook, Susan and Judy S. Tsou, Editors. *Cecilia reclaimed: feminist perspectives on gender and music*. Urbana: University of Illinois Press, 1994.

Cooper, Barry. *Beethoven*: The master musicians series. Oxford: Oxford University Press, 2000.

Cooper, Barry. *Beethoven and the creative process*. Oxford: Clarendon Press, 1990.

Cooper, Barry. *Beethoven's folksong settings: chronology, sources, style*. Cambridge: Cambridge University Press, 1991.

Cooper, Barry. *The Beethoven compendium: a guide to Beethoven's life and music*. London: Thames and Hudson, 1991.

Cooper, Martin. *Beethoven: the last decade, 1817–1827*. London: Oxford University Press, 1970.

Cooper, Martin. *Judgements of value: selected writings on music*. Oxford; New York: Oxford University Press, 1988.

Cooper, Martin. *Ideas and music*. London: Barrie and Rockliff, 1965.

Cooper, Victoria L. *The house of Novello: the practice and policy of a Victorian music publisher, 1829–1866*. Aldershot, Hants: Ashgate, 2003.

Coover, James. *Music at auction: Puttick and Simpson (of London), 1794–1971: being an annotated, chronological list of sales of musical materials. Warren, Michigan: Harmonie Park Press, 1988.

Copland, Aaron. *Copland on music.* London: Deutsch, 1961.

Corredor, J. Ma. *Conversations with Casals.* London: Hutchinson, 1956.

Cott, Jonathan. *Stockhausen: conversations with the composer.* London: Picador, 1974.

Cottrell, Stephen. *Professional music making in London: ethnography and experience.* Aldershot: Ashgate, 2004.

Cowell, Henry. *Charles Ives and his music.* New York: Oxford University Press, 1955.

Cowling, Elizabeth. *The cello.* London: Batsford, 1983.

Crabbe, John. *Beethoven's empire of the mind.* Newbury: Lovell Baines, 1982.

Craft, Robert. *An improbable life: memoirs.* Nashville: Vanderbilt University Press, 2002.

Craft, Robert, Editor. *Stravinsky: selected correspondence.* London: Faber and Faber, 3 Vols. 1982–1985.

Craw, Howard Allen. *A biography and thematic catalog of the works of J. L. Dussek: 1760–1812.* Ann Arbor: Michigan, 1965.

Crawford, Richard, R. Allen Lott and Carol J. Oja, Editors. *A Celebration of American music: words and music in honor of H. Wiley Hitchcock.* Ann Arbor: University of Michigan Press, 1990.

Craxton, Harold and Tovey, Donald Francis. *Beethoven: Sonatas for Pianoforte.* London: The Associated Board, [1931].

Crichton, Ronald: Editor. *The memoirs of Ethel Smyth.* New York: Viking, 1987.

Crist, Stephen A. and Roberta M. Marvin, Editors. *Historical musicology: sources, methods, interpretations.* Rochester, New York: University of Rochester Press, 2004.

Crofton, Ian and Donald Fraser, Editors. *A dictionary of musical quotations.* London: Croom Helm, 1985.

Crompton, Louis, Editor. *Shaw, Bernard: The great composers: reviews and bombardments.* Berkeley; London: University of California Press, 1978.

Csicserry-Ronay, Elizabeth, Translator and Editor. *Hector Berlioz: The art of music and other essays: (A travers chants).* Bloomington: Indiana University Press, 1994.

Curtiss, Mina Kirstein. *Bizet and his world.* London: Secker & Warburg, 1959.

Cuyler, Louise Elvira. *The symphony.* New York: Harcourt Brace Jovanovich, 1973.

Dahlhaus, Carl. *Ludwig van Beethoven: approaches to his music.* Oxford: Clarendon Press, 1991.

Dahlhaus, Carl. *Nineteenth-century music.* Translated by J. Bradford Robinson. Berkeley; London: University of California Press, 1989.

Daniels, Robin. *Conversations with Cardus.* London: Gollancz, 1976.

Daniels, Robin. Conversations with Menuhin. London: Macdonald General Books, 1979.

Day, James. *Vaughan Williams.* London: Dent, 1961.

Davies, Peter Maxwell. *Studies from two decades*. Selected and introduced by Stephen Pruslin. London: Boosey & Hawkes, 1979.

Dean, Winton. *Georges Bizet: his life and work*. London: J.M. Dent, 1965.

Deas, Stewart. *In defence of Hanslick*. London: Williams and Norgate, 1940.

Debussy, Claude. *Debussy on music*. London: Secker & Warburg, 1977.

Delbanco, Nicholas. *The Beaux Arts Trio*. London: Gollancz, 1985.

Demény, Janos, Editor. *Béla Bartók: letters*. London: Faber and Faber, 1971.

Dent, Edward Joseph. *Selected essays*. Edited by Hugh Taylor. Cambridge; New York: Cambridge University Press, 1979.

Deutsch, Otto Erich. *Mozart: a documentary biography*. London: Adam & Charles Black, 1965.

Deutsch, Otto Erich. *Schubert: a documentary biography*. London: J.M. Dent, 1946

Deutsch, Otto Erich. *Schubert: memoirs by his friends*. London: Adam & Charles Black, 1958.

Dibble, Jeremy. *C. Hubert H. Parry: his life and music*. Oxford: Clarendon Press, 1992.

Dibble, Jeremy. *Charles Villiers Stanford: man and musician*. Oxford: Oxford University Press, 2002.

Donakowski, Conrad L. *A muse for the masses: ritual and music in an age of democratic revolution, 1770–1870*. Chicago: University of Chicago Press, 1977.

Dower, Catherine. *Alfred Einstein on music: selected music criticisms*. New York: Greenwood Press, 1991.

Downs, Philip G. *Classical music: the era of Haydn, Mozart, and Beethoven*. New York: W.W. Norton, 1992.

Drabkin, William. *Beethoven: Missa Solemnis*. Cambridge: Cambridge University Press, 1991.

Dreyfus, Kay. *The farthest north of humanness: letters of Percy Grainger, 1901–1914*. South Melbourne; Basingstoke: Macmillan, 1985.

Dubal, David, Editor. *Remembering Horowitz: 125 pianists recall a legend*. New York: Schirmer Books, 1993.

Dubal, David. *The world of the concert pianist*. London: Victor Gollancz, 1985.

Dvořák, Otakar. *Antonín Dvořák, my father*. Spillville, Iowa: Czech Historical Research Center, 1993.

Dyson, George. *The progress of music*. London: Oxford University Press, Humphrey Milford, 1932.

Eastaugh, Kenneth. *Havergal Brian: the making of a composer*. London: Harrap, 1976.

Edwards, Allen. *Flawed words and stubborn sounds: a conversation with Elliott Carter*. New York: Norton & Company, 1971.

Edwards, Frederick George. *Musical haunts in London*. London: J. Curwen & Sons, 1895.

Ehrlich, Cyril. *First philharmonic: a history of the Royal Philharmonic Society*. Oxford: Clarendon Press, 1995.

Einstein, Alfred. *A short history of music*. London: Cassell and Company Ltd., 1948.

Einstein, Alfred. *Essays on music*. London: Faber and Faber, 1958.

Einstein, Alfred. *Mozart: his character, his work*. London: Cassell and Company Ltd., 1946.

Einstein, Alfred. *Music in the Romantic era*. London: J.M. Dent Ltd., 1947.

Ekman, Karl. *Jean Sibelius, his life and personality*. New York: Tudor Publishing. Co., 1945.

Elgar, Edward. *A future for English music: and other lectures*, Edited by Percy M. Young. London: Dobson, 1968.

Elkin, Robert. *Queen's Hall, 1893–1941*. London: Rider, 1944.

Ella, John. *Musical sketches, abroad and at home: with original music by Mozart, Czerny, Graun, etc., vocal cadenzas and other musical illustrations*. London: Ridgway, Vol. 1., 1869.

Ellis, William Ashton. *The family letters of Richard Wagner*. Edited and translated by William Ashton Ellis and enlarged with introduction and notes by John Deathridge. Basingstoke: Macmillan, 1991.

Ellis, William Ashton. *Richard Wagner's prose works: Vol. 1, The art-work of the future*. Edited and translated by William Ashton Ellis. London: Kegan Paul, Trench, Trübner, 1895.

Ellis, William Ashton. *Richard Wagner's prose works: Vol. 2, Opera and drama*. Edited and translated by William Ashton Ellis. London: Kegan Paul, Trench, Trübner, 1900.

Ellis, William Ashton. *Richard Wagner's prose works: Vol. 3, The theatre*. Edited and translated by William Ashton Ellis. London: Kegan Paul, Trench, Trübner, 1907.

Ellis, William Ashton. *Richard Wagner's prose works: Vol. 4, Art and politics*. Edited and translated by William Ashton Ellis. London: Kegan Paul, Trench, Trübner, 1895.

Ellis, William Ashton. *Richard Wagner's prose works: Vol. 5, Actors and singers*. Edited and translated by William Ashton Ellis. London: Kegan Paul, Trench, Trübner, 1896.

Ellis, William Ashton. *Richard Wagner's prose works: Vol. 6, Religion and art*. Edited and translated by William Ashton Ellis. London: Kegan Paul, Trench, Trübner, 1897.

Ellis, William Ashton. *Richard Wagner's prose works: Vol. 7, In Paris and Dresden*. Edited and translated by William Ashton Ellis. London: Kegan Paul, Trench, Trübner, 1898.

Ellis, William Ashton. *Richard Wagner's prose works: Vol. 8, Posthumous*. Edited and translated by William Ashton Ellis. London: Kegan Paul, Trench, Trübner, 1899.

Elterlein, Ernst von. *Beethoven's pianoforte sonatas: explained for the lovers of the musical art*. London: W. Reeves, 1898.

Engel, Carl. *Musical myths and facts*. London: Novello, Ewer & Co.; New York: J.L. Peters, 1876.

Eosze, László. *Zoltán Kodály: his life and work*. London: Collet's, 1962.

Etter, Brian K. *From classicism to modernism: Western musical culture and the metaphysics of order*. Aldershot: Ashgate, 2001.

Ewen, David. *From Bach to Stravinsky: the history of music by its foremost critics.* New York, Greenwood Press, 1968.

Ewen, David. *Romain Rolland's Essays on music.* New York: Dover Publications, 1959.

Fay, Amy. *Music-study in Germany: from the home correspondence of Amy Fay.* New York: Dover Publications, 1965.

Fenby, Eric. *Delius as I knew him.* London: Quality Press, 1936.

Ferguson, Donald Nivison. *Masterworks of the orchestral repertoire: a guide for listeners.* Minneapolis: University of Minnesota Press, 1954.

Fétis, François-Joseph. *Curiosités historiques de la musique: complément nécessaire de la Musique mise à la portée de tout le monde.* Paris: Janet et Cotelle, 1830.

Fifield, Christopher. *Max Bruch: his life and works.* London: Gollancz, 1988.

Fifield, Christopher. *True artist and true friend: a biography of Hans Richter.* Oxford: Clarendon Press, 1993.

Finson, Jon and R. Larry Todd, Editors. *Mendelssohn and Schumann: essays on their music and its context.* Durham, N.C.: Duke University Press, 1984.

Fischer, Edwin. *Beethoven's pianoforte sonatas: a guide for students & amateurs.* London: Faber and Faber, 1959.

Fischer, Edwin. *Reflections on music.* London: Williams and Norgate, 1951.

Fischer, Hans Conrad and Erich Kock. *Ludwig van Beethoven: a study in text and pictures.* London: Macmillan; New York, St. Martin's Press, 1972.

Fischmann, Zdenka E. *Janáček-Newmarch correspondence. 1st limited and numbered edition.* Rockville, MD: Kabel Publishers, 1986.

Fitzlyon, April. *Maria Malibran: diva of the romantic age.* London: Souvenir Press, 1987.

FitzLyon, April. *The price of genius: a life of Pauline Viardot.* London: John Calder, 1964.

Forbes, Elliot, Editor. *Thayer's life of Beethoven.* Princeton, New Jersey: Princeton University Press, 1967.

Foreman, Lewis. *Bax: a composer and his times.* London: Scolar Press, 1983.

Foreman, Lewis, Editor. *Farewell, my youth, and other writings by Arnold Bax.* Aldershot: Scolar Press, 1992.

Foster, Myles Birket. *History of the Philharmonic Society of London, 1813–1912: a record of a hundred years' work in the cause of music.* London: Bodley Head, 1912.

Foulds, John. *Music today: its heritage from the past, and legacy to the future.* London: I. Nicholson and Watson, limited, 1934.

Frank, Mortimer H. *Arturo Toscanini: the NBC years.* Portland, Oregon: Amadeus Press, 2002.

Fraser, Andrew Alastair. *Essays on music.* London: Oxford University Press, H. Milford, 1930.

Frohlich, Martha. *Beethoven's Appassionata' sonata.* Oxford: Clarendon Press, 1991.

Gal, Hans. *The golden age of Vienna.* London: Max Parrish & Co. Limited, 1948.

Gal, Hans. *The musician's world:*

great composers in their letters. London: Thames and Hudson, 1965.

Galatopoulos, Stelios. *Bellini: life, times, music*. London: Sanctuary, 2002.

Garden, Edward and Nigel Gottrei, Editors. *'To my best friend': correspondence between Tchaikovsky and Nadezhda von Meck, 1876–1878*. Oxford: Clarendon Press, 1993.

Geck, Martin. Beethoven. London: Haus, 2003.

Gerig, Reginald. *Famous pianists & their technique*. Washington: R. B. Luce, 1974.

Gilliam, Bryan. *The life of Richard Strauss*. Cambridge: Cambridge University Press, 1999.

Gilliam, Bryan, Editor. *Richard Strauss and his world*. Princeton, New Jersey: Princeton University Press, 1992.

Gillies, Malcolm and Bruce Clunies Ross, Editors. *Grainger on music*. Oxford; New York: Oxford University Press, 1999.

Gillies, Malcolm and David Pear, Editors. *The all-round man: selected letters of Percy Grainger, 1914–1961*. Oxford: Clarendon Press, 1994.

Gillies, Malcolm, Editor. *The Bartók companion*. London: Faber and Faber, 1993.

Gillmor, Alan M. *Erik Satie*. Basingstoke: Macmillan Press, 1988.

Glehn, M. E. *Goethe and Mendelssohn : (1821–1831)*. London: Macmillan, 1874.

Glowacki, John, Editor. *Paul A. Pisk: Essays in his honor*. Austin, Texas: University of Texas, 1966

Gollancz, Victor. *Journey towards music: a memoir*. London: Victor Gollancz Ltd., 1964.

Good, Edwin Marshall. *Giraffes, black dragons, and other pianos: a technological history from Cristofori to the modern concert grand*. Stanford, California: Stanford University Press, 1982.

Gordon, David. *Musical visitors to Britain*. London: Routledge, 2005.

Gordon, Stewart. *A history of keyboard literature: music for the piano and its forerunners*. Schirmer Books: New York: London : Prentice Hall International, 1996.

Gorrell, Lorraine. *The nineteenth-century German lied*. Portland, Oregon: Amadeus Press, 1993.

Goss, Glenda D. *Jean Sibelius: the Hämeenlinna letters: scenes from a musical life, 1875–1895*. Esbo, Finland: Schildts, 1997.

Goss, Madeleine. *Bolero: the life of Maurice Ravel*. New York: Tudor, 1945.

Gotch, Rosamund Brunel, Editor. *Mendelssohn and his friends in Kensington: letters from Fanny and Sophy Horsley, written 1833–36*. London: Oxford University Press, 1938.

Gounod, Charles. *Charles Gounod; autobiographical reminiscences: with family letters and notes on music; from the French*. London: William Heinemann, 1896.

Grabs, Manfred, Editor. *Hanns Eisler: a rebel in music; selected writings*. Berlin: Seven Seas Publishers, 1978.

Grace, Harvey. *A musician at large*. London: Oxford University Press, H. Milford, 1928.

(La) Grange, Henry-Louis de. *Gustav Mahler*. Oxford: Oxford University Press, 1995.

Graves, Charles L. *Hubert Parry: his life and works*. London: Macmillan, 1926.

Graves, Charles L. *Post-Victorian music: with other studies and sketches*. London: Macmillan and Co., limited, 1911.

Graves, Charles L. *The life & letters of Sir George Grove, Hon. D.C.L. (Durham), Hon. LL.D. (Glasgow), formerly director of the Royal college of music*. London: Macmillan and Co., Ltd.; New York: The Macmillan Co., 1903.

Gray, Cecil. *Musical chairs, or, between two stools: being the life and memoirs of Cecil Gray*. London: Home & Van Thal, 1948.

Gregor-Dellin and Dietrich Mack, Editors. *Cosima Wagner's diaries.: Vol. 1, 1869 - 1877*. London: Collins, 1978-1980.

Griffiths, Paul. *Modern music: the avant-garde since 1945*. London: J. M. Dent & Sons Ltd., 1981.

Griffiths, Paul. *Olivier Messiaen and the music of time*. London: Faber and Faber, 1985.

Griffiths, Paul. *Peter Maxwell Davies*. London: Robson Books, 1988.

Griffiths, Paul. *The sea on fire: Jean Barraqué*. Rochester, New York: Woodbridge: University of Rochester Press, 2003.

Griffiths, Paul. *The string quartet*. London: Thames and Hudson, 1983.

Grout, Donald Jay and Claude V. Palisca, Editors. *A history of Western music*. London: J. M. Dent, 1988.

Grove, George. *Beethoven and his nine symphonies*. London: Novello, Ewer, 1896.

Grover, Ralph Scott. *Ernest Chausson: the man and his music*. London: The Athlone Press, 1980.

Grover, Ralph Scott. *The music of Edmund Rubbra*. Aldershot: Scolar Press, 1993.

Grun, Bernard. *Alban Berg: letters to his wife*. Edited and translated by Bernard Grun. London: Faber and Faber, 1971.

Gutman, David. *Prokofiev*. London: Omnibus Press, 1990.

Hadow, William Henry. *Collected essays*. London: H. Milford at the Oxford University Press, 1928.

Hadow, William Henry. *Beethoven's Op. 18 Quartets*. London: H. Milford at the Oxford University Press, 1926.

Haggin, Bernard H. *Music observed*. New York: Oxford University Press, 1964.

Hailey, Christopher. *Franz Schreker, 1878–1934: a cultural biography*. Cambridge: Cambridge University Press, 1993.

Hall, Michael. *Leaving home: a conducted tour of twentieth-century music with Simon Rattle*. London: Faber and Faber, 1996.

Hall, Patricia and Friedemann Sallis, Editors. (Brief Description): *A handbook to twentieth-century musical sketches*. Cambridge: Cambridge University Press, 2004.

Hallé, C. E. *Life and letters of Sir Charles Hallé: being an autobiography (1819–1860) with correspondence and diaries*. London: Smith, Elder & Co., 1896.

Halstead, Jill. *The woman composer: creativity and the gendered politics of musical composition.* Aldershot: Ashgate, 1997.

Hamburger, Michael, Editor and Translator. *Beethoven letters, journals, and conversations.* New York: Thames and Hudson, 1951.

Hammelmann, Hanns A. and Ewald Osers. *The correspondence between Richard Strauss and Hugo von Hofmannsthal.* London: Collins, 1961.

Hanson, Lawrence and Elisabeth Hanson. *Tchaikovsky: the man behind the music.* New York: Dodd, Mead & Co, 1967.

Harding, James. *Massenet.* London: J. M. Dent & Sons Ltd., 1970.

Harding, James. *Saint-Saëns and his circle.* London: Chapman & Hall, 1965.

Harding, Rosamond E. M. *Origins of musical time and expression.* London: Oxford University Press, 1938.

Harman, Alec with Anthony Milner and Wilfrid Mellers. *Man and his music: the story of musical experience in the West.* London: Barrie & Jenkins, 1988.

Harper, Nancy Lee. *Manuel de Falla: his life and music.* Lanham, Maryland; London: The Scarecrow Press, 2005.

Hartmann, Arthur. *'Claude Debussy as I knew him' and other writings of Arthur Hartmann.* Edited by Samuel Hsu, Sidney Grolnic, and Mark Peters. Rochester, New York; Woodbridge: University of Rochester Press, 2003.

Haugen, Einar and Camilla Cai. *Ole Bull: Norway's romantic musician and cosmopolitan patriot.* Madison: The University of Wisconsin Press, 1993.

Headington, Christopher. *The Bodley Head history of Western music.* London: The Bodley Head, 1974.

Heartz, Daniel. *Music in European capitals: the galant style, 1720–1780.* New York; London: W. W. Norton, 2003.

Hedley, Arthur, Editor. *Selected correspondence of Fryderyk Chopin: abridged from Fryderyk Chopin's correspondence.* London: Heinemann, 1962.

Heiles, Anne Mischakoff. *Mischa Mischakoff: journeys of a concertmaster.* Sterling Heights, Michigan: Harmonie Park Press, 2006.

Henderson, Sanya Shoilevska. *Alex North, film composer: a biography, with musical analyses of a Streetcar named desire, Spartacus, The misfits, Under the volcano, and Prizzi's honor.* Jefferson, N.C.; London: McFarland, 2003.

Henschel, George. *Personal recollections of Johannes Brahms: some of his letters to and pages from a journal kept by George Henschel.* Boston: R G. Badger, 1907.

Henze, Hans Werner. *Bohemian fifths: an autobiography.* London: Faber and Faber, 1998.

Henze, Hans Werner. *Music and politics: collected writings 1953–81.* London: Faber and Faber, 1982.

Herbert, May, Translator. *Early letters of Robert Schumann.* London: George Bell and Sons, 1888.

Heyman, Barbara B. *Samuel Barber:*

the composer and his music. New York: Oxford University Press, 1992.

Heyworth, Peter. *Otto Klemperer, his life and times.* Cambridge: Cambridge University Press, 2 Vols. 1983–1996.

Hildebrandt, Dieter. *Pianoforte: a social history of the piano.* London: Hutchinson, 1988.

Hill, Peter. *The Messiaen companion.* London: Faber and Faber, 1995.

Hill, Peter and Nigel Simeone. *Messiaen.* New Haven Connecticut; London: Yale University Press, 2005.

Hiller, Ferdinand. *Mendelssohn: Letters and recollections.* New York: Vienna House, 1972.

Hines, Robert Stephan. *The orchestral composer's point of view: essays on twentieth-century music by those who wrote it.* Norman: University of Oklahoma Press, 1970.

Ho, Allan B. *Shostakovich reconsidered.* London: Toccata Press, 1998.

Hodeir, André. *Since Debussy: a view of contemporary music.* New York: Da Capo Press, 1975.

Holmes, Edward. *The life of Mozart: including his correspondence.* London: Chapman and Hall, 1845.

Holmes, John L. *Composers on composers.* New York: Greenwood Press, 1990.

Hopkins, Anthony. *The concertgoer's companion.* London: J.M. Dent & Sons Ltd., 1984.

Hopkins, Anthony. *The seven concertos of Beethoven.* Aldershot: Scolar Press, 1996.

Holt, Richard. *Nicolas Medtner (1879–1951): a tribute to his art and personality.* London: D. Dobson, 1955.

Honegger, Arthur. *I am a composer.* London: Faber and Faber, 1966.

Hoover, Kathleen and John Cage. *Virgil Thomson: his life and music.* New York; London: T. Yoseloff, 1959.

Horgan, Paul. *Encounters with Stravinsky: a personal record.* London: The Bodley Head, 1972.

Horowitz, Joseph. *Conversations with Arrau.* London: Collins, 1982.

Horowitz, Joseph. Understanding Toscanini. London: Faber and Faber, 1987.

Horwood, Wally. *Adolphe Sax, 1814–1894: his life and legacy.* Bramley: Bramley Books, 1980.

Howie, Crawford. *Anton Bruckner: a documentary biography.* Lewiston, N.Y.; Lampeter: Edwin Mellen Press, 2002.

Hueffer, Francis. *Correspondence of Wagner and Liszt.* New York: Greenwood Press, 2 Vols.1969.

Hughes, Spike. *The Toscanini legacy: a critical study of Arturo Toscanini's performances of Beethoven, Verdi, and other composers.* London: Putnam, 1959.

Hullah, Annette. *Theodor Leschetizky.* London and New York: J. Land & Co., 1906.

Le Huray, Peter and James Day, Editors. *Music and aesthetics in the eighteenth and early-nineteenth centuries.* Cambridge: Cambridge University Press, 1988.

D' Indy, Vincent. *César Franck.* New York: Dover Publications, 1965.

Jacobs, Arthur. *Arthur Sullivan: A

Victorian musician. Aldershot: Scolar Press, 1992.

Jahn, Otto. *Life of Mozart.* London: Novello, Ewer & Co., 1882.

Jefferson, Alan. *Sir Thomas Beecham: a centenary tribute.* London: World Records Ltd., 1979.

Jezic, Diane. *The musical migration and Ernst Toch.* Ames: Iowa State University Press, 1989.

Johnson, Douglas Porter, Editor. *The Beethoven sketchbooks: history, reconstruction, inventory.* Oxford: Clarendon, 1985.

Johnson, Stephen. *Bruckner remembered.* London: Faber and Faber, 1998.

Jones, David, Wyn. *Beethoven: Pastoral symphony.* Cambridge: Cambridge University Press, 1995.

Jones, David Wyn. *The life of Beethoven.* Cambridge: Cambridge University Press, 1998.

Jones, David Wyn. *The symphony in Beethoven's Vienna.* Cambridge: Cambridge University Press, 2006.

Jones, J. Barrie, Editor. *Gabriel Fauré: a life in letters.* London: Batsford, 1989.

Jones, Peter Ward, Editor and Translator. *The Mendelssohns on honeymoon: the 1837 diary of Felix and Cécile Mendelssohn Bartholdy, together with letters to their families.* Oxford: Clarendon Press, 1997.

Jones, Timothy. *Beethoven, the Moonlight and other sonatas, Op. 27 and Op. 31.* Cambridge; New York, N.Y.: Cambridge University Press, 1999.

Kalischer, A. C., Editor. *Beethoven's letters: a critical edition.* London: J. M. Dent, 1909.

Kárpáti, János. *Bartók's chamber music.* Stuyvesant, New York: Pendragon Press, 1994.

Keefe, Simon P. *The Cambridge companion to the concerto.* Cambridge, New York, N.Y.: Cambridge University Press, 2005.

Keller, Hans. *The great Haydn quartets: their interpretation.* London: J. M. Dent, 1986.

Keller, Hans, Editor. *The memoirs of Carl Flesch.* New York: Macmillan, 1958.

Keller, Hans, and Christopher Wintle. *Beethoven's string quartets in F minor, Op. 95 and C minor, Op. 131: two studies.* Nottingham: Department of Music, University of Nottingham, 1995.

Kelly, Thomas Forrest. *First nights at the opera: five musical premiers.* New Haven: Yale University Press, 2004.

Kennedy, Michael. *Adrian Boult.* London: Hamish Hamilton, 1987.

Kennedy, Michael. *Barbirolli, conductor laureate: the authorised biography.* London: Hart-Davis, MacGibbon, 1973.

Kennedy, Michael, Editor. *The autobiography of Charles Hallé; with correspondence and diaries.* London: Paul Elek, 1972.

Kennedy, Michael. *Hallé tradition: a century of music.* Manchester: Manchester University Press, 1960.

Kennedy, Michael. *The works of Ralph Vaughan Williams.* London: Oxford University Press, 1964.

Kemp, Ian. *Tippett: the composer and his music.* London; New York: Eulenburg Books, 1984.

Kerman, Joseph. *The Beethoven quartets.* London: Oxford University Press, 1967, c1966.

Kerman, Joseph. *Write all these down: essays on music.* Berkeley, California; London: University of California Press, 1994.

Kildea, Paul, Editor. *Britten on music.* Oxford: Oxford University Press, 2003.

Kinderman, William. *Beethoven.* Oxford: Oxford University Press, 1997.

Kinderman, William. *Beethoven's Diabelli variations.* Oxford: Clarendon Press; New York: Oxford University Press, 1987.

Kinderman, William, Editor. *The string quartets of Beethoven.* Urbana, Ilinois: University of Illinois Press, 2005.

King, Alec Hyatt. *Musical pursuits: selected essays.* London: British Library, 1987.

Kirby, F. E. *Music for piano: a short history.* Amadeus Press: Portland, 1995.

Kirkpatrick, John, Editor. *Charles E. Ives: Memos.* New York: W.W. Norton, 1972.

Knapp, Raymond. *Brahms and the challenge of the symphony.* Stuyvesant, N.Y.: Pendragon Press, c.1997.

Knight, Frida. *Cambridge music: from the Middle Ages to modern times.* Cambridge, England.: New York: Oleander Press, 1980.

Knight, Max, Translator. *A confidential matter: the letters of Richard Strauss and Stefan Zweig, 1931–1935.* Berkeley; London: University of California Press, 1977.

Kok, Alexander. *A voice in the dark: the philharmonia years.* Ampleforth: Emerson Edition, 2002.

Kopelson, Kevin. *Beethoven's kiss: pianism, perversion, and the mastery of desire.* Stanford, California: Stanford University Press, 1996.

Kostelanetz, Richard, Editor. *Aaron Copland: a reader; selected writings 1923–1972.* New York; London: Routledge, 2003.

Kostelanetz, Richard. *Conversing with Cage.* New York; London: Routledge, 2003.

Kostelanetz, Richard. *On innovative musicians.* New York: Limelight Editions, 1989.

Kostelanetz, Richard, Editor. *Virgil Thomson: a reader ; selected writings, 1924–1984.* New York; London: Routledge, 2002.

Kowalke, Kim H. *Kurt Weill in Europe.* Ann Arbor, Michigan: UMI Research Press, 1979.

Krehbiel, Henry Edward. *The pianoforte and its music.* New York: Cooper Square Publishers, 1971.

Kruseman, Philip, Editor. *Beethoven's own words.* London: Hinrichsen Edition, 1948.

Kurtz, Michael. *Stockhausen: a biography.* London: Faber and Faber, 1992.

Lam, Basil. *Beethoven string quartets.* Seattle: University of Washington Press, 1975.

Lambert, Constant. *Music ho!: a study of music in decline.* London: Faber and Faber, Ltd. 1934.

Landon, H. C. Robbins. *Beethoven: a documentary study.* London: Thames and Hudson, 1970.

Landon, H. C. Robbins. *Beethoven: his life, work and world.*

Landon, H. C. Robbins. *Essays on the Viennese classical style: Gluck, Haydn, Mozart, Beethoven.* London: Barrie & Rockliff The Cresset Press, 1970.

Landon, H. C. Robbins. *Haydn: chronicle and works/Haydn, the late years, 1801–1809.* Bloomington: Indiana University Press, 1977.

Landon, H. C. Robbins. *Haydn: his life and music.* London: Thames and Hudson, 1988.

Landon, H. C. Robbins. *Haydn in England, 1791–1795.* London: Thames and Hudson, 1976.

Landon, H. C. Robbins. *Haydn: the years of 'The creation', 1796–800.* London: Thames and Hudson, 1977.

Landon, H. C. Robbins. *Mozart: the golden years, 1781–1791.* New York: Schirmer Books, 1989.

Landon, H. C. Robbins. *1791, Mozart's last year.* London: Thames and Hudson, 1988.

Landon, H. C. Robbins *The collected correspondence and London notebooks of Joseph Haydn.* London: Barrie and Rockliff, 1959.

Landon, H. C. Robbins: Editor. *The Mozart companion. London: Faber, 1956.*

Landowska, Wanda. *Music of the past.* London: Geoffrey Bles, 1926.

Lang, Paul Henry. *Musicology and performance.* New Haven: Yale University Press, 1997.

Lang, Paul Henry. *The creative world of Beethoven.* New York: W. W. Norton 1971.

Laurence, Dan H., Editor. *Shaw's music: the complete musical criticism in three volumes.* London: Max Reinhardt, the Bodley Head, 1981.

Lawford-Hinrichsen, Irene. *Music publishing and patronage: C. F. Peters, 1800 to the Holocaust.* Kenton: Edition Press, 2000.

Layton, Robert, Editor. *A guide to the concerto.* Oxford: Oxford University Press, 1996.

Layton, Robert, Editor. *A guide to the symphony.* Oxford: Oxford University Press, 1995.

Lebrecht, Norman. *The maestro myth: great conductors in pursuit of power.* London: Simon & Schuster, 1991.

Lee, Ernest Markham. *The story of the symphony.* London: Scott Publishing Co., 1916.

Leibowitz, Herbert A., Editor. *Musical impressions: selections from Paul Rosenfeld's criticism.* London: G. Allen & Unwin, 1970.

Lenrow, Elbert, Editor and Translator. *The letters of Richard Wagner to Anton Pusinelli.* New York: Vienna House, 1972.

Leonard, Maurice. *Kathleen: the life of Kathleen Ferrier: 1912–1953.* London: Hutchinson, 1988.

Lesure, François and Roger Nichols, Editors. *Debussy, letters.* London: Faber and Faber, 1987.

Letellier, Robert Ignatius, Editor and Translator. *The diaries of Giacomo Meyerbeer.* Madison: Fairleigh Dickinson University Press; London: Associated University Presses, 4 Vols., 1999–2004.

Levas, Santeri. *Sibelius: a personal portrait.* London: J. M. Dent, 1972.

Levy, Alan Howard. *Edward MacDowell, an American master.* Lanham, Md. & London: Scarecrow Press, 1998.

Levy, David Benjamin. *Beethoven: the Ninth Symphony.* New Haven, Connecticut; London: Yale University Press, 2003.

Leyda, Jay and Sergi Bertensson. *The Musorgsky reader: a life of Modeste Petrovich Musorgsky in letters and documents.* New York: W.W. Norton, 1947.

Lewis, Thomas P., Editor. *Raymond Leppard on music: an anthology of critical and personal writings.* White Plains, N.Y.: Pro/Am Music Resources, 1993.

Liébert, Georges. *Nietzsche and music.* Chicago: University of Chicago Press, 2004.

Liszt, Franz. *An artist's journey: lettres d'un bachelier ès musique, 1835–1841.* Chicago: University of Chicago Press, 1989.

Litzmann, Berthold, Editor. *Clara Schumann: an artist's life, based on material found in diaries and letters.* London: Macmillan; Leipzig: Breitkopf & Härtel, 2 Vols. 1913.

Litzmann, Berthold, Editor. *Letters of Clara Schumann and Johannes Brahms, 1853–1896.* New York, Vienna House. 2 Vols. 1971.

Lloyd, Stephen. *William Walton: muse of fire.* Woodbridge, Suffolk: The Boydell Press, 2001.

Locke, Ralph P. and Cyrilla Barr, Editors. *Cultivating music in America: women patrons and activists since 1860.* Berkeley: University of California Press, 1997.

Lockspeiser, Edward. *Debussy: his life and mind.* London: Cassell. 2 Vols. 1962–1965.

Lockspeiser, Edward. *The literary clef: an anthology of letters and writings by French composers.* London: J. Calder. 1958.

Lockwood, Lewis, Editor. *Beethoven essays: studies in honor of Elliot Forbes.* Cambridge, Massachusetts: Harvard University Department of Music: Distributed by Harvard University Press, 1984.

Lockwood, Lewis and Mark Kroll, Editors. *The Beethoven violin sonatas: history, criticism, performance.* Urbana: University of Illinois Press, 2004.

Loft, Abram. *Violin and keyboard: the duo repertoire.* New York: Grossman Publishers. 2 Vols. 1973.

Longyear, Rey Morgan. *Nineteenth-century romanticism in music.* Englewood Cliffs: Prentice-Hall, 1969.

Lowe, C. Egerton. *Beethoven's pianoforte sonatas: hints on their rendering, form, etc., with appendices on definition of sonata, music forms, ornaments, pianoforte pedals, and how to discover keys.* London: Novello, 1929.

Macdonald, Hugh, Editor. *Berlioz: Selected letters.* London: Faber and Faber, 1995.

Macdonald, Malcolm, Editor. *Havergal Brian on music: selections from his journalism: Volume One, British music.* London: Toccata Press, 1986.

MacDonald, Malcolm. *Varèse: astronomer in sound.* London: Kahn & Averill, 2003.

MacDowell, Edward. *Critical and historical essays: lectures delivered at Columbia University.* Edited by W. J. Baltzell. London: Elkin; Boston: A.P. Schmidt, 1912.

MacFarren, Walter. Memories: an autobiography. London: Walter Scott Publishing Co.,1905.

Mackenzie, Alexander Campbell. *A musician's narrative.* London: Cassell and company, Ltd, 1927.

McCarthy, Margaret William, Editor. *More letters of Amy Fay: the American years, 1879–1916.* Detroit: Information Coordinators, 1986.

McClary, Susan. *Feminine endings: music, gender, and sexuality.* Minneapolis: University of Minnesota Press, 1991.

McClatchie, Stephen, Editor and Translator. *The Mahler family letters.* Oxford: Oxford University Press, 2006.

McVeigh, Simon. *Concert life in London from Mozart to Haydn.* Cambridge: Cambridge University Press, 1993.

Mahler, Alma. *Gustav Mahler: memories and letters.* Enlarged edition revised and edited and with and introduction by Donald Mitchell. London: John Murray, 1968.

Mai, François Martin. *Diagnosing genius: the life and death of Beethoven.* Montreal; London: McGill-Queen's University Press, 2007.

Del Mar, Norman. *Orchestral variations: confusion and error in the orchestral repertoire.* London: Eulenburg, 1981.

Del Mar, Norman. *Richard Strauss: a critical commentary on his life and works.* London: Barrie & Jenkins. 3 Vols. 1978.

(La) Mara [pseudonym]. *Letters of Franz Liszt.* London: H. Grevel & Co., 2 Vols. 1894.

Marek, George Richard. *Puccini.* London: Cassell & Co., 1952.

Marek, George Richard. *Toscanini.* London: Vision, 1976.

(De) Marliave, Joseph. *Beethoven's quartets.* New York: Dover Publications (reprint), 1961.

Martin, George Whitney. *Verdi: his music, life and times.* London: Macmillan, 1965.

Martner, Knud, Editor. *Selected letters of Gustav Mahler.* London; Boston: Faber and Faber, 1979.

Martyn, Barrie. *Nicolas Medtner: his life and music.* Aldershot: Scolar Press, 1995.

Martyn, Barrie. *Rachmaninoff: composer, pianist, conductor.* Aldershot: Scolar, 1990.

Massenet, Jules. *My recollections.* Westport, Connecticut: Greenwood Press.1970.

Matheopoulos, Helena. *Maestro: encounters with conductors of today.* London: Hutchinson, 1982.

Matthews, Denis. *Beethoven.* London: J. M. Dent, 1985.

Matthews, Denis. *Beethoven piano sonatas.* London: British Broadcasting Corporation, 1967.

Matthews, Denis. *In pursuit of music.* London: Victor Gollancz Ltd., 1968.

Matthews, Denis. *Keyboard music.* Newton Abbot: London David & Charles, 1972.

Mellers, Wilfrid Howard. *Caliban reborn: renewal in twentieth-century music.* London: Victor Gollancz, 1967.

Mellers, Wilfrid Howard. *The sonata principle (from c. 1750).* London: Rockliff, 1957.

Mendelssohn Bartholdy. *Letters from Italy and Switzerland.* London: Longman, Green, Longman, and Roberts, 1862.

Mendelssohn Bartholdy, Paul. *Letters of Felix Mendelssohn Bartholdy, from 1833 to 1847.* London: Longman, Green, Longman, Roberts, & Green, 1864.

Menuhin, Yehudi and Curtis W. Davis. *The music of man.* London: Macdonald and Jane's, 1979.

Menuhin, Yehudi. *Theme and variations.* London: Heinemann Educational Books Ltd., 1972.

Menuhin, Yehudi. *Unfinished journey.* London: Macdonald and Jane's, 1977.

Messian, Olivier. *Music and color: conversations with Claude Samuel.* Portland, Oregon: Amadeus, 1994.

Miall, Anthony. *Musical bumps.* London: J.M. Dent & Sons Ltd, 1981.

Michotte, Edmond. *Richard Wagner's visit to Rossini (Paris 1860): and, An evening at Rossini's in Beau-Sejour (Passy), 1858.* Chicago; London: University of Chicago Press, 1982.

Mies, Paul. *Beethoven's sketches: an analysis of his style based on a study of his sketchbooks.*
New York: Johnson Reprint, 1969.

Milhaud, Darius. *My happy life.* London: Boyars, 1995.

Miller, Mina. *The Nielsen companion.* London: Faber and Faber, 1994.

Milsom, David. *Theory and practice in late nineteenth-century violin performance: an examination of style in performance, 1850–1900.* Aldershot: Ashgate, 2003.

Mitchell, Donald, Editor. *Letters from a life: the selected letters and diaries of Benjamin Britten 1913–1976.* London: Faber and Faber. 3 Vols., 1991.

Mitchell, Donald and Hans Keller, Editors. *Music survey: new series 1949–1952.* London: Faber Music in association with Faber & Faber, 1981.

Mitchell, Jon C. *A comprehensive biography of composer Gustav Holst, with correspondence and diary excerpts: including his American years.* Lewiston, New York: Edwin Mellen Press, 2001.

Moldenhauer, Hans. *Anton von Webern: a chronicle of his life and work.* London: Victor Gollancz, 1978.

Monrad-Johansen. Edvard Grieg. New York: Tudor Publishing Co., 1945.

Moore, Gerald. *Am I too loud?: memoirs of an accompanist.* London: Hamish Hamilton, 1962.

Moore, Gerald. *Farewell recital: further memoirs.* Harmondsworth: Penguin Books, 1979.

Moore, Gerald. *Furthermoore: interludes in an accompanist's life.* London: Hamish Hamilton, 1983.

Moore, Jerrold Northrop. *Edward Elgar: a creative life.* Oxford: Oxford University Press, 1984.

Moore, Jerrold Northrop. *Elgar, Edward. The windflower letters: correspondence with Alice Caroline Stuart Wortley and her family.* Oxford: Clarendon

Press; New York: Oxford University Press, 1989.

Moore, Jerrold Northrop. *Elgar, Edward. Edward Elgar: letters of a lifetime.* Oxford: Clarendon Press; New York: Oxford University Press, 1990.

Moore, Jerrold Northrop. *Elgar, Edward. Elgar and his publishers: letters of a creative life.* Oxford: Clarendon, 1987.

Moreux, Serge. *Béla Bartók.* London: Harvill Press, 1953.

Morgan, Kenneth. *Fritz Reiner, maestro and martinet.* Urbana: University of Illinois Press, 2005.

Cone, Edward T., Editor. *Music, a view from Delft: selected essays.* Chicago: University of Chicago Press, 1989.

Morgan, Robert P. *Twentieth-century music: a history of musical style in modern Europe and America.* New York: Norton, 1991.

Morgenstern, Sam., Editor. *Composers on music: an anthology of composers' writings.* London: Faber & Faber, 1956.

Morrow, Mary Sue. *Concert life in Haydn's Vienna: aspects of a developing musical and social institution.* Stuyvesant, New York: Pendragon Press, 1989.

Moscheles, Felix, Editor and Translator. *Letters from Felix Mendelssohn-Bartholdy to Ignaz and Charlotte Moscheles.* London: Trübner and Co., 1888.

Mudge, Richard B., Translator. *Glinka, Mikhail Ivanovich: Memoirs.* Norman: University of Oklahoma Press, 1963.

Munch, Charles. *I am a conductor.* New York: Oxford University Press, 1955.

Mundy, Simon. *Bernard Haitink: a working life.* London: Robson Books, 1987.

Musgrave, Michael. *The musical life of the Crystal Palace.* Cambridge: Cambridge University Press, 1995.

Music & Letters. *Beethoven: special number.* London: Music & Letters, 1927.

Musical Times. *Special Issue.* John A. Fuller-Maitland London: Vol. VIII, No. 2, 1927.

Myers, Rollo H., Editor. *Twentieth-century music.* London: Calder and Boyars, 1960.

National Gallery (Great Britain). *Music performed at the National Gallery concerts, 10th October 1939 to 10th April 1946.* London: Privately printed, 1948.

Nattiez, Jean-Jacques, Editor. *Orientations: collected writings — Pierre Boulez.* London: Faber and Faber, 1986.

Nauhaus, Gerd, Editor. *The marriage diaries of Robert & Clara Schumann.* London: Robson Books, 1994.

Nectoux, Jean Michel. *Gabriel Fauré: a musical life.* Translated by Roger Nichols. Cambridge: Cambridge University Press, 1991.

Nettl, Paul. *Beethoven handbook.* Westport, Connecticut: Greenwood Press, 1975.

Neumayr, Anton. *Music and medicine.* Bloomington, Illinois: Medi-Ed Press, 1994–1997

Newbould, Brian. *Schubert and the symphony: a new perspective.* Surbiton: Toccata Press, 1992.

Newlin, Dika. *Schoenberg remembered: diaries and recollections (1938–76).* New York: Pendragon Press, 1980.

Newman, Ernest. *From the world of music: essays from 'The Sunday Times'.* London: J. Calder, 1956.

Newman, Ernest. Hugo Wolf. New York: Dover Publications, 1966.

Newman, Ernest, Annotated and Translated. *Memoirs of Hector Berlioz from 1803 to 1865, comprising his travels in Germany, Italy, Russia, and England.* New York: Knopf, 1932.

Newman, Ernest. *More essays from the world of music: essays from the 'Sunday Times'.* London: John Calder, 1958.

Newman, Ernest. *Musical studies.* London; New York: John Lane, 1910.

Newman, Ernest. *Testament of music: essays and papers.* London: Putnam, 1962.

Newman, Richard. *Alma Rosé: Vienna to Auschwitz.* Portland, Oregon: Amadeus Press, 2000.

Newman, William S. *The sonata in the classic era.* Chapel Hill: University of North Carolina Press 1963.

Newman, William S. *The sonata in the Classic era.* New York; London: W.W. Norton, 1983.

Newmarch, Rosa Harriet. *Henry J. Wood.* London & New York: John Lane, 1904.

Nicholas, Jeremy. *Godowsky: the pianists' pianist; a biography of Leopold Godowsky.* Hexham: Appian Publications & Recordings, 1989.

Nichols, Roger. *Debussy remembered.* London: Faber and Faber, 1992.

Nichols, Roger. *Mendelssohn remembered.* London: Faber and Faber, 1997.

Nichols, Roger. *Ravel remembered.* London: Faber and Faber, 1987.

Niecks, Frederick. *Robert Schumann.* London: J. M. Dent, 1925.

Nielsen, Carl. *Living music.* Copenhagen, Wilhelm Hansen, 1968.

Nielsen, Carl. *My childhood.* Copenhagen, Wilhelm Hansen, 1972.

Nikolska, Irina. *Conversations with Witold Lutoslawski, (1987–92).* Stockholm: Melos, 1994.

Nohl, Ludwig. *Beethoven depicted by his contemporaries.* London: Reeves, 1880.

De Nora, Tia. *Beethoven and the construction of genius: musical politics in Vienna, 1792–1803.* Berkeley: University of California Press, 1997.

Norton, Spencer, Editor and Translator. *Music in my time: the memoirs of Alfredo Casella.* Norman: University of Oklahoma Press, 1955.

Nottebohm, Gustav. *Two Beethoven sketchbooks: a description with musical extracts.* London: Gollancz, 1979.

Oakeley, Edward Murray. *The life of Sir Herbert Stanley Oakeley.* London: George Allen, 1904.

Lucas, Brenda and Michael Kerr. *Virtuoso: the story of John Ogdon.* London: H. Hamilton, 1981.

Oliver, Michael, Editor. *Settling the score: a journey through the music of the twentieth century.* London: Faber and Faber, 1999.

Olleson, Philip. *Samuel Wesley: the man and his music.* Woodbridge: Boydell Press, 2003.

Olleson, Philip, Editor. *The letters of Samuel Wesley: professional* and social correspondence, 1797–1837. Oxford; New York: Oxford University Press, 2001.

Olmstead, Andrea. *Conversations with Roger Sessions.* Boston: Northeastern University Press, 1987.

Orenstein, Arbie, Editor. *A Ravel reader: correspondence, articles, interviews.* New York: Columbia University Press, 1990.

Orenstein, Arbie. *Ravel: man and musician.* New York: Columbia University Press, 1975.

Orledge, Robert. *Charles Koechlin (1867–1950): his life and works.* New York: Harwood Academic Publishers, 1989.

Orledge, Robert. *Gabriel Fauré.* London: Eulenburg Books, 1979.

Orledge, Robert. *Satie remembered.* London: Faber and Faber, 1995.

Orledge, Robert. *Satie the composer.* Cambridge: Cambridge University Press, 1990.

Orlova, Alexandra. *Glinka's life in music: a chronicle.* Ann Arbor: UMI Research Press, 1988.

Orlova, Alexandra. *Musorgsky's days and works: a biography in documents.* Ann Arbor: UMI Research Press, 1983.

Orlova, Alexandra. *Tchaikovsky: a self-portrait.* Oxford: Oxford University Press, 1990.

Osborne, Charles, Editor and Translator. *Letters of Giuseppe Verdi.* London: Victor Gollancz, 1971.

Osmond-Smith David, Editor and Translator. *Luciano Berio: Two interviews with Rossana Dalmonte and Bálint András Varga.* New York; London: Boyars, 1985.

Ouellette, Fernand. *Edgard Varèse.* London: Calder & Boyars, 1973.

Paderewski, Ignacy Jan and Mary Lawton. *The Paderewski memoirs.* London: Collins, 1939.

Page, Tim: Editor. *The Glenn Gould reader.* London: Faber and Faber, 1987.

Page, Tim. *Music from the road: views and reviews, 1978–1992.* New York; Oxford: Oxford University Press, 1992.

Page, Tim and Vanessa Weeks, Editors. *Selected letters of Virgil Thomson.* New York: Summit Books, 1988.

Page, Tim. *Tim Page on music: views and reviews.* Portland, Oregon: Amadeus Press, 2002.

Palmer, Christopher. *Herbert Howells, (1892–1983): a celebration.* London: Thames, 1996.

Palmer, Christopher, Editor. *Sergei Prokofiev: Soviet diary 1927 and other writings.* London: Faber and Faber, 1991.

Palmer, Fiona M. *Domenico Dragonetti in England (1794–1846): the career of a double bass virtuoso.* Oxford: Clarendon, 1997.

Palmieri, Robert, Editor. *Encyclopedia of the piano.* New York: Garland, 1996.

Panufnik, Andrzej. *Composing myself.* London: Methuen, 1987.

Parsons, James, Editor. *The Cambridge companion to the Lied.* Cambridge: Cambridge University Press, 2004.

Paynter, John, Editor. *Between old worlds and new: occasional writings on music by Wilfrid Mellers.* London: Cygnus Arts, 1997.

Pestelli, Giorgio. *The age of Mozart and Beethoven.* Cambridge:

Cambridge University Press, 1984.

Peyser, Joan. *Bernstein: a biography: revised & updated.* New York: Billboard Books, 1998.

Phillips-Matz, Mary Jane. *Verdi: a biography.* Oxford: Oxford University Press, 1993.

Piggott, Patrick. *The life and music of John Field, 1782–1837: creator of the nocturne.* London: Faber and Faber, 1973.

Plantinga, Leon. *Beethoven's concertos: history, style, performance.* New York: Norton, 1999.

Plantinga, Leon. *Clementi: his life and music.* London: Oxford University Press, 1977.

Plantinga, Leon. *Romantic music: a history of musical style in nineteenth-century Europe.* New York; London: Norton, 1984.

Plaskin, Glenn. *Horowitz: a biography of Vladimir Horowitz.* London: Macdonald, 1983.

Pleasants, Henry, Editor and Translator. *Hanslick, Eduard: Music criticisms, 1846–99.* Baltimore: Penguin Books, 1963.

Pleasants, Henry, Editor and Translator. *Hanslick's music criticisms.* New York: Dover Publications, 1988.

Pleasants, Henry, Editor and Translator. *The music criticism of Hugo Wolf.* New York: Holmes & Meier Publishers, 1978.

Pleasants, Henry, Editor and Translator. *The musical journeys of Louis Spohr.* Norman: University of Oklahoma Press, 1961.

Pollack, Howard. *Aaron Copland: the life and work of an uncommon man.* New York: Henry Holt, 1999.

Poulenc, Francis. *My friends and myself.* London: Dennis Dobson, 1978.

Powell, Richard, Mrs. *Edward Elgar: memories of a variation.* Aldershot, Hants, England: Scolar Press; Brookfield, Vermont, USA: Ashgate Publishing. Co., 1994.

Poznansky, Alexander, Editor. *Tchaikovsky through others' eyes.* Bloomington: Indiana University Press, 1999.

Praeger, Ferdinand. *Wagner as I knew him.* London; New York: Longmans, Green, 1892.

Previn, Andre. *Anthony Hopkins. Music face to face.* London, Hamish Hamilton, 1971.

Prieberg, Fred K. *Trial of strength: Wilhelm Furtwängler and the Third Reich.* London: Quartet, 1991.

Procter-Gregg, Humphrey. *Beecham remembered.* London: Duckworth, 1976.

Prokofiev, Sergey. *Prokofiev by Prokofiev: a composer's memoir.* London: Macdonald and Jane's, 1979.

Rachmaninoff, Sergei. *Rachmaninoff's recollections told to Oskar von Riesemann.* London: George Allen & Unwin, 1934.

Radcliffe, Philip. *Beethoven's string quartets.* Cambridge: Cambridge University Press, 1978.

Radcliffe, Philip. *Piano Music in: The Age of Beethoven, The New Oxford History of Music, Vol. VIII.* Gerald Abraham, (Editor), 1988, p. 340.

Ratner, Leonard G. *Romantic music: sound and syntax.* New York: Schirmer Books, 1992.

Raynor, Henry. *A social history of music: from the middle ages to*

Beethoven. London: Barrie & Jenkins, 1972.

Rees, Brian. *Camille Saint-Saëns: a life.* London: Chatto & Windus, 1999.

Reich, Willi, Editor. *Anton Webern: The path to the new music.* London; Bryn Mawr: Theodore Presser in association with Universal Edition, 1963.

Reid, Charles. *John Barbirolli: a biography.* London, Hamish Hamilton, 1971.

Reid, Charles. *Malcolm Sargent: a biography.* London: Hamilton, 1968.

Rennert, Jonathan. *William Crotch (1775–1847): composer, artist, teacher.* Lavenham: Terence Dalton, 1975.

Rice, John A. *Antonio Salieri and Viennese Opera.* Chicago, Illinois: University of Chicago Press, 1998.

Rice, John A. *Empress Marie Therese and music at the Viennese court, 1792–1807.* Cambridge: Cambridge University Press, 2003.

Richards, Fiona. *The Music of John Ireland.* Aldershot: Ashgate, 2000.

Rigby, Charles. *Sir Charles Hallé: a portrait for today.* Manchester: Dolphin Press, 1952.

Ringer, Alexander, Editor. *The early Romantic era: between Revolutions; 1789 and 1848.* Basingstoke: Macmillan, 1990.

Roberts, John P.L. and Ghyslaine Guertin, Editors. *Glenn Gould: Selected letters.* Toronto; Oxford: Oxford University Press, 1992.

Robertson, Alec. *More than music.* London: Collins, 1961.

Robinson, Harlow, Editor and Translator. *Selected letters of Sergei Prokofiev.* Boston: Northeastern University Press, 1998.

Robinson, Harlow. *Sergei Prokofiev: a biography.* London: Hale, 1987.

Robinson, Paul A. *Ludwig van Beethoven, Fidelio.* Cambridge: Cambridge University Press, 1996.

Robinson, Suzanne, Editor. *Michael Tippett: music and literature.* Aldershot: Ashgate, 2002.

Rochberg, George. *The aesthetics of survival: a composer's view of twentieth-century music.* Ann Arbor, Michigan: University of Michigan Press, 2004.

Rodmell, Paul. *Charles Villiers Stanford.* Aldershot: Ashgate, 2002.

Roeder, Michael Thomas. *A history of the concerto.* Portland, Oregon: Amadeus Press, 1994.

Rohr, Deborah Adams. *The careers of British musicians, 1750–1850: a profession of artisans.* Cambridge: Cambridge University Press, 2001.

Rolland, Romain. *Goethe and Beethoven.* New York; London: Blom, 1968.

Rolland, Romain. *Beethoven and Handel.* London: Waverley Book Co., 1917.

Rolland, Romain. *Beethoven the creator.* Garden City, New York: Garden City Pub., 1937.

Roscow, Gregory, Editor. *Bliss on music: selected writings of Arthur Bliss, 1920–1975.* Oxford: Oxford University Press, 1991.

Rosen, Charles. *Beethoven's piano sonatas: a short companion.* New Haven, Connecticut:

Rosen, Charles. *Critical entertainments: music old and new.* Cambridge, Massachusetts; London: Harvard University Press, 2000.

Rosen, Charles. *The classical style: Haydn, Mozart, Beethoven.* London: Faber and Faber, 1976.

Rosen, Charles. *The romantic generation.* Cambridge, Massachusetts: Harvard University Press, 1995.

Rosenthal, Albi. *Obiter scripta: essays, lectures, articles, interviews and reviews on music, and other subjects.* Oxford: Offox Press; Lanham: Scarecrow Press, 2000.

Rostal, Max. *Beethoven: the sonatas for piano and violin; thoughts on their interpretation.* London: Toccata Press, 1985.

Rostropovich, Mstislav and Galina Vishnevskaya. *Russia, music, and liberty.* Portland, Oregan: Amadeus Press, 1995.

Rubinstein, Arthur. *My many years.* London: Jonathan Cape, 1980.

Rubinstein, Arthur. *My young years.* London: Jonathan Cape, 1973.

Rumph, Stephen C. *Beethoven after Napoleon: political romanticism in the late works.* Berkeley; London: University of California Press, 2004.

Rye, Matthew Rye. *Notes to the BBC Radio Three Beethoven Experience, Friday 10 June 2005,* www.bbc.co.uk/radio3/Beethoven.

Sachs, Harvey. *Toscanini.* London: Weidenfeld and Nicholson, 1978.

Sachs, Joel. *Kapellmeister Hummel in England and France.* Detroit: Information Coordinators, 1977.

Saffle, Michael, Editor. *Liszt and his world: proceedings of the International Liszt Conference held at Virginia Polytechnic Institute and State University, 20–23 May 1993.* Stuyvesant, New York: Pendragon Press, 1998.

Safránek, Milos. *Bohuslav Martinu, his life and works.* London: Allan Wingate, 1962.

Saint-Saëns, Camille. *Outspoken essays on music.* Westport, Connecticut: Greenwood Press, 1970.

Saussine, Renée de. *Paganini.* Westport, Connecticut: Greenwood Press, 1976.

Sayers, W. C. Berwick. *Samuel Coleridge-Taylor, musician: his life and letters.* London; New York: Cassell and Co., 1915.

Schaarwächter, Jürgen. *HB: aspects of Havergal Brian.* Aldershot: Ashgate, 1997.

Schafer, R. Murray. *E.T.A. Hoffmann and music.* Toronto: University of Toronto Press, 1975.

Schafer, R. Murray, Editor. *Ezra Pound and music: the complete criticism.* London: Faber and Faber, 1978.

Schat, Peter. *The tone clock.* Chur, Switzerland; Langhorne, Pa.: Harwood Academic Publishers, 1993.

Schenk, Erich. *Mozart and his times.* Edited and Translated by Richard and Clara Winstin. London: Secker & Warburg, 1960.

Schindler, Anton Felix. *Beethoven as I knew him.* Edited by Donald W. MacArdle and Translated by Constance S. Jolly from the

German edition of 1860 London: Faber and Faber, 1966.

Schlosser, Johann. *Beethoven: the first biography, 1827.* Edited by Barry Cooper. Portland, Oregon: Amadeus Press, 1996.

Schnabel, Artur. *My life and music.* London: Longmans, 1961.

Schnittke, Alfred. *A Schnittke reader.* Bloomington: Indiana University Press, 2002.

Scholes, Percy Alfred. *Crotchets: a few short musical notes.* London: John Lane, 1924.

Schonberg, Harold C. *The great pianists.* London: Victor Gollancz, 1964.

Schrade, Leo. *Beethoven in France: the growth of an idea.* New Haven; London: Yale University Press, H. Milford, Oxford University Press, 1942.

Schrade, Leo. *Tragedy in the art of music.* Cambridge, Massachusetts: Harvard University Press, 1964.

Schuh, Willi. *Richard Strauss: a chronicle of the early years 1864–1898.* Cambridge: Cambridge University Press, 1982.

Schuh, Willi, Editor. *Richard Strauss: Recollections and reflections.* London; New York: Boosey & Hawkes, 1953.

Schuller, Gunther. *Musings: the musical worlds of Gunther Schuller.* New York: Oxford University Press, 1986.

Schumann, Robert. *Music and musicians: essays and criticisms.* London: William Reeves, 1877.

Schuttenhelm, Editor. *Selected letters of Michael Tippett.* London: Faber and Faber, 2005.

Schwartz, Elliott. *Music since 1945: issues, materials, and literature.* New York: Schirmer Books, 1993.

Scott, Marion M. *Beethoven: (The master musicians).* London: Dent, 1940.

Scott-Sutherland, Colin. *Arnold Bax.* London: J. M. Dent, 1973.

Searle, Muriel V. *John Ireland: the man and his music.* Tunbridge Wells: Midas Books, 1979.

Secrest, Meryle. *Leonard Bernstein: a life.* London: Bloomsbury, 1995.

Seeger, Charles. *Studies in musicology II, 1929–1979.* Edited by Anne M. Pescatello. Berkeley; London: University of California Press, 1994.

Selden-Goth, Gisela, Editor. *Felix Mendelssohn: letters.* London: Paul Elek Publishers Ltd, 1946.

Senner, Wayne M., Robin Wallace and William Meredith, Editors. *The critical reception of Beethoven's compositions by his German contemporaries.* Lincoln: University of Nebraska Press, in association with the American Beethoven Society and the Ira F. Brilliant Center for Beethoven Studies, San José State University, 1999.

Seroff, Victor I. *Rachmaninoff.* London: Cassell & Company, 1951.

Sessions, Roger. *Questions about music.* Cambridge, Massachusetts: Harvard University Press, 1970.

Sessions, Roger. *The musical experience of composer, performer, listener.* New York: Atheneum, 1966, 1950.

Seyfried, Ignaz von. *Louis van Beethoven's Studies in thoroughbass, counterpoint and the art of scientific composition.* Leipzig; New-York: Schuberth and Company, 1853.

Sharma, Bhesham R. *Music and culture in the age of mechanical reproduction.* New York: Peter Lang, 2000.

Shaw, Bernard. *How to become a musical critic.* London: R. Hart Davis, 1960.

Shaw, Bernard. *London music in 1888–89 as heard by Corno di Bassetto (later known as Bernard Shaw): with some further autobiographical particulars.* London: Constable and Company, 1937.

Shaw, Bernard. *Music in London, 1890–1894.* London: Constable and Company Limited, 3 Vols., 1932.

Shedlock, John South. *Beethoven's pianoforte sonatas: the origin and respective values of various readings.* London: Augener Ltd., 1918.

Shedlock, John South. *The pianoforte sonata: its origin and development.* London: Methuen, 1895.

Shepherd, Arthur. *The string quartets of Ludwig van Beethoven.* Cleveland: H. Carr, The Printing Press, 1935.

Sheppard, Leslie and Herbert R. Axelrod. *Paganini: containing a portfolio of drawings by Vido Polikarpus.* Neptune City, New Jersey: Paganiniana Publications, 1979.

Short, Michael. *Gustav Holst: the man and his music.* Oxford: Oxford University Press, 1990.

Shostakovich, Dmitry. *Dmitry Shostakovich: about himself and his times.* Moscow: Progress Publishers, 1981.

Simpson, John Palgrave. *Carl Maria von Weber: the life of an artist, from the German of his son Baron, Max Maria von Weber.* London: Chapman and Hall, 1865.

Simpson, Robert. *Beethoven symphonies.* London: British Broadcasting Corporation, 1970.

Sipe, Thomas. *Beethoven: Eroica symphony.* Cambridge: Cambridge University Press, 1998.

Sitwell, Sacheverell. *Mozart.* Edinburgh: Peter Davies Limited, 1932.

Skelton, Geoffrey. *Paul Hindemith: the man behind the music; a biography.* London: Victor Gollancz, 1975.

Smallman, Basil. *The piano trio: its history, technique, and repertoire.* Oxford: Clarendon Press; Oxford; New York: Oxford University Press, 1990.

Smidak, Emil. *Isaak-Ignaz Moscheles: the life of the composer and his encounters with Beethoven, Liszt, Chopin, and Mendelssohn.* Aldershot, Hampshire, England: Scolar Press; Brookfield, Vermont, USA: Gower Publishing Co., 1989.

Smith, Barry. *Peter Warlock: the life of Philip Heseltine.* Oxford: Oxford University Press, 1994.

Smith, Joan Allen. *Schoenberg and his circle: a Viennese portrait.* New York: Schirmer Books, London: Collier Macmillan, 1986.

Smith, Richard Langham, Editor. *Debussy on music: the critical writings of the great French composer Claude Debussy.* London: Secker & Warburg, 1977.

Smith, Ronald. *Alkan.* London: Kahn and Averill, 1976.

Snowman, Daniel. *The Amadeus Quartet: the men and the music.* London: Robson Books, 1981.

Solomon, Maynard. *Beethoven.* New York: Schirmer, 1977.

Solomon, Maynard. *Beethoven essays.* Cambridge, Massachusetts; London: Harvard University Press, 1988.

Solomon, Maynard. *Late Beethoven: music, thought, imagination.* Berkeley; London: University of California Press, 2003.

Solomon, Maynard. *Mozart: a life.* London: Hutchinson, 1995.

Sonneck, Oscar George Theodore. *Beethoven: impressions of contemporaries.* London: Oxford University Press, 1927.

Spalding, Albert. *Rise to follow: an autobiography.* London: Frederick Muller Ltd., 1946.

Spohr, Louis. *Louis Spohr's autobiography.* London: Longman, Green, Longman, Roberts, & Green, 1865.

Stafford, William. *Mozart myths: a critical reassessment.* Stanford, California: Stanford University Press, 1991.

Stanford, Charles Villiers. *Interludes: records and reflections.* London: John Murray, 1922.

Stanley, Glen, Editor. *The Cambridge companion to Beethoven.* Cambridge; New York: Cambridge University Press, 2000

Stedman, Preston. *The symphony.* Englewood Cliffs, New Jersey; London: Prentice-Hall, 1979.

Stedron, Bohumír, Editor and Translator. *Leos Janácek: letters and reminiscences.* Prague: Artia, 1955.

Stein, Erwin, Editor. *Arnold Schoenberg: letters.* London: Faber and Faber, 1964.

Stein, Erwin. *Orpheus in new guises.* London: Rockliff, 1953.

Stein, Jack Madison. *Poem and music in the German lied from Gluck to Hugo Wolf.* Cambridge, Massachusetts: Harvard University Press, 1971.

Stein, Leonard, Editor. *Style and idea: selected writings of Arnold Schoenberg.* London: Faber and Faber, 1975.

Steinberg, Michael P. *Listening to reason: culture, subjectivity, and nineteenth-century music.* Princeton, New Jersey: Princeton University Press, 2004.

Steinberg, Michael. *The concerto: a listener's guide.* New York: Oxford University Press, 1998.

Steinberg, Michael. *The symphony: a listener's guide.* Oxford; New York: Oxford University Press, 1995.

Sternfeld, Frederick William. *Goethe and music: a list of parodies and Goethe's relationship to music; a list of references.* New York: Da Capo Press, 1979.

Stivender, David. *Mascagni: an autobiography compiled, edited and translated from original sources.* New York: Pro/Am Music Resources; London: Kahn & Averill, 1988.

Stone, Else and Kurt Stone, Editors. *The writings of Elliott Carter: an American composer looks at modern music.* Bloomington: Indiana University Press, 1977.

Stowell, Robin. *Beethoven: violin concerto.* Cambridge: Cambridge University Press, 1998.

Stowell, Robin: Editor. *The Cambridge companion to the cello.*

Cambridge: Cambridge University Press, 1999.

Stowell, Robin: Editor. *The Cambridge companion to the string quartet.* Cambridge: Cambridge University Press, 2003.

Stratton, Stephen Samuel. *Mendelssohn.* London: J.M. Dent & Co.; New York: E.P. Dutton & Co., 1901.

Straus, Joseph N. *Remaking the past: musical modernism and the influence of the tonal tradition.* Cambridge, Massachusetts: Harvard University Press, 1990.

Stravinsky, Igor. *An autobiography.* London: Calder and Boyars, 1975.

Stravinsky, Igor. *Themes and conclusions.* London: Faber and Faber, 1972.

Stravinsky, Igor and Robert Craft. *Conversations with Igor Stravinsky.* London: Faber and Faber, 1959.

Stravinsky, Igor and Robert Craft. *Dialogues and a diary.* London: Faber and Faber 1968.

Stravinsky, Igor and Robert Craft. *Memories and commentaries.* London: Faber and Faber, 2002.

Strunk, Oliver. *Source readings in music history, 4: The Classic era.* London: Faber and Faber 1981.

Sullivan, Blair, Editor. *The echo of music: essays in honor of Marie Louise Göllner.* Warren, Michigan: Harmonie Park Press, 2004.

Sullivan, Jack, Editor. *Words on music: from Addison to Barzun.* Athens: Ohio University Press, 1990.

Symonette, Lys and Kim H. Kowalke, Editors and Translators. *Speak low (when you speak love): the letters of Kurt Weill and Lotte Lenya.* London: Hamish Hamilton, 1996.

Swalin, Benjamin F. *The violin concerto: a study in German romanticism.* New York, Da Capo Press, 1973.

Szigeti, Joseph. *With strings attached: reminiscences and reflections.* London: Cassell & Co. Ltd, 1949.

Tanner, Michael, Editor. *Notebooks, 1924–1954: Wilhelm Furtwängler.* London: Quartet Books, 1989.

Taylor, Robert, Editor. *Furtwängler on music: essays and addresses.* Aldershot: Scolar, 1991.

Taylor, Ronald. *Kurt Weill: composer in a divided world.* London: Simon & Schuster, 1991.

Tchaikovsky, Peter Ilich. *Letters to his family: an autobiography.* Translated by Galina von Meck. London: Dennis Dobson, 1981.

Tertis, Lionel. *My viola and I: a complete autobiography; with, 'Beauty of tone in string playing', and other essays.* London: Paul Elek, 1974.

Thayer, Alexander Wheelock. *Salieri: rival of Mozart.* Edited by Theodore Albrecht. Kansas City, Missouri: Philharmonia of Greater Kansas City, 1989.

Thomas, Michael Tilson. *Viva voce: conversations with Edward Seckerson.* London: Faber and Faber 1994.

Thomson, Andrew. *Vincent d'Indy and his world.* Oxford: Clarendon Press, 1996.

Thomson, Virgil. *The musical scene.* New York: Greenwood Press, 1968.

Thomson, Virgil. *Virgil Thomson.*

London: Weidenfeld & Nicolson, 1967.

Tillard, Françoise. *Fanny Mendelssohn*. Amadeus Press: Portland, 1996.

Tilmouth, Michael, Editor. *Donald Francis Tovey: The classics of music: talks, essays, and other writings previously uncollected*. Oxford: Oxford University Press, 2001.

Tippett, Michael. *Moving into Aquarius*. London: Routledge and Kegan Paul, 1959.

Tippett, Michael. *Those twentieth century blues: an autobiography*. London: Hutchinson, 1991.

Todd, R. Larry, Editor. *Nineteenth-century piano music*. New York; London: Routledge, 2004.

Todd, R. Larry, Editor. *Schumann and his world*. Princeton: Princeton University Press, 1994.

Tommasini, Anthony. *Virgil Thomson: composer on the aisle*. New York: W.W. Norton, 1997.

Tortelier, Paul. *A self-portrait: in conversation with David Blum*. London: Heinemann, 1984.

Tovey, Donald Francis. *A Companion to Beethoven's Pianoforte Sonatas*. Revised by Barry Cooper. London: The Associated Board, [1931], 1998.

Tovey, Donald Francis. *Beethoven*. London: Oxford University Press, 1944.

Tovey, Donald Francis. *Essays and lectures on music*. London: Oxford University Press, 1949.

Tovey, Donald Francis. *Essays in musical analysis*. London: Oxford University Press, H. Milford, 7 Vols., 1935–41.

Tovey, Donald Francis. *The forms of music: musical articles from The Encyclopaedia Britannica*. London: Oxford University Press, 1944.

Toye, Francis. *Giuseppe Verdi: his life and works*. London: William Heinemann Ltd., 1931.

Truscott, Harold. *Beethoven's late string quartets*. London: Dobson, 1968.

Tyler, William R. *The letters of Franz Liszt to Olga von Meyendorff, 1871–1886, in the Mildred Bliss Collection at Dumbarton Oaks*. Translated by William R. Tyler. Washington: Dumbarton Oaks, Trustees for Harvard University; Cambridge, Massachusetts: distributed by Harvard University Press, 1979.

Tyrrell, John. *Janácek: years of a life. Vol. 1, (1854–1914) The lonely blackbird*. London: Faber and Faber, 2006.

Tyrrell, John, Editor and Translator. *My life with Janácek: the memoirs of Zdenka Janácková*. London: Faber and Faber, 1998.

Tyson, Alan, Editor. *Beethoven studies 2*. Cambridge: Cambridge University Press, 1977.

Tyson, Alan, Editor. *Beethoven studies 3*. Cambridge: Cambridge University Press, 1982.

Tyson, Alan. *Mozart: studies of the autograph scores*. Cambridge, Massachusetts; London: Harvard University Press, 1987.

Tyson, Alan. *The authentic English editions of Beethoven*. London: Faber and Faber, 1963.

Underwood, J. A., Editor. *Gabriel Fauré: his life through his letters*. London: Marion Boyars, 1984.

Vechten, Carl van, Editor. *Nikolay, Rimsky-Korsakov: My musical *life*. London: Martin Secker & Warburg Ltd., 1942.

Vinton, John. *Essays after a dictionary: music and culture at the close of Western civilization.* Lewisburg: Bucknell University Press, 1977.

Volkov, Solomon, Editor. *Testimony: the memoirs of Dmitri Shostakovich.* London: Faber and Faber, 1981.

Volta, Ornella, Editor. *A mammal's notebook: collected writings of Erik Satie.* London: Atlas Press, 1996.

Wagner, Richard. Beethoven: *With [a] supplement from the philosophical works of A. Schopenhauer.* Translated by E. Dannreuther. London: Reeves, 1893.

Wagner, Richard. *My life.* London: Constable and Company Ltd., 1911.

Walden, Valerie. *One hundred years of violoncello: a history of technique and performance practice, 1740–1840.* Cambridge: Cambridge University Press, 1998.

Walker, Alan. *Franz Liszt. Volume 1, The virtuoso years: 1811–1847.* New York: Alfred A. Knopf, 1983.

Walker, Alan. *Franz Liszt. Volume 2, The Weimar years: 1848–1861.* London: Faber and Faber, 1989.

Walker, Alan. *Franz Liszt. Volume 3, The final years, 1861–1886.* London: Faber and Faber, 1997.

Walker, Bettina. *My musical experiences.* London: Richard Bentley and Son, 1890.

Walker, Ernest. *Free thought and the musician, and other essays.* London; New York: Oxford University Press, 1946.

Walker, Frank. *Hugo Wolf: a biography.* London: J. M. Dent, 1951.

Walker, Frank. *The man Verdi.* London: Dent, 1962.

Wallace, Grace, [Lady Wallace]. *Beethoven's letters (1790–1826): from the collection of Dr. Ludwig Nohl. Also his letters to the Archduke Rudolph, Cardinal-Archbishop of Olmutz, K.W., from the collection of Dr. Ludwig Ritter Von Kölchel.* London: Longmans, Green, 2 Vols., 1866.

Wallace, Robin. *Beethoven's critics: aesthetic dilemmas and resolutions during the composer's lifetime.* Cambridge; New York: Cambridge University Press, 1986.

Walter, Bruno. *Theme and variations: an autobiography.* London: H. Hamilton, 1948.

Warrack, John Hamilton. *Writings on music.* Cambridge: Cambridge University Press, 1981.

Wasielewski, Wilhelm Joseph von. *Life of Robert Schumann: with letters, 1833–1852.* London: William Reeves, 1878.

Watkins, Glenn. *Proof through the night: music and the Great War.* Berkeley: University of California Press, 2003.

Watkins, Glenn. *Pyramids at the Louvre: music, culture, and collage from Stravinsky to the postmodernists.* Cambridge, Massachusetts; London: Belknap Press of Harvard University Press, 1994.

Watkins, Glenn. *Soundings: music in the twentieth century.* New York: Schirmer Books London: Collier Macmillan, 1988.

Watson, Derek. *Liszt.* London: J. M. Dent, 1989.

Weaver, William, Editor. *The Verdi-Boito correspondence.* Chicago; London: University of Chicago Press, 1994.

Wegeler, Franz. *Remembering Beethoven: the biographical notes of Franz Wegeler and Ferdinand Ries.* London: Andre Deutsch, 1988.

Weingartner, Felix. *Buffets and rewards: a musician's reminiscences.* London: Hutchinson & Co., 1937.

Weinstock, Herbert. *Rossini: a biography.* New York: Limelight, 1987.

Weiss, Piero and Richard Taruskin. *Music in the Western World: a history in documents.* New York: Schirmer; London: Collier Macmillan, 1984.

Weissweiler, Eva *The complete correspondence of Clara and Robert Schumann.* New York: Peter Lang, 2 Vols., 1994.

Whittaker, William Gillies. *Collected essays.* London: Oxford University Press, 1940.

Whittall, Arnold. *Exploring twentieth-century music: tradition and innovation.* Cambridge; New York: Cambridge University Press, 2003.

Whittall, Arnold. *Music since the First World War.* London: J. M. Dent, 1977.

Whitton, Kenneth S. *Lieder: an introduction to German song.* London: Julia MacRae, 1984.

Wightman, Alistair, Editor. *Szymanowski on music: selected writings of Karol Szymanowski.* London: Toccata Press, 1999.

Wilhelm, Kurt. *Richard Strauss: an intimate portrait.* London: Thames and Hudson, 1999.

Will, Richard James. *The characteristic symphony in the age of Haydn and Beethoven.* Cambridge: Cambridge University Press, 2002.

Willetts, Pamela J. *Beethoven and England: an account of sources in the British Museum.* London: British Museum, 1970.

Williams, Adrian, Editor and Translator. *Liszt, Franz: Selected letters.* Oxford: Clarendon Press, 1998.

Williams, Adrian. *Portrait of Liszt: by himself and his contemporaries.* Oxford: Clarendon Press, 1990.

Williams, Ralph Vaughan. *Heirs and rebels: letters written to each other and occasional writings on music.* London; New York: Oxford University Press, 1959.

Williams, Ralph Vaughan. *Some thoughts on Beethoven's Choral symphony: with writings on other musical subjects.* London; Oxford University Press, 1953.

Williams, Ralph Vaughan. *The making of music.* Ithaca, New York: Cornell University Press, 1955.

Williams, Ursula Vaughan. *R.V.W.: a biography of Ralph Vaughan Williams.* London: Oxford University Press, 1964.

Wilson, Conrad. *Notes on Beethoven: 20 crucial works.* Edinburgh: Saint Andrew Press, 2003.

Wilson, Elizabeth. *Shostakovich: a life remembered.* Princeton, New Jersey: Princeton University Press, 1994.

Winter, Robert, Editor. *Beethoven, performers, and critics: the International Beethoven Congress, Detroit, 1977.* Detroit: Wayne State University Press, 1980.

Winter, Robert. *Compositional origins of Beethoven's opus 131.* Ann Arbor, Michigan: UMI Research Press, 1982.

Winter, Robert and Robert Martin, Editors. *The Beethoven quartet companion.* Berkeley: University of California Press, 1994.

Wolf, Eugene K. and Edward H. Roesner, Editors. *Studies in musical sources and style: essays in honor of Jan LaRue.* Madison, Wisconsin: A-R Editions, 1990.

Wolff, Christoph and Robert Riggs. *The string quartets of Haydn, Mozart and Beethoven: studies of the autograph manuscripts: a conference at Isham Memorial Library, March 15–17, 1979.* Cambridge, Massachusetts: Department of Music, Harvard University, 1980.

Wolff, Konrad. *Masters of the keyboard: individual style elements in the piano music of Bach, Haydn, Mozart, Beethoven, Schubert, Chopin, and Brahms.* Bloomington: Indiana University Press, 1990.

Wörner, Karl Heinrich. *Stockhausen: life and work.* London: Faber, 1973.

Wright, Donald, Editor. *Cardus on music: a centenary collection.* London: Hamish Hamilton, 1988.

Wyndham, Henry Saxe. *August Manns and the Saturday concerts: a memoir and a retrospect.* London and Felling-on-Tyne, New York, The Walter Scott Publishing Co., Ltd., 1909.

Yastrebtsev, V.V. Edited and Translated by Florence Jonas. *Reminiscences of Rimsky-Korsakov.* New York: Columbia University Press, 1985.

Yates, Peter. *Twentieth century music: its evolution from the end of the harmonic era into the present era of sound.* London: Allen & Unwin Ltd., 1968.

Young, Percy M. *Beethoven: a Victorian tribute based on the papers of Sir George Smart.* London: D. Dobson, 1976.

Young, Percy M. *George Grove, 1820–1900: a biography.* London: Macmillan, 1980.

Young, Percy M. *Letters of Edward Elgar and other writings.* London: Geoffrey Bles, 1956.

Young, Percy M., Editor. *Letters to Nimrod: Edward Elgar to August Jaeger, 1897–1908.* London: Dennis Dobson, 1965.

Young, Percy M. *The concert tradition: from the middle ages to the twentieth century.* London: Routledge and Kegan Paul, 1965.

Young, Rob, Editor. *(Brief Description): Undercurrents: the hidden wiring of modern music.* London; New York, N.Y.: Continuum, 2002.

Yourke, Electra Slonimsky, Editor. *Nicolas Slonimsky: writings on music.* New York, N.Y.; London: Routledge, 4 Vols. 2003-2005.

Slonimsky, Nicolas. *The great composers and their works.* Edited by Electra Slonimsky Yourke. New York: Schirmer Books, 2 Vols. 2000.

Ysaÿe, Antoine. *Ysaÿe: his life, work and influence.* London: W. Heinemann, 1947.

Zamoyski, Adam. *Paderewski.* London: Collins, 1982.

Zegers, Mirjam, Editor. *Louis Andriessen: The art of stealing time.* Todmorden: Arc Music, 2002.

Zemanova, Mirka, Editor. *Janáček's uncollected essays on music.* London: Marion Boyars, 1989.

INDEX

The order adopted for the listing of the individual entries in this index is chronological - according to the sequential unfolding of the events under discussion. Thereby, the reader is provided with both a guide to the contents discussed in the main text and a time-line of the principal events bearing on Beethoven's life and work.

SELECTED WRITINGS PP. 1-28
Allgemeine musikalische Zeitung (AMZ)
Wilhelm Altmann
Paul Bekker
John Blacking
Leon Botstein
Joseph Braunstein
Barry Cooper
Basil Deane
Philip G. Downs
Donald Jay Grout, and Claude V. Palisca
(Sir) George Grove
George Hogarth
David Wyn Jones
William Kinderman
Gustav Mahler
Stedman Preston
Maynard Solomon
Michael Steinberg
Coriander Stuttard
Donald Francis Tovey
Paul Webster
Ralph Vaughan Williams

BEETHOVEN AND BONN PP. 29-37
Accounts of youth
Electoral musical establishment
Christian Gottlob Neefe
Dressler Variations (WoO 63)
Kurfürsten Sonatas, WoO 47
Piano Concerto in E-flat major, WoO 4
Cantata Death of the Emperor Joseph II, WoO 87
Carl Ludwig Junker
Cramer's Magazin der Musik
Bonn Court orchestra
Joseph Haydn, meeting with
Cantata Emperor Leopold II, WoO 88
Beethoven's Stammbuch, signatories to
Ferdinand von Waldstein
Ritterballet

BEETHOVEN AND VIENNA PP. 38-68
Maximilian Franz, obligations to
Haydn relationship with
Nikolaus Simrock
Piano Sonatas, Op. 2
Prince Karl Lichnowsky
Gottfried Freiherr van Swieten
Gesellschaft der Associierten Kavaliere
Vienna's nobility
Beethoven's début as orchestral composer
Redoutensaal
Antonio Salieri
Paul Wranitzky
Viennese Tonkünstier-Sozietät
Artaria & Co.
Count Moritz Lichnowsky
Anton Schindler, recollections of
Allgemeine musikalische Zeitung - (AmZ)
Beethoven's finances and domestic circumstances
Residences
Elisabeth von Kissow
Johann Andreas Streicher
Franz Gerhard Wegeler
Contemporary symphonists
Baron Johann Kaspar Risbeck
Burgtheater and Kärntnertortheater
European concert theatres
Vienna's Augarten
Joseph Johann Baptist Wölfl
Daniel Gottlieb Steibelt
Johann Albrechtsberger
Anton Diabelli
Haydn, Beethoven's respect for
Johann Baptist Schenk
Ferdinand Ries, recollections of
Beethoven, concert pianist
Nikolaus Johann van Beethoven
Kaspar Karl van Beethoven
Breitkopf and Härtel, business with
Johann von Schönfeld
Nikolaus von Zmeskall
Karl Amenda
AmZ's views of Beethoven's music
2 April 1800 Beethoven's (Akademie)

BEETHOVEN: A CONTEMPORARY PORTRAIT PP. 69-91
Baron Carl Friedrich Kübeck, recollections of
Therese von Brunswick
Carl Czerny
Ignaz von Seyfried
Beethoven conducting
Hector Berlioz Mémoires
Gottfried Christoph Härtel
Gandolph von Stainhauser
C. F. Riedl
Joseph Neesen
Christian Horneman
Joseph Mähler
Alexander Thayer
Daniel Steibelt
Count Moritz Fries
Gesellschaft der Musikfreunde
Ferdinand Ries
Joseph Gelinek

Carl Maria von Weber
Wenzel Tomaschek
Johann Aloys Schlosser
Johann Baptist Cramer
Beethoven onset of deafness
Luigi Galvani and galvanism
Countess Gillette Guicciadi
Reflections on Beethoven's deafness: Bedřich Smetana, Gabriel Fauré, Michael Berkeley, William Kinderman, Maynard Solomon, Electra Yourke

BEETHOVEN: A NEW PATH
PP. 92-110

1798-1802, compositions for
Wenzel Krumpholz, recollections of
Beethoven and the orchestra
Orchestra, expansion of
Beethoven's orchestral sound
Gottfried Wilhelm Fink, views of
Ferdinand Gotthelf Hand's Asthetik der Tonkunst
Gian Francesco Malipiero
Wilhelm Furtwängler
Authentic performance: Clive Brown,
Sir Roger Norrington, Otto Klemperer
Ignaz Schuppanzigh
Franz Clement
Norman Del Mar
Johann Nepomuk Maelzel's metronome
Beethoven's metronome markings
Louis Spohr, advent of baton technique
Joseph Wielder
Beethoven conducting, impressions of: Carl Czerny, Ignaz Moscheles, Johann Friedrich Reichardt, Ferdinand Ries, Ignaz von Seyfried, Louis Spohr

SYMPHONY NO. 1 CREATION ORIGINS PP. 111-129

Sketch sources
Kafka Miscellany
Kerman, Miscellany
C minor Symphony, origins of
Willy Hesse, realisation
C major Symphony, origins of
Beethoven's symphonic contemporaries:
Paul Wranitzky, Joseph Leopold Eybler, Antonio Casimir Cartellieri
Gustav Nottebohm
Alfred Peter Brown
Haydn and Mozart, influence of
Bonn period, sketch origins
Prague-Berlin period, sketch origins
Beethoven's working method
Fritz Stein
Jena Symphony
H. C. Robbins Landon, researches
First Symphony, sketch origins
Beethoven, working method
Gustav Nottebohm
Roger Sessions, Charles Eliot Norton Professor
1799 - 1800, work on Op. 21

PUBLISHERS AND PUBLICATION PP. 130-147

Franz Anton Hoffmeister, negotiations with Hoffmeister and Kühnel - Bureau de Musique
Title Page to Op. 21
Dedicatee, Elector Maximilian Franz
Gottfried Christof Härtel, negotiations with Breitkopf and Härtel.
Allgemeine musikalische Zeitung, Beethoven's relationship with
Copyright infringement
Carl van Beethoven, transactions with publishers
First Symphony performed 2 April 1800
Beethoven's creativity, related works composed
Publication of Op. 21 in parts

Beethoven's tempi
Nikolaus Winkel, chronometer
Johann Maelzel, metronome
Ignaz von Moscl
Ferdinand Ries
Missa Solemnis
Baron Gottfried van Swieten, revised dedicatee to Op. 21
Title Page to Op. 21, revised
Cianchettini and Sperati, English score edition of First Symphony

Symphony No. 1 Reception History pp. 148-197
Akademie Concert held 2 April 1800
Paul Wranitzky, role of
AmZ response to
Maynard Solomon
Donald Tovey
March 1803 concert
Zeitung für die Elegante Welt, response to
Cantata Christus am Ölberge
1804, performances
Gewandhaus Orchestra
Felix Mendelsohn
Ferdinand Hiller, views of
1805 music season
Herr von Würth concert
Eroica Symphony, premier
Beethoven's audiences
Sébastien Érard, gift of piano
1806, views of AmZ
1807-08, Liebhaber-Concerte
Paris, Concerts Français
François-Antoine Habeneck
Gesellschaft von Musikfreunden
Giuseppe Cambini
1812, Munich concert season
Piano transcriptions
1819-20, Vienna concert season Concerts Spirituels
Gesellschaft der Musikfreunde, record of symphonic performances
13 November 1822, full-score publication of Op. 21 announced
Cianchettini and Sperati, English full-score publication of Op. 21
Beethoven's English publishers
Amadeus Wendt, music criticism
Post 1827 piano transcriptions
Franz Liszt
1828, Paris Société des Concerts
François-Antoine Habeneck
Castil-Blaze, Journal des débats
Leo Schrade
Philharmonic Society, early history of
Beethoven repertoire
Felix Mendelsohn
Chrystal Palace, concerts
Wilhelm Furtwängler, recollections of
Sir Herbert Hamilton Harty
Otto Klemperer, recollections o

Musicology pp. 198-222
FIRST MOVEMENT
   Adagio molto - Allegro con brio
SECOND MOVEMENT
   Andante cantabile con moto
THIRD MOVEMENT
   Menuetto - Allegro molto e vivace
Fourth Movement
   Adagio - Allegro molto e vivace

ABOUT THE AUTHOR

Terence M. Russell graduated with first class honours in architecture and was a nominee for the coveted Silver Medal of the Royal Institute of British Architects. He is a Fellow of the Royal Incorporation of Architects in Scotland (retired), was formerly Reader in the School of Arts, Culture and Environment at the University of Edinburgh, a Fellow of the British Higher Education Academy, and Senior Assessor to the Scottish Higher Education Funding Council. Alongside his professional work in the field of architecture – embracing practice, teaching and research – he has maintained a lifetime's interest in the music and musicology of Beethoven. He has an equal admiration for the work of Franz Schubert and was for many years an active member of the Schubert Institute, UK. His book writings in the field of architecture include the following:

The Built Environment: A Subject Index, Gregg Publishing (1989):
- Vol. 1: Town planning and urbanism, architecture, gardens and landscape design
- Vol. 2: Environmental technology, constructional engineering, building and materials
- Vol. 3: Decorative art and industrial design, international exhibitions and collections, recreational and performing arts
- Vol. 4: Public health, municipal services, community welfare

Architecture in the Encyclopédie of Diderot and D'Alemebert: The Letterpress Articles and Selected Engravings, Scolar Press (1993)

The Encyclopaedic Dictionary in the Eighteenth Century: Architecture, Arts and Crafts, Scolar Press (1997):
- Vol. 1: John Harris, Lexicon Technicum
- Vol. 2: Ephraim Chambers, Cyclopaedia
- Vol. 3: The Builder's Dictionary
- Vol. 4: Samuel Johnson, A Dictionary of the English Language
- Vol. 5: A Society of Gentlemen, Encyclopaedia Britannica

Gardens and Landscapes in the Encyclopédie of Diderot and D'Alemebert: The Letterpress Articles and Selected Engravings, 2 Vols., Ashgate (1999)

The Napoleonic Survey of Egypt: The Monuments and Customs of Egypt, 2 Vols., Ashgate (2001)

The Discovery of Egypt: Vivant Denon's Travels with Napoleon's Army, History Press (2005)